New Technology Policy and
Social Innovations in the Firm

T0347401

New Technology Policy and Social Innovations in the Firm

Edited by
Jorge Niosi

Routledge
Taylor & Francis Group

LONDON AND NEW YORK

First published 1994 by Pinter Publishers Ltd.

2 Park Square, Milton Park, Abingdon, Oxon OX14 4RN
711 Third Avenue, New York, NY 10017, USA

Routledge is an imprint of the Taylor & Francis Group, an informa business

First issued in paperback 2016

British Library Cataloguing in Publication Data

A CIP catalogue record for this book is available from the British Library

ISBN 978-1-85567-259-8 (hbk)
ISBN 978-1-138-97714-3 (pbk)

Library of Congress Cataloging-in-Publication Data

New technology policy and social innovations in the firm / edited by
  Jorge Niosi.
    p.   cm.
  Includes bibliographical references and index.
  ISBN 1-85567-259-6
  1. Technological innovations – Management.   2. Organizational
  change.   3. Research, Industrial.   4. Technology and state.
  5. Information technology.   I. Niosi, Jorge.
  HD42.N485   1994
  658.5'14–dc20   94–15090
                                                              CIP

Typeset by Mayhew Typesetting, Rhayader, Powys

Contents

List of contributors

Paolo Saviotti, Lecturer, Department of Economics, University of Manchester, UK

P. Gummett, Lecturer, Department of Government, University of Manchester, UK

Michael Crow, Professor and Vice Provost, Science and Technology, Columbia University, USA

Réjean Landry, Professor, Department of Political Science, Université Laval, Canada

Weijian Shan, Associate Professor, Wharton School, University of Pennsylvania, USA

Jorge Niosi, Professor, Department of Administrative Science, Université du Québec à Montréal and Director, Center for Interdisciplinary Research on Science and Technology (CIRST), UQAM and Université de Montréal, Canada

Michel Delapierre, Director, LAREA-CEREM, Université de Paris, Nanterre, France

Terutomo Ozawa, Professor, Department of Economics, Colorado State University, USA

Jonathan Morris, Lecturer, Cardiff Business School, Wales, UK

Thomas Durand, École Centrale, Paris, France

Harland Prechel, Associate Professor, Department of Sociology, Texas A & M University, USA

Pierre Dubois, Directeur de Recherche, CNRS, France

Pierre-A. Julien, Professor, Department of Economics and Administration, Université du Québec à Trois-Rivières, Canada

Introduction: Technical and organizational change in Western enterprises and the policy environment

Jorge Niosi

During the post-war period, national innovation policies in major industrial countries were built around a set of basic assumptions. One was that the production of basic science was a governmental responsibility and that science would naturally flow to industrial firms and become incorporated into new products and new processes, through R&D activities in the firms; this flow would take place without any major inefficiencies and losses, even if science was supposed to be an activity exclusively guided by academic curiosity. Business would be able to understand and seize the opportunities brought by the development of government-funded science. A second assumption was that mission-oriented R&D activities performed or funded by the state (particularly in military and space technologies) would have natural spin-offs on civilian technology. This was particularly true for countries like the United States, the United Kingdom and France, where defence R&D was a major component of the total research effort. Both assumptions supported a third one, namely that government only needed to give general financial support to business in order to maintain R&D activities; innovations would be at a sub-optimal level without government incentives because of their risky and uncertain outcomes. Except for specific missions, governments would remain aloof from the innovation process and leave the markets to choose the technology developments.

In the 1980s, these assumptions were severely challenged, and there has been a major shift in technology policy in all industrialized countries. This shift had several major causes. The first was the decline of government technological support to defence-related industries which until 1985 represented more than 50 per cent of all federal research and development public expenditures in countries like the United States, the United Kingdom and France. With the end of the cold war, defence expenditures (and also military R&D expenditures) have declined. These expenditures had represented an undeclared industrial policy, since R&D in many high-technology industries, like aerospace, computers, new materials and transportation equipment had been subsidized under the umbrella of defence support. Additionally, opportunity costs and the scanty spin-offs of military research were observed in several countries, as were the non-commercial habits acquired by advanced-technology corporations, lethargic after decades of cost-plus military contracts with governments with their excessive emphasis on products and performance instead of process and costs.[1] The need for an open commercially oriented technology policy was now more evident if some of these high technology sectors were to survive. Also, the returns from space research seemed less evident as giant R&D programs, like the space shuttle in the United States, proved ill-fated and excessively expensive. Thus, under the Clinton administration, the US has been steadily shifting R&D public funds to support the development of commercial technology. All across the industrialized world, defence programs are being cut and often replaced by civilian enterprises.

The second factor which was to change policies was the growing consciousness that the commercially oriented technology policy of countries like Japan, Germany and Korea was resulting in their industrial pre-eminence in the world markets. This commercially oriented policy subsidized civilian innovation, and technology diffusion, more than basic science and military technology. The results were mammoth surpluses in these countries' trade balances, in comparison to deficits in countries like the United States, the United Kingdom or France.

Finally, it seemed also evident that, compared to the West, Japan and the Asian NICs (Newly Industrialized Countries) had different patterns of technology policy and social institutions to support technological innovation such as government-supported technical cooperation among firms and between universities, firms and government laboratories. Instead of letting the market decide the number and types of linkages between these, governments started promoting collaborative research between them. Technology policy is more and more oriented towards collaborative research, diffusion and commercial goals. Governments support collaborative R&D for several reasons, including a desire to avoid the wasteful duplication of efforts in risky, costly and uncertain areas; to accelerate innovation that will create critical masses of R&D resources; to save public funds by avoiding the subsidization of competing research-oriented companies; and to assume the transaction costs of collaboration. All industrial countries have developed an impressive numbers of programmes to support collaborative research. In the European Community there are ESPRIT, RACE, JOULE, BRITE, EURAM, JESSI and others; in the United States the government has cleared the way for collaborative research through the National Cooperative Research Act of 1984, and then through the conversion of the Defense Advanced Research Projects Agency (DARPA) into ARPA, charged to support critical technologies. In the 1980s, Canada (at both the federal and provincial levels) created more than one hundred programmes aimed at the public promotion of collaborative research.

Several authors in Europe, the United States and Canada have developed the concept of national systems of innovation to understand the relationships between national policy objectives, public and private institutions within which innovation takes place and their performance.[2] The concept links technology policy with social institutions for innovation, both at the macro level and at the firm level. In the West there has been a massive adoption of different technological collaboration schemes by private firms. It is believed that government policies have originated this movement, but many of the largest technological alliances have been developed without government support.

The new private institutions accompanying technological change are more far-reaching than mere collaborative research. The way in which research and development is conducted is now radically changing. In the post-war period, the sequential model of relationships between functional departments inside the corporation was developed: R&D activities produced innovations in products and processes, then handed them on to manufacturers who applied them; then these were commercialized through the marketing arms of the companies with the assistance of finance and advertising. This sequential model was highly inefficient: many of the novelties produced by the R&D departments could not be manufactured (because the specific productive assets of the corporation were not taken into consideration by the R&D labs) or could not be marketed (because the commercial strategy of the firm was ignored by the R&D department). Many of these inventions, thus, never became commercially viable and represented costly failures for the company. Again, horizontal communications within the companies, and eventually the organization of inter-departmental groups for the development of new products represented better organizational 'routines'.[3] The origins of these social innovations may be found in the practice of Japanese firms. In the 1980s, Western companies began to catch up and develop similar schemes for the management of technological change and innovation. Inter-departmental Business Development Groups, concurrent engineering and the multiplication of interfaces between functions through horizontal communications are on the rise. This change has profound implications for many other organizational areas: job perimeters become less defined, hierarchies lose their precise contours, collective contracts are less explicit.

The new Japanese management methods go far beyond the development of horizontal communications or technological cooperation between independent firms. They include just-in-time (JIT) systems, total quality-control circles, the multiplication of statistical methods for process control and others. JIT systems were first implemented by Toyota, tentatively in the 1930s and 1940s, and more consciously and systematically in the 1950s and 1960s. Afterwards, they found their way into the practice of a large number of Japanese firms and then were adopted by an increasing number of Western firms.[4] The goal of JIT is to reduce almost to zero the stocks of raw materials and semi-manufactured parts and components held at a factory, and thus eliminate the capital invested in inventories and labour lost in materials handling. Through a continuous flow of inputs from suppliers, JIT reduces the negative impact of product diversity on manufacturing costs. It also forces the assembler to collaborate with its suppliers in order to improve quality, to conduct collaborative research with them for the production of new or improved goods and to train its workers for a diversity of products and tasks. JIT is thus linked to polyvalent workers and less-specialized machines.

Total quality control (TQC) of products and processes is not a Japanese innovation in management. It is based on the studies and writings of the Americans W. Edwards Deming and Joseph M. Juran. Deming, who lectured in Japan in the late 1940s and early 1950s, brought practical statistical methods and principles to Japanese manufacturing. He was soon followed by Juran, who extended quality control to engineering methods. The Japanese immediately understood the importance of these ideas. In the 1960s Professor Kaoru Ishikawa introduced the quality control circles and suggested merging the best of American ideas with Japanese organizational principles and European craftsmanship. TQC diffused and improved in Japan before it was transferred back to the United States and Western Europe.[5]

The links between technological change and organizational change have not been thoroughly studied, partially due to the speed through which the generic technological revolution developed in the last twenty years. Technological determinism would argue that technical change forces firms to adapt their organizations and skill designs in order to use the best available technology. Organizational choice theories would suggest that firms are free to vary, adapt and refuse different types of institutions and norms on the basis of their own managerial strategies.[6] An evolutionary approach, the one most authors in this volume prefer, would maintain that firms adopt, incorporate, transform and develop both technologies and organizational routines according to their past internal resources (path dependency) and their environmental constraints. In a competitive environment, firms do not have the choice of adopting or not adopting more efficient technologies or organizational forms because they run the risk that some competitor so doing may drive them out of the market. Also, the adoption of new and better organizational forms depends on the previous routines and techniques firms already possess. Many firms disappear because they are unable to adopt, let along understand, the processes of technological or organizational change that take place in their own markets.[7]

Contents of this volume

This book puts forward the thesis that public and private institutions related to science and technology form a system, under government leadership and general guidance, and that this is an evolutionary process.

All major industrial countries, including Canada up to a certain point, are now discussing the future of their technology policy. Part I of this book presents the state of the debates and institutional change in three industrial countries. P. Paolo Saviotti and Philip Gummet present a short theoretical justification of the concept of a national system of innovation in an evolutionary perspective, based on concepts like multistability, path dependency and irreversibility. They then proceed to describe the characteristics of the British innovation system in the 1990s. Michael Crow offers a clear overview of the evolution of the US national system of innovation up to the early 1990s, and analyses the most recent changes in the technology policy of the United States. He suggests that countries evolve from a purely military science and technology policy (type I), to a commercial policy that puts civilian industry objectives at the forefront (type II), towards a comprehensive science and technology policy that also takes the environment and the quality of life into consideration. In the new conditions of the end of the cold war, the United States should be moving from type I to type II, Réjean Landry presents a transaction-cost analysis of Canadian technology policy, a policy reoriented towards the creation of networks between private enterprises, universities and government laboratories.

Government intervention stimulated institutional change in private companies, but private and public firms have themselves taken a lead in organizing new institutions for technical innovation and adopting new technology. The latter parts of the book study some of these major changes, starting with the most important of them all, the development of technical alliances. Part II presents the state of technological alliances in Canada (Jorge Niosi), Japan (Terutomo Ozawa), the United States (Weijian Shan) and the European Union (Michel Delapierre). Niosi dismisses the usefulness of most neoclassical economic theories, as well as theories in industrial economics. He finds management, and transaction cost explanations useful but believes they need to be articulated in a more explicit evolutionary framework allowing for selection, variation and changes in the routine arsenal of firms; alliances are a specific case of routine, adopted by firms to cope with turbulence in the technological environment and renewed competition in product markets. Ozawa links the growth of international alliances of Japanese firms to the rise of information-intensive industries and foreign direct investments (FDI). Alliances are a new type of strategic behaviour that arrives after the three post-war stages of labour-intensive FDI, resource-intensive FDI and capital-intensive FDI. Only the most advanced industrial countries are conducting international technological strategic alliances; the adoption of this type of behaviour by Japanese firms indicates their increased sophistication in the conduct of R&D activities. Weijian Shan analyses the factors that lie behind the choice of organizational forms (independent operations vs. cooperation) in high-technology firms. Using a sample of US biotechnology start-ups, Shan finds that the size, age and strategy of the firms, and the market conditions under which they operate, are all correlated with their propensity to cooperate with other companies. Like Niosi, he believes that a new, eclectic theoretical framework needs to be built to understand inter-firm cooperation. Delapierre analyses the European alliances of the 1980s in the information-processing industries (electronics), and finds that a majority of these alliances are international in scope, that most of them are conducted within the EC (both characteristics probably due to the impact of the EC cooperative programmes) and secondly with US firms and that R&D production and commercialization are their main areas.

Part III proceeds with other major institutional changes within the firm. The set of these company strategies is what some authors (including Jonathan Morris in this volume) called 'Japanization'. They include total quality management, horizontal communications in the firm and inter-departmental groups (of which concurrent engineering is a particular case), JIT, permanent and polyvalent training of the labour force. Morris finds that Japanization occurs both through Japanese foreign direct investment and through imitation by Western firms of Japanese practices, and he compares the extent of these changes in Canadian and British industries. The adoption of concurrent engineering, though the name was coined in the United States in the mid-1980s, came at the beginnings of the 1980s through the imitation of Japanese routines. Thomas Durand analyses the characteristics and limitations of this social innovation in the Western context. Harland Prechel shows in a detailed case study of an American steel firm that manufacturing flexibility was obtained through a centralization of both decision-making and information-gathering systems. He then demonstrates that the introduction of advanced computing technology and flexibility can co-exist with vertical flows of information, a rather different form of organization in comparison to the stylized Japanese firms. Pierre Dubois shows a similar pattern in the German, French and Italian clothing and information industries: increased computerization does not bring additional competitiveness to the European firms because power relationships between managers and employees remain basically unaltered, in what he calls 'taylorist-style participation'. The building of a network of external linkages is a useful social form for the gathering of information, particularly for small and medium-sized enterprises (SMEs). Pierre-A. Julien shows that network building (especially with suppliers and customers) and technical training are the most important sources of technological information for SMEs and conditions for the adoption of new technology. Both themes are high on the agenda of social innovations in technology management.

The chapters show that the imitation of competitors' routines is a complex endeavour and that most often the new practice is a mix of previous and new traits; new embodied technologies can more easily be transferred than social institutions, showing evolutionary patterns of imitation, selection of successful practices and abandonment of unsuccessful ones.

Notes

1. In the United Kingdom, see H. Ergas: 'Does Technology Policy Matter?' in B.R. Guile and H. Brooks (eds), *Technology and Global Industry*, Washington DC, National Academy Press, 1987, pp. 191–245. For France, see F. Chesnais (ed.), *Compétitivité internationale et industrie militaire*, Paris, Économica, 1990. For the United States, see S. Melman, *Profits Without Production*, New York, Knopf, 1983.
2. C. Freeman, *Technology Policy and Economic Performance. Lesson from Japan*, London, Pinter, 1987 and 'Japan. A New National System of Innovation?' in G. Dosi *et al.* (eds), *Technical Change and Economic Theory*, London, Pinter, 1988. B.-A. Lundvall, *National Systems of Innovation*, London, Pinter, 1992. R. Nelson, 'Institutions supporting technical change in the United States', in G. Dosi *et al.* (eds) (op. cit.). R. Nelson (ed.), *National Innovation Systems*, New York, Oxford University Press, 1993. J. Niosi, P. Saviotti, B. Bellon and M. Crow, 'National Systems of Innovation. In Search of a Workable Concept', *Technology in Society*, Vol. 15, 1993, pp. 207–27.
3. For the concept of 'routine', see R. Nelson and S. Winter, *An Evolutionary Theory of Economic Change*, Boston, The Belknap Press, 1982.
4. J.C. Abegglen and G. Stalk Jr., *Kaisha. The Japanese Corporation*, New York, Basic Books, 1985, Chap. 5; D. Hutchins, *Just in Time*, Aldershot, Gower Technical Press, 1988.
5. W. Edwards Deming, *Out of the Crisis*, Cambridge, Cambridge University Press, 1986; J.M. Juran, *Juran's New Quality Road Map*, New York, Free Press, 1991;

K. Ishikawa, *What is Total Quality Control. The Japanese Way*, Englewood Cliffs, N.J., Prentice Hall, 1985.

6. See the technological determinism approach in L. Winner, *The Whale and the Reactor*, Chicago, The University of Chicago Press, 1986. The organizational choice theory appears in J. Child, 'Managerial Strategies, New Technology and the Labour Process', in D. Knights et al. (eds), *Job Redesign: Critical Perspectives on the Labour Process*, Aldershot, Gower, 1985.

7. R. Nelson and S. Winter, *An Evolutionary Theory of Economic Change*, op. cit; P.P. Saviotti and J.S. Metcalfe (eds), *Evolutionary Theories of Economic and Technological Change*, Chur, Harwood, 1991.

Part I:
New technology policy in industrialized countries

1 Britain's evolving technology policy: the end of defence domination

Pier Paolo Saviotti and Philip Gummett

1.1. Introduction

Important changes have recently taken place in the international environment in which technology policy is formulated and implemented. These environmental changes have considerable implications for technology policies and in the institutions underpinning them in the UK and in other countries. This chapter aims at reassessing policies for technology in the new international environment characterized by the above-mentioned changes in the light of these developments. It also tries to do so within a theoretical framework that goes beyond the empiricism that characterizes much policy formulation in general and technology policy in particular.

This empiricism has been imposed by the limitations of our knowledge in the relevant areas. However, it limits both the usefulness and the scope of policies, as well as our understanding of these matters. It is, therefore, desirable to try and develop, even if only *ex-post*, theories which shed light on policy matters and increase the rationality of policy making. The specific reasons for the empiricism of technology policy are related both to the relative novelty of this policy area, which did not exist explicitly before the 1960s, and to the types of theories which were then available to support policy making. We therefore begin with a brief review of some of the foundations of orthodox economic theories and the results of more recent studies of technological change, in particular, those falling within the school of evolutionary theories.

In particular, the concept of National System of Innovation (NSI) will be used as a framework for analysis. Such a concept has been recently proposed by students of technological policy, but it bears some resemblance to concepts previously proposed by theorists of economic development. We shall explore the theoretical foundations of the concept of NSI and the use made of networks in elucidating it. The concept of NSI is considered a useful interpretive device, but at the moment it is only very broadly defined. In order to make it more useful for technology policy analysis it needs to be further developed. Our second goal is to contribute to the clarification of the concept of NSI and of its implications.

The main changes which have taken place recently in the international environment of technology policies are the growing internationalization of firms' operations and the collapse of the Soviet system. The former has been accompanied by different types of collaboration between firms, generally having a substantial technological content. The latter is accelerating pre-existing pressures on the balance between military and civilian research and development (R&D) and technology.

In what follows, then, we begin by reviewing the relevant economic theory literature, before going on to examine the concept of NSIs. In particular, the implications of the present trend towards internationalization are examined in terms of the balance between convergence and divergence in the world economic system. Subsequently, the UK NSI is examined, with particular reference to the possible effects of the transformation in the international security environment since 1989: in Britain, more than in most other countries, the NSI is dominated by investment in military technology. The acute pressure on that investment today makes it a particularly interesting research site for the application of the concepts developed here.

1.2. Some policy implications of evolutionary theories of economic and technological change

It is understandable that orthodox economic theories, based on the concept of equilibrium and on a representation of technological change founded exclusively on its efficiency-increasing properties, could be of only limited use in the formulation of technology policies. Technology was assumed to be exogenous to the economic system. In other words, it had economic consequences but no economic origin. In this way most of the problems related to either the sponsorship or to the control of technology were automatically excluded from this theoretical background (Coombs *et al.*, 1987). Studies of innovation and of technological change developed in the last twenty years have partly bridged this gap. A selection of concepts which are relevant for technology policy will be presented here.

The early studies of technological innovation were articulated around the dichotomy demand pull–technology push (Mowery and Rosenberg, 1979; Freeman, 1982; Coombs *et al.*, 1987). This dichotomy turned out to be an oversimplification and gave way to a richer array of concepts describing patterns of technological change such as dominant designs (Abernathy and Utterback, 1975, 1978), natural trajectories and technological regimes (Nelson and Winter, 1977), technological guideposts (Sahal, 1981a, 1981b, 1985) and technological paradigms (Dosi, 1982). In turn such concepts have been incorporated into an attempt to construct an evolutionary theory of economic and technological change (Nelson and Winter, 1982; Dosi *et al.*, 1988).

Dominant designs, technological regimes and technological guideposts imply that after a given configuration, for example a set of technological characteristics (Saviotti and Metcalfe, 1984), is chosen, subsequent examples of technological development will be improved variants of that configuration, sharing with it some central and defining elements. A paradigm will be constituted by these shared elements of the technology and by the knowledge possessed by engineers, designers and manufacturing firms. Routines and decision rules will be part of this paradigm (Nelson and Winter, 1982). The implication of these concepts is that progress and adaptation to demand/

selection environment will take place almost continuously within established boundaries, while radical changes, leading to a replacement paradigm, will be infrequent.

The evolutionary theories which will be used here have a generally Schumpeterian flavour but have benefited from contributions coming from a number of other disciplines and research traditions. In particular biology, systems theory, irreversible thermodynamics and organization theory made important contributions to modern evolutionary theories of economic and technological change (Saviotti and Metcalfe, 1991).

From a Schumpeterian matrix we shall use the fundamental role of innovations (as opposed to routine activities) in stimulating long-term economic development and the discontinuous nature of the introduction of innovations. From system theory and irreversible thermodynamics we borrow the concept of an open system – exchanging matter, energy and information with its environment (Von Bertalanffy, 1950). Open systems may undergo discontinuous transitions to states of increasing order and complexity, as they are moved away from equilibrium. In other words, as the flow of matter, energy and information between the system and its environment increases, the system itself may undergo transitions to states of greater order and complexity

These transitions have a number of important properties. First, the number of states after the transition can be greater than that before the transition. Hence, even if one started from one steady state, the number of steady states could be greater after the transition. This property is called *multistability* and can be represented by means of a *bifurcation diagram* (Prigogine and Stengers, 1984; Allen, 1982). Second, when in the vicinity of a transition, the system undergoes stochastic fluctuations and its behaviour becomes indeterminate. In other words, it is not certain to which of the possible states the transition will lead. In proximity of a transition, when the behaviour of the system becomes indeterminate due to fluctuations, historical accidents can influence the final state of the system. According to this property, called *path dependency*, the outcome of a transition depends on the path followed to reach the final state. A particular application of this general situation to processes of technological choice has been given by Arthur (1983, 1988, 1989). He argues that in circumstances of increasing returns to adoption, a technology which is not necessarily the 'best' may be chosen from a set of competing ones. In the period of transition from the old to the new technology historical events (fluctuations) may steer the choice towards an inferior technology, which would then be stabilized by increasing returns. In other words, as any policy maker has always known, but as economists have consistently refused to admit, history matters. Third, the transition of open systems is *irreversible*, in the sense that it is not possible to return to a previous state of the system without introducing some change in the external environment.

These features of open systems have very important policy implications. Multistability implies that several system configurations may be stable. We can translate this into terms relevant for technology policy by saying that more than one institutional configuration and set of related policies may be stable. Thus institutional imitation is not necessarily the answer to technology policy problems. The answer has to come from some criterion of coherence/synergism of the institutions. Moreover, the concept of path dependency implies that the final (steady) state(s) achieved varies depending on the path followed. The socioeconomic structures and policies of the past shape, address and limit those of the future.

A related set of considerations refers to the nature of technological knowledge. First, this is often likely to be *local* (David, 1975; Nelson and Winter, 1982). In other words, this knowledge becomes progressively ineffective for dealing with situations which differ more and more from those for which it was created. According to David, the local character is partly responsible for the irreversible and path-dependent character of technological transformations. According to Nelson and Winter the same local character means that the probability of a successful innovation is greater in the neighbourhood of an existing technology. Consequently, technological knowledge is *specific*, and the locus of this specificity is the firm or producing institution. Furthermore, technological knowledge is *cumulative* and may be *tacit* or *codified* (Teece, 1981; Nelson and Winter, 1982), and therefore be either difficult or easy to communicate.

At least part of technological knowledge will be local, tacit, specific, and cumulative. These features imply that the state of technological knowledge of a set of institutions at a given time is path dependent. A general outcome of evolutionary theories is reinforced by considerations about the nature of technological knowledge. We can then expect that the technological knowledge of different firms, which constitutes a substantial part of their *knowledge base*, has a number of features which are specific to each firm. The nature of knowledge is also related to its appropriability and transferability. Tacit, specific knowledge will be easy to appropriate but difficult to transfer.

Naturally not all technological knowledge is local, tacit and specific. The outcome of basic research is likely to be codified and to resemble a latent public good. The institutions responsible for the generation of this type of knowledge are among the most important in determining the performance of a country as an innovator and constitute a necessary addition to the basic Schumpeterian model of economic development (Nelson, 1988, 1990).

At least part of the institutions involved in generating innovations will have a knowledge base which is local, tacit, specific and cumulative. These features will tend to differentiate the knowledge bases of different firms. On the other hand, advances in basic scientific and technological knowledge will constitute a common and unifying trend among all participating institutions.

1.3. National systems of innovation

Economic and technological development are characterized by a number of general trends. For example, the percentage of the labour force employed in agriculture declines with industrialization, which is accompanied by increasing incomes per capita. Also, and more recently, R&D expenditures as a percentage of GDP have tended to increase as the income per capita of the country increases. Likewise, the ratio of R&D expenditures to TBP (technological balance of payments) increases with income per capita. In addition to these and to other tendencies common to most countries, a number of features are quite specific to each country as a producer. Areas of strength in technology and in trade are often quite country-specific. This specificity cannot be explained by factor endowments, but it is more likely to be caused by specific institutional configurations and by the cumulative, local and specific character of the knowledge that the institutions possess. Thus, firms which are good in particular sectors are not scattered at random but concentrated in particular countries (Dosi *et al.* 1990; Porter, 1990).

The national character of technological 'asymmetries' means that the firms and other institutions contributing to the generation of innovations in one country do not act independently but are linked in some kind of network. In other words, these institutions constitute a system that some authors have called a National System of Innovation (NSI) (Lundvall, 1986, 1988; Freeman, 1987, 1988; Nelson, 1988, 1990; Freeman and Lundvall, 1990). A number of antecedents for conceptualizing production systems in systemic terms exist, especially in the French research tradition. Examples of such concepts are national production systems (Perroux, 1955, quoted in Dosi *et al.* 1990) and 'filières' (Dosi *et al.* 1990). Also, the concept of vertically integrated sectors (Pasinetti, 1981) presents some similarities with these.

A National System of Innovation can be defined as 'that combination of institutions which is influential in creating and implementing a country's innovation potential and their patterns of interaction'. Some of its features can be derived from our consideration of evolutionary theories. First, each country, being an open system, will have steady states characterized by some degree of order and structure. Such order and structure could not exist in a system which was a random assembly of independent institutions. Order and structure necessarily imply institutional interaction. Second, changes in the structure of the system are likely to be infrequent. This does not exclude incremental improvements but tends to consider radical changes in the institutions and in patterns of institutional interaction as having a low probability under most circumstances. Adaptation to environmental changes without any fundamental change in the structure of the system is an example of hysteresis or homeostasis (Ashby, 1956). Third, multistability implies that NSIs can produce comparable outcomes, that is products and services which are traded in world markets, starting from specific institutional realities. From the viewpoint of technology policy it is, therefore, particularly important to understand the relationship between common outcomes and the specific patterns of institutional interaction which characterize each NSI.

Adapting these concepts to technology policy we can say that the outputs of each NSI will need to be comparable. Each country produces at least a number of products and services which are traded internationally and chosen by users/consumers on the basis of uniform criteria. Trends in demand and in technology common to most countries function as output constraints for individual NSIs, specifying what can be successfully produced and sold and what not. Each NSI adapts to common output constraints using its own, specific national institutional configuration. Thus new technologies are introduced by small high-technology firms in the USA but by large firms (often multinationals) in Japan and in Germany. New output constraints are created by technological leaders and imitated by other countries. In other words, we have simultaneously one trend towards specificity and differentiation and another trend towards homogenization. Each NSI can be expected to react to output constraints by modifying incrementally existing institutions and patterns of institutional interactions. In other words, common outcomes and output constraints can be achieved by means of a multiplicity of institutional configurations/structures of NSIs. Also, such a mechanism leads obviously to path dependency.

The multiplicity of institutional configurations referred to above is an example of multistability. Multistability implies that more than one state/institutional configuration may be stable. Structures which are intermediate between the stable steady states are themselves not necessarily stable.

1.4. National systems of innovation and networks

The stability of the institutional configuration corresponding to a particular NSI is probably due to some form of institutional *coherence* or *synergism*. In order to understand this better we can represent an NSI by means of a *network* (or a group of interconnected networks) of institutions, where the interactions represent links between the different nodes of the network. Networks can be of different complexity and intensity of interaction. Furthermore, a transition between different NSIs is likely to imply a radical restructuring of existing networks, determined by a change of the participating institutions and/or of the links between them.

The network concept has been used in different research traditions for various purposes. For example both sociologists (Burt *et al.*, 1983; Callon, 1989, 1992) and political scientists (Wright, 1988) have used the concept in different ways. The considerations that follow are not a review of these different concepts but rely predominantly on the ideas of Callon *et al.* We shall consider networks generally as having three poles: a scientific pole, a techno-industrial one and a market pole. In our case we might add a defence pole. In the network actors exchange intermediaries, which can be capital goods, disembodied information or documents of any kind, technical artifacts, trained personnel and their skills, and funds supporting innovation. Actors may have to perform translations on intermediaries in order to reinterpret and divert them from their intended purpose in order to produce new texts, new instruments and new machines.

Networks of these types can converge, disperse or be integrated, and they can be short, long or incomplete. Converging networks are characterized by close links between actors (high connectivity). An actor can at any time mobilize the skills within a strongly converging network without having to embark upon adaptations, translations or costly decodings (Callon, 1990; OECD, 1992, pp. 82–3). In dispersed networks, which have low density, translations are required but are not yet firmly in place. It is difficult for actors to mobilize the rest of the network. Long networks span the range of activities from basic research to users uninterruptedly. Short networks cover only a part of the range but are not incomplete. In incomplete networks one or more poles are either missing or underdeveloped.

Using slightly more economic terminology one could say that actors

perform activities (transformation of inputs into outputs) and exchange intermediaries in order to coordinate their own and other institutions' activities. The exchange of intermediaries constitutes an important part of the links in a network. A change in existing networks can then be a change in actors, in links and in activities.

Networks by definition must have a minimum of stability, but in the middle or long run they may change, and so they must be analysed dynamically. Thus networks can be static, flexible or in the process of branching out (OECD, 1992; Imai and Baba, 1991). During network changes actors fluctuate between attachment and detachment. The former is related to competence, procedural rationality, limited yet perfect information, predictability and incremental innovation, existing technological trajectories. The latter is related to flexibility, uncertainty, risk, variable factor combinations, radical innovation and market creation.

A very important question arises here about the efficiency and the stability of network structures. Efficiency refers to the transformation of the existing resources of a country into successful innovations. More specifically, an NSI will be efficient to the extent that it achieves its intended goal(s) with the minimum possible use of resources. Stability refers to the persistence of a given NSI in presence of fluctuations in the external environment. The two concepts are not synonymous nor are they entirely unconnected. A stable NSI cannot be extremely inefficient for very long but needs not be the 'best' in order to survive for quite reasonable periods of time. The conditions leading to efficiency/stability are among the most important aspects of an NSI.

The previous problems can be analysed in terms of the internal interactions of the network. Each institution involved in the network produces some form of generalized output, which does not have to be conceived here in a strict economic sense. For example, output can be laws, financial packages, the outcome of an R&D project or programme etc. The output of each institution is then used as an input by one (or more) other institutions in the network. The network can then be expected to be stable if the output of each institution constitutes an *appropriate* input for the other institutions.

We can note here that the stability of a network is related to the stability of the environment in which it is embedded. A very stable environment will lead to very stable networks and vice versa. Furthermore, changes in networks can take place in different ways. For example, there can be a change in actors, activities and links or in some of them only. These different types of changes may be extended to all the network or involve only a part of it. Examples of adaptation strategies to an environmental change could then be: (a) the same actors preserve the same links, but perform different activities; (b) the same links are preserved by different actors performing the same activities; and (c) new links are established by new actors performing a modified version of the old activities.

Two concepts are relevant in this context. The first is that of *technological system* (Carlsson and Stankiewicz, 1991; Carlsson, 1992). Such a system is defined as a network of agents interacting in a specific technology area under a particular institutional infrastructure for the purpose of generating, diffusing and utilizing technological knowledge. The second is that of

Techno Economic Network (TEN) (Callon *et al.*, 1990; Laredo, 1991). A TEN is defined as a coordinated set of heterogeneous actors – laboratories, technical research centres, financial organizations, users and public authorities, which participate collectively in the development and diffusion of innovations, and which organizes, via numerous interactions, the relationship between research and the market-place. Both of these concepts stress the interactions between the units of the economic system and are related more or less directly to the concept of network.

1.5. Convergence, divergence and NSI

The concept of NSI implies that inter-country differences in innovative performance, procedures and structures are greater than the intra-country differences of the same variables. In turn, these differences can be related to differential barriers to the flow of information, artefacts, people etc. between different nation states as compared to the barriers internal to each of them. Furthermore, NSIs show varying performance (rates of economic growth, trade performance, etc.) and a very high degree of institutional specificity. We can, therefore, characterize different NSIs in terms of their asymmetries at the levels of structure and performance.

Some scholars have argued that recent trends towards internationalization and globalization could diminish the national specificity of innovation systems and, in the long run, make the same concept of NSI meaningless. However, the position taken here is that, while these trends could lead to some degree of convergence, they would not necessarily lead to a complete homogeneity of the various NSIs.

Consider, for example, the consequences of the fact that differences in performance create inducements for change for the less successful NSIs. In other words, an innovating country achieving low rates of economic growth is likely to 'observe' the structure and behaviour of the more successful NSIs and to imitate them to a certain extent. An example of such an induced diffusion of practices is the attempt by other countries to imitate Japanese procedures of quality control and just-in-time. While some form of behaviour may diffuse, it is also possible to achieve similar outcomes by different means, as the concept of multistability implies, and as numerous examples demonstrate. Therefore, even forms of imitation and diffusion induced by differences in performance do not necessarily lead to complete homogeneity and convergence.

More fundamentally, the degree of homogeneity/asymmetry among NSIs is determined by the balance between convergence and divergence in the world economic system. Imitation, diffusion, technology transfer and trade are phenomena which contribute to convergence. On the other hand, innovations do not spring up at random but originate in particular places. The economic rewards for such innovations tend to remain, sometimes for a long time, in the country/NSI which created them. Hence, innovation creates heterogeneity/asymmetry/divergence while imitation/technology transfer/ diffusion and trade lead to convergence/homogenization. Whether the world system tends to converge or to diverge depends on the balance between these two trends and not only on the increase of phenomena leading to convergence. For example, it is quite conceivable that an increased rate of innovation (carrying increased divergence with it) will accompany the growing internationalization that the world economy is experiencing. The outcome would be determined by the balance between the increases in the rates of convergence and divergence.

This situation can be represented in more general terms. Following Prigogine and Stengers (1984), we can classify all the phenomena taking place in an economic system as 'generalized forces' and 'fluxes' (p. 135). Generalized forces (for example, chemical reactions, innovations etc) produce *local* outcomes and give rise to asymmetries. In this way generalized forces create a diffusion potential, which 'causes' fluxes. The morphology of the system and its degree of heterogeneity are determined by the balance between forces and fluxes.

These considerations can be given a more concrete form by reference to the concepts of technological system and of Techno Economic Network (TEN). The technological systems studied by Carlsson (1992) tend to show a high degree of technological rather than national specificity. To the extent that the productive system of an economy can be represented by a set of technological systems, one can expect similar patterns of development internationally. These would lead to a growing international convergence, although national specificity would still exist at the level of institutions and policies. A similar situation exists concerning the use of networks in comparative policy studies (Wilks and Wright, 1987), where a greater emphasis is placed on inter-sectoral differences than on inter-country differences. On the other hand, TENs contain actors who are likely to have different degrees of national specificity. Thus industrial firms are likely to experience greater pressures towards international convergence than are universities or government research laboratories.

These two examples add some flesh to the more general considerations about convergence and divergence presented above. However, while it is possible to establish in general that growing pressures towards convergence do not necessarily lead to a greater degree of convergence, the particular mechanisms by which convergence and divergence are obtained deserve greater attention and are rich in policy implications.

It is also possible to say something more definite about the future development of NSIs. One of us (Saviotti, 1988, 1991, 1992) has argued that the growth in output variety of an economic system is a necessary requirement for the long-term continuation of economic growth and development. This growing output variety is generated by means of specialization and of the emergence of completely new products. The presence of an ever-increasing output variety creates increasing possibilities for the specialization and differentiation of NSIs. Hence, if the rate of growth of output variety is at least as great as that of diffusion/convergence, constant or growing asymmetries may remain among NSIs in the world economic system.

Asymmetries are likely to remain more pronounced at the level of institutional structures than of performance. Countries with considerably different political systems can achieve similar economic performance. Even if firms in these countries were to acquire very similar practices, the state institutions in each of them would still show a very high degree of specificity. Although such a statement is difficult to make in any quantitative sense, the degree of asymmetry among institutional structures is likely to remain higher than among the performance of NSIs. In summary, the concept of National System of Innovation and some of its features follow naturally from the foundations of evolutionary theories, while they could not be foreseen on the basis of orthodox economics.

Naturally, in order to be able to exploit it fully, we need to articulate more completely the concept of NSI. This goal can be achieved both by *ex-ante* analysis of the concept itself and by studies of particular NSIs. The following is an example of the latter approach.

1.6. Application of the NSI concept to the UK

In this section, we briefly describe the UK NSI before considering in more detail how the concepts developed within the NSI approach can illuminate current developments within the UK arising from changes on the international security scene.

1.6.1. Overview of structure

As we discuss below, changes were introduced into the machinery for British science and technology policy following the April 1992 elections. The significance of these changes is not yet clear. We therefore describe here the position prior to 1992 and then update as far as is possible.

The structure of British government machinery for science and technology (S&T), at least until 1992, could be described as decentralized or, at best, loosely coordinated. There has been no overall R&D or S&T or innovation budget: each ministry functions largely autonomously, with decisions about levels and directions of R&D/S&T being made within the framework of each ministry's own goals. A web of inter-departmental committees, up to and including cabinet level, does, however, attempt to coordinate activities across the board. There has been continuous resistance to the idea of a centralizing Ministry of Science/R&D for reasons to do with beliefs about clear lines off accountability and the view that science is not in itself a primary function of government (and therefore not requiring its own ministry) in the same way as, say, defence or education (Gummett, 1980).

On the industrial side, firms generally function independently of government; this is true even of utilities (electricity, gas, water etc), which in many other countries are part of the state sector but in Britain have been steadily privatized. The state sector in the UK is now quite small. British firms are frequently criticized for under-spending on innovation, compared with their main competitors, and for thinking too much in the short term. This is not true of certain sectors (for example pharmaceuticals; also those related to defence, where however, it is mainly government money that is spent on R&D). Whatever the reasons, it is clear that in manufacturing, despite certain strengths (Williams, 1991), British industry is generally weak, and this is especially so in key 'bread and butter' sectors such as consumer electronics, cars, telecommunications, machine tools and mechanical engineering generally.

It is important to note that, under Britain's liberal economic regime, including the high degree to which firms are quoted on the stock market, firms are liable to take-over with much greater ease than in, say, France (where family ownership and networks of relations with banks impede hostile takeovers), Germany (banks) and Japan (Keiretsu). This is often said to be an important factor in 'short-termism'.

The third important sector is higher education institutions (HEIs). These comprise some forty-five older universities and a slightly larger number of polytechnics, most of which were recently upgraded to universities. These, together with research council institutes (many co-located at HEIs), perform the bulk of the basic/strategic research and are, of course, the main training ground for actors in the NSI. In general, the universities aim at non-vocational education. Moreover, British education is highly specialized, which some would say builds rigidities into the NSI. Further down the system in the schools, science and maths have been underemphasized in the past and British society/culture generally values practical and engineering skills less than some of its competitors.

Britain also has an active body of independent contract research organizations (Duckworth 1991). There are said to be more of these in the UK, pro rata, than in any other European country. These bodies have the potential to act as key agents in the process of technology transfer, because of their regular contact with a wide range of organizations and the fact that their services are drawn upon precisely because firms recognize that they need to 'import' capabilities that they lack.

Figure 1.1 shows the main flows of funds for research and development, distinguishing between sources of funds and performers of R&D. Figure 1.3 shows the relations between the main sets of actors.

1.6.2. Finance

As Figure 1.2 shows, government funding for research and development is dominated by that from the Ministry of Defence (MOD). This has been true for decades and remains so despite an active debate over the past few years which seems now to have reached a consensus that much of what has been classified for statistical purposes as defence R&D is not in fact true R&D according to the OECD's Frascati definitions. (Williams, 1992; National Audit Office, 1991). This non-R&D expenditure has, nevertheless, been for innovation-related activities, and so the precise outcome of this debate need not concern us since our focus is on innovation rather than purely on R&D.

It is worth adding that, in the past but less so today, there was a heavy emphasis on atomic energy and aviation (both, of course, defence-related) and generally on high technology. The emphasis, in Ergas's terms, has been mission-oriented rather than diffusion-oriented (Ergas, 1986). In this respect, commentators have noted at various times in recent decades a

SECTORS PROVIDING THE FUNDS
(£billion)

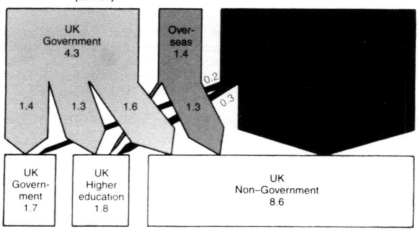

SECTORS CARRYING OUT THE WORK

Figure 1.1   Total R&D performed in the United Kingdom (GERD) in each sector according to source of finance, 1990 (Total GERD in 1990 = £12.1 bn)

Source: Cabinet Office, *Annual Review of Government Funded Research and Development* 1992 (London, HMSO, 1992)

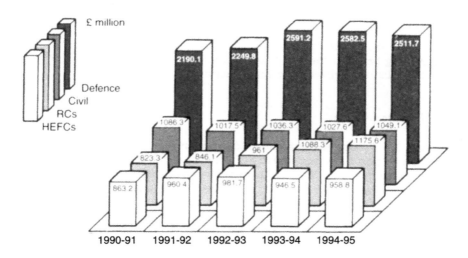

Figure 1.2   Trends in planned government R&D expenditure 1990–1 to 1994–5 (cash terms)

Notes: HEFCs = Higher Education Funding Councils; RCs = Research Councils

Source: See Figure 1.1

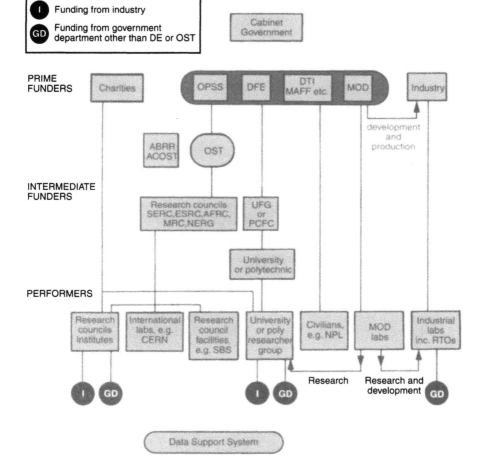

Figure 1.3 Organization of research in the UK

Notes:

OPSS	= Office of Public Service and Science	AFRC	= Agriculture and Food Research Council
DFE	= Department for Education		
DTI	= Department of Trade and Industry	MRC	= Medical Research Council
MAFF	= Ministry of Agriculture, Fisheries and Food	NERC	= Natural Environment Research Council
MOD	= Ministry of Defence	UFC	= Universities Funding Council
ABRC	= Advisory Board for the Research Councils	PCFC	= Polytechnics and Colleges Funding Council
ACOST	= Advisory Council on Science and Technology	CERN	= Centre Européene de la Recherche Nucléaire
OST	= Office of Science and Technology	NPL	= National Physical Laboratory
SERC	= Science and Engineering Research Council	RTOs	= Research and Technology Organizations
ESRC	= Economic and Social Research Council	SRS	= Synchrotron Radiation Source (Daresbury Laboratory)

Source: See Figure 1.1

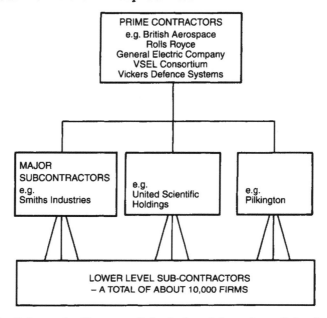

Figure 1.4   Schematic diagram of the industrial section of the defence element in the British NSI

distinct mismatch between the levels of investment in R&D in different industrial sectors and the actual economic significance of those sectors (Williams, 1991, quoting Maddock (1975)).

1.6.3. Policies

In terms of *policies for innovation*, key features of the UK scene in recent years include:

(i)   The striking separation between the development of technologies for civil and military purposes – probably carried further than in any other European country (ACOST, 1989); and the relative increase in support for military R&D in recent years.

(ii) A variety of initiatives to develop new technologies, often at the same time, integrating different sectors – for example the National Electronics Research Initiatives and other 'Advanced Technology Programmes' in, for example, advanced robotics, high-temperature superconductivity and safety-critical software; the 'Small Firms Merit Award for Research'; the LINK Programme for encouraging joint industrial–university research; and Alvey, the fifth-generation computer and IT programme, involving collaboration between government, industry and HEIs. (Details are given in successive editions of the Department of Trade and Industry entry in Cabinet Office, 1991.) It is clear, however, that the main source of long-term support for relatively applied areas has been MOD. Examples include the aircraft sector in general (Gummett,

1992), support over many years for electronics from the Controllerate of Valves and Devices and its successor bodies (Dickson 1983), and as a more recent and specific case, support for gallium arsenide technology, which is now coming into commercial application.

(iii) The Thatcher years saw a reaction against government intervention in, and support for, the private sector. Support for so-called 'near market' R&D was sharply reduced. The Department of Trade and Industry (DTI), especially from 1988 under successive secretaries of state (Young, Ridley and Lilley), refocused on policies that, it was hoped, would stimulate 'enterprise'. This entailed a move in the direction of what Ergas (1986) has called enabling or diffusion-oriented policies. (See also Walker, 1991; Saviotti, 1991; Edgerton and Hughes 1989). Even the British Technology Group, successor to the National Research Development Corporation (a body set up in 1949 to finance the step between invention and the market-place) was privatized.

(iv) At the same time, there has been a marked shift towards taking advantage of European Community research and development programmes, for which British firms and HEIs have been among the most energetic bidders. Thus, great interest has been shown in the EC Framework programmes and in other EC programmes (mainly under the Structural Fund) that support innovation (in the latter case through such measures as training schemes or regional aid) (Findlay, 1991). At the industrial level, too, firms (civil and defence) anticipated the Single Market by engaging in substantial cross-border mergers and alliances, thus internationalizing their technology and marketing bases, a point we will come back to later in discussing how 'national' a national innovation system can be.

1.6.4. *The Office of Public Service and Science*

To complete this review, we should mention the surprise establishment, following the April 1992 election, of a new Office of Public Service and Science (OPSS), within the Cabinet Office, and headed by a cabinet minister. The OPSS is served by an Office of Science and Technology (OST), based on a strengthened version of the previous Cabinet Office Science and Technology Secretariat and headed by the chief scientific adviser to the government. A White Paper, spelling out the powers of, and policies to be pursued by, the OPSS was in preparation at the time of writing, and until it is published one cannot say how far the traditional British machinery of government in this field has really been changed. All that is clear thus far is that responsibility for the research councils has been transferred from the former Department of Education and Science (now the Department for Education) to the OPSS. Whether the new Office will really have a strong central coordinating role, such as would permit it, for example, to pull together the industrial investments of the DTI and the MOD, remains unclear but seems unlikely.

1.7. The UK defence sector and the NSI

We can illustrate certain features of the British NSI with reference to recent developments in the field of defence procurement. The UK organizes the development, design and production of defence equipment through an arm of the Ministry of Defence called the procurement Executive. Set up in the early 1970s, this body assumed responsibility from the former separate service and supply ministries, and from the Atomic Energy Authority, for all areas of conventional and nuclear weapons R&D and procurement. It in turn responds to operational requirements set by the Defence Staffs in the Ministry of Defence who act as 'customers' for research programmes and development projects.

The Procurement Executive is the largest single customer of British industry, with a budget of £10,298m in the Supply Estimates for 1992–3, of which £2,769m net was scheduled for R&D. Its weight within the NSI is therefore considerable, even allowing for what (as mentioned earlier) now seems to be the acknowledged fact that the declared R&D figures contain a substantial element of spending which, although innovation related, is not R&D according to the OECD's Frascati definition. Its 1992–3 budget for research (as distinct from development) of £474m is comparable in size to that of the main civil governmental sources of research funds such as the research councils. The justification of this level of spending has traditionally been couched in terms of a wide range of defence objectives and a preference for a high degree of independence in meeting the equipment needs of those objectives.

The relations between the Procurement Executive and the defence industry underwent a significant change from the mid-1980s. The government began, within a framework of Thatcherism, to place increased emphasis on 'value for money' in all areas of public spending, defence not excluded. Steps were taken to shift the balance between cost-plus and fixed-price contracts; to increase the number of contracts that were awarded competitively; and to require firms to put their own money at risk over defence contracts. Steps were also taken to extend these reforms to the European level.

The result has been a toughening of the competitive environment for defence firms, and a growing volume of criticism from many industrialists of the ministry for its alleged failure to realize the need for partnership and stability in the long-term development and maintenance of technological capabilities. It is clear that, in the perception of industry, the old relations (networks) of trust and cooperation between themselves and the Ministry of Defence had been replaced by a more straightforward commercial relationship. The moves in 1990–2 to establish a Defence Research Agency (comprising the four main non-nuclear research establishments of MOD), operating relatively independently of the ministry under a contractual relationship, and free to compete with industry for defence research contracts, exacerbated this tension (Gummett, 1991a - POST report).

In response to these pressures, but also to a general overcapacity on the European level, and to the indirect effects on the defence industry of moves towards the Single Market, British firms have been among the most active in another key development of recent years, the international restructuring of the arms industry, leading to the formation of new, international networks of firms, linked by complementary needs for risk capital, technology, and access to national markets. It should be emphasized that international restructuring (as opposed to mere collaboration) has come to the defence sector later than to the rest of industry, with defence still being regarded as a sector of unusual strategic significance by governments, who therefore remain active in policing foreign interventions. Hence, in part, the interest in applying the NSI concept to the defence sector, since it presents the possibility of some sharp test cases.

This international restructuring has been particularly active in the electronics and aerospace sectors. Restructuring of the warship and land-equipment industries has, in the UK as elsewhere, tended so far to remain within national boundaries, although even this is changing: plans are now afoot for an Anglo–French frigate; and in land systems, the British GKN and French GIAT are studying the possibility of a joint venture to seek common solutions for the British and French markets for armoured fighting vehicles.

One pattern of behaviour has been of major defence contractors taking over second-tier firms elsewhere (Walker and Gummett, 1989). Examples include British Aerospace's purchase of Ballast Nedam (a Dutch construction company with interests in Saudi Arabia which had potential to underpin BAe's support facilities in connection with major arms deals with Saudi Arabia); BAe's purchase of Steinheil Optronik (Germany); Plessey's acquisition of the Electronics Systems Division of Singer, of Nash Engineering and of Sippican (all USA), and its bid for Harris Corporation (blocked by the Pentagon); and GEC's purchase of Astronics (part of Lear Sigler, USA) and of a significant holding (along with Daimler Benz) in Matra (France).

Of greater significance, however, have been the moves to establish joint-venture companies among the major players on the European scene, particularly between British and French, and French and German, firms. British Aerospace and Thomson-CSF (numbers one and two in defence sales in Europe) planned a merger of their missile divisions, only to postpone it at the last moment (and BAe are reported to be again exploring the possibility of some international arrangement for their missile division). GEC-Marconi (number three in Europe) and Aérospatiale (number six) have reached an agreement on missiles. GEC has another agreement with Dassault on avionics and in May 1991 announced a plan with Thomson-CSF jointly to develop and make radars for the generation of aircraft after the European Fighter Aircraft (EFA). More recently, BAe and Dassault have begun studies of a post-EFA airframe which, if it progressed far, would have organizational consequences. In aeroengines, where international collaboration has a longer history, Rolls-Royce is involved in multiple ventures with European and US firms. Between France and Germany, finally, Aérospatiale and MBB (Germany) have a longstanding missile collaboration and have also now merged their helicopter interests in a joint venture, Eurocopter.

These industrial networking moves have occurred in parallel with a shift at governmental level under which the focus of the UK's competition policy has moved from the national to the international, and especially European, level. This has been reflected in two main ways: first, through the 1987 Anglo–French reciprocal purchasing initiative, under which both countries have taken steps to encourage firms from the other country to bid for defence contracts; and second, through the 1988 Action Plan of the

Independent European Programme Group (IEPG) (comprising the European members of NATO, plus France, minus Iceland) which aimed towards a European free-trade area in defence equipment. Britain has also joined in the IEPG's 'EUCLID' programme of collaborative defence research projects (Walker and Gummett, 1989). More recently still, it has lent its weight to US proposals for improved trade within the entire NATO alliance.

So far, it has to be said, none of these initiatives has had much effect. But evidence from the government's attitude towards successive attempts by GEC to take over Plessey go some way to support the claim of a shift in outlook. Thus, a bid in 1986 by GEC for Plessey was opposed by the MOD on the grounds that the resulting firm would hold 75 per cent of MOD electronics contracts (Monopolies and Mergers Commission, 1986). Yet in 1989 a joint GEC–Siemens bid for Plessey was successful, and in 1990 GEC was allowed to buy Ferranti Defence Systems, resulting in a degree of national concentration in this sector probably higher than that which MOD had blocked in 1986. The official explanation of this change of heart was that by 1989 competition on a European scale was held to be an adequate substitute for competition purely within the UK (though there was also some suspicion that settling the future of the troubled Ferranti company was crucial to resolving the vexed question of the contract for the radar for EFA, without which, in turn, the future of the aircraft as a whole might have been jeopardized). In any event, the rules of the game for British defence firms, in respect of concentration and competition, do appear to have changed in the latter 1980s.

In discussing changes in the rules of the game, and the composition of networks, we should not overlook the European Commission, which has recently begun to flex its muscles over defence issues, particularly in relation to defence industrial affairs. It is notable that major firms (BAe, Aéro-spatiale, for example) are putting considerable effort into liaison with the Commission, through dedicated staff and, in some cases, Brussels offices. Parts of the Commission clearly fall within these firms' networks, even if only defensively – in the sense of staving off unwanted interventions – though in the case of aerospace, as we shall see in a moment, there is also evidence of more positive lobbying.

One important issue will be how the Commission would respond to possible claims that support for defence R&D could be used as a means of state aid for industry in ways that might be regarded as unfair. Also notable was a report in November 1991 that the EC Competition Commissioner, Sir Leon Brittan, would henceforth be scrutinizing defence contract awards to see whether the national security exemption under Article 223 of the Treaty of Rome was being used as 'a device to protect so-called dual-use production with primarily civil applications' (Reed, 1991).

Given the reluctance of various governments to rescind Article 223, there may nevertheless be scope to restrict its application to a narrower range of unequivocally defence-related items, thus extending the scope of EU competition and public procurement policy into defence contracts, even if not to all such contracts. Such a step would bring these contracts within a legal framework, representing a much strong regime than that of the IEPG.

It remains to be seen whether such an outcome is achievable in the present climate, and it should also be recalled that historically, free trade has always been advocated by those most likely to benefit from it, which in this case would be the countries of Europe with the strongest defence industries.

A particular sector which the Commission is seeking authority to support is aerospace. The Commission argues that aerospace is exceptional in that it is the only industry where the state provides more than 50 per cent of R&D expenditure, and that:

Taking account of the consequences of the reduction in defence budgets on research in the military area and the technology transfer within dual undertakings, it could be useful for the sector as a whole, if the Community, while respecting the principle of subsidiarity, were to support increased research in those areas common to both the military and the civil. [Commission of the European Communities, 1990, para. 5.2 and Annex 6]

Appeals for help have been voiced by representatives of the aerospace industries in the UK an France. Thus, *The Guardian* published on 4 October 1991 a letter, dated 17 June 1991, from Sir Roland Smith, then chairman of British Aerospace, to the then leader of the UK Opposition, Neil Kinnock, in which he complained of the damage that MOD policies were doing to British manufacturing industry. Similarly, Henri Martre, chairman of Aérospatiale, called for greater EC support for the aerospace industry through research and technology contracts (Betts, 1991). Further fruit of this activity appeared in April 1992, in a Commission document that called for various measures to support the sector, one of which was the inclusion of the field of aeronautics and air transport in the Fourth Framework Programme (1994–8) and substantial increases in civil expenditure on research and technology to compensate for the effects of reductions in defence spending (Commission of the European Communities, 1992).

Another feature of changes in defence innovation networks arises from the structure of defence production and the distribution within it of relevant knowledge and capabilities which itself is a product of the path dependency of the firms concerned. Increasingly, the prime contractor, at the top of a hierarchy of subcontractors, functions as design and management authority, systems integrator and final assembler. Detailed understanding of the technologies that are to be integrated and assembled lies primarily with the subcontractors, and the lengthy processes that go into acquiring it make it implausible that the prime contractor could bypass its suppliers. The complexity of the technologies that make up sub-assemblies means that the fraction of value-added by the suppliers is growing (Edmonds *et al.*, 1990 estimate it to be generally more than 50 per cent), increasing the dependence of the prime on its suppliers and squeezing its profit margins. Just such a concern was voiced by the chairman of Vickers Defence Systems (the British tank manufacturer) who, at a conference on manufacturing strategies in May 1990, warned that companies faced a range of threats, 'not only from their direct competitors but also from suppliers developing technologies that form the core of the final product' (Leadbeater, 1990). This is particularly an issue in electronics, where economies of scale give an increasing advantage to the major civil suppliers over small defence suppliers, and where it has already been accepted for some years that, in the field of Very Large Scale Integration, military electronics must use civil components, albeit in modified form. As budgetary pressures grow, the appeal of defence equipment that is developed on the back of civil technologies will also grow. So too will the risk to defence firms that civilian holders of technology will move sideways into defence markets. To a degree this is already happening, as shown by IBM's success (teamed with an established defence contractor) in winning the contract to manage the electronics package in the EH101 helicopter project.

1.8. Conclusions

In this chapter there is a tension between the general character of the first part and the more applied character of the second part. The applicability of the theoretical concepts of the first part to the analysis of the UK NSI is for the moment limited. We are stretching their interpretive capacity in order to develop them and to prepare a better set of tools for subsequent studies. Such concepts can lead, for example, to the establishment more accurate maps of existing networks and to the study of the factors determining their stability.

These brief observations on developments within the dominant part of the British NSI, that concerned with defence research and development and production, raise a number of points that we can now put in more formal terms within the framework of the NSI approach. The first question to be asked about such a system concerns the separation of civilian and military networks. As has been shown before, at present they are largely separated in the UK. Doubts have been expressed about this arrangement and there are people in the MOD arguing for more use of dual-use approaches. In this situation intra-network links are obviously stronger and much more developed than inter-network links. Defence firms tend to operate in networks comprising hierarchies of contractors, many of whom are accustomed to working with each other over time. In particular, the prime contractors hardly change over long periods. Another important dimension of the networks is the relations between firms and relevant parts of the MOD (especially technical directorates and research establishments). In the past, these were often said to be (too) close and cosy. The second question concerns the stability and permanence of networks. The answer has already been anticipated above. The main actors, links and activities have remained the same, with the only changes taking place in the lower hierarchical layers of contractors.

Existing networks have been stable for a long time, but have they been efficient? The question is a complex one, and there are at least two parts to it: first, how 'good' are the goals of the networks, and second, how efficiently have existing goals been achieved? Both parts raise considerable difficulties when the goals of the network(s) are anything other than the production of a tangible and constant output. On balance one could say that, although efficiency was not considered ideal, as is demonstrated by the MOD procurement reforms, the British R&D/technology defence networks are close to European best practice. Concerning the setting of the goals, while in the past these may have been unchallenged for a long time, the great changes taking place in the international environment are likely to demand the setting of new ones.

The next question concerns the inducements and barriers to change. Changes have already taken place and more are likely to follow. For example, there has been criticism in the past of the difficulty of entry for new firms, and the MOD has taken steps to encourage more small firms to work as subcontractors. The changes in procurement introduced by the MOD were intended to weaken established links and to create greater competitiveness. Perhaps the most relevant change in recent years has arisen from internationalization. Attempts to open up the European arms market; companies' pre-emptive steps against the effects of 1992; and the globalization of technology have led to the formation of international networks on a greatly increased scale.

Existing networks within the UK span predominantly the MOD and the contractor firms, with more limited links to the academic system. Most of the R&D performed in the defence sector is development. On the other hand incipient European networks are mostly confined to academic institutions and to civil R&D/technology, with secondary participation by firms and a limited commitment to defence R&D. Both types of networks are incomplete, since they contain some of the poles in a very limited manner, and short, since they do not encompass the whole range of activities from basic research to development. This character of the defence-related networks may change in future if civil technology becomes a more frequent source of military technologies and if more technologies become dependent on basic research.

The actual changes which have taken place have arisen, and will arise in future, from the balance between inducements and barriers. In this sense there are important questions about the scope available to firms as they formulate strategies to cope with the downturn in defence spending. Their existing networks have tended to lock them in, at the levels of marketing, sales and production standards, to government (specifically, the Procurement Executive but also to foreign governments). In Britain, perhaps more than in some other countries, the break during the Thatcher years in the old cosy relations between firms and the MOD may have prepared them better for the harsher environment in which they find themselves now, but the fact remains that in selling defence equipment their customers are governments, who differ in many respects from commercial customers. To the extent that the colder climate under Thatcher caused some firms at least to broaden their horizons and diversify away from defence, they will now be in a stronger position.

Moving from a position of being geared to supply only governments raises various issues of path dependence in terms of technological capabilities acquired (and their applicability in other markets), the 'unlearning' of production procedures and standards appropriate to defence and the learning of new ones, and (crucially) the marketing orientation and skills. These transformations of the knowledge, technology and marketing bases are further complicated by the technological challenges mentioned above. For the prime contractors, especially, these require the formation of new networks in order to be able to incorporate technologies that fall outside the scope of the prime itself. Managing their relations with their suppliers in ways that both successfully import the necessary technologies without at the same time leading to undue dependence on the supplier (or that could even put the supplier in a position to turn the tables on the prime and itself bid for the prime role) has become a key management task. The complexity of escaping from the consequences of path dependency, of building new networks and of acquiring new codified and tacit skills generally militates against easy diversification away from defence, let alone complete conversion of production at the plant level from defence to civil markets.

The international dimension of this process adds further complexity. It cannot be avoided for several reasons. One is the potential role of the European Commission as a player in the networks, if only on the regulatory rather than the promotional side. More fundamentally, however, the process of concentration in the European defence sector has not yet gone as far as in the USA. Too many players are chasing too few orders, so survival demands collaboration in some form or another. In addition, the smaller size of European orders demands a reduction in the number of production lines if anything like US economies of scale are to be achieved. The politics of these networks further demand not only the satisfaction of the major firms and their governments but also the smaller ones. Without the latter, European-wide orders for many defence products would again become too small to achieve significant economies of scale. In that event, smaller countries would ask themselves why they should buy expensive European products when they could buy cheaper ones from America. The result would be to undermine the European market entirely.

One of the interesting features of the UK government's response to these developments has been its carelessness (at least until now) about the need to retain a British technology base in more than a few areas of extreme security sensitivity (such as nuclear weapons, cryptography, and chemical and biological defences). Its emphasis instead has been on obtaining value for money for the taxpayer, with at least a rhetorical willingness to go abroad to find it, whatever the risk to the stability and survival of the NSI. This can be contrasted with, say, the French approach (Hébert 1991; Chesnais 1992) or the Japanese approach to innovation more generally, described by Friedman and Samuels as being one of 'indigenisation, diffusion and nurturing' of key technologies (Friedman and Samuels, 1992). There have been some informal signs of a partial change of heart on this point, at least to the extent of considering the longer-term implications of any individual procurement decision, but the overall UK philosophy remains unchanged.

Within this policy framework, there is a problem over how the Ministry of Defence is to maintain technological dynamism in the defence field. To the extent that the NSI has, at least for defence purposes, functioned fairly effectively in the past, how is that effectiveness to be maintained into the future? How should the MOD intervene in the burgeoning new industrial networks to protect a national interest that is defined in such a minimalist way? How should it respond to arguments (POST report) that support of the civil technological base is now an essential part of maintaining capabilities relevant to defence purposes? After all, given the separateness of the military and civil parts of the NSI hitherto, any military support for civil activity would represent a significant change.

Again, international comparisons are interesting. In France, for instance, the house journal of the counterpart to the Procurement Executive recently argued that

Le temps n'est plus où les contraintes de secret et de spécificité conduisaient la Défense à mener des recherches isolément, en espérant, peut-être, des 'retombées' civiles. Les conditions économiques et techniques d'aujourd'hui imposent de mener recherches et développements en pensant dualité: ce que je cherche n'existe-t-il pas ailleurs? ce que je trouverai ne sera-t-il pas utile ailleurs?

This same theme of supporting 'dual-use' technology has been taken up strongly in the United States, both in the Office of Technology Assessment (OTA, 1989) and in a major academic study at Harvard (Alic *et al.*, 1992), though a policy framework in the USA similar to that in the UK nevertheless prevails. (See also POST report.)

There has, nevertheless, been some movement in the UK. The then procurement minister said in September 1991

In the future I see the MOD making increased use of commercial off-the-shelf technology wherever we can. Our R&D will be increasingly targeted on producing military derivatives of basically civil technology, and on those areas where civil technology is not suitable or simply does not exist. In the constantly extending border area between military and civil technology there will be scope for MOD to become a more eclectic – though discriminating – patron and customer of work with potential for civil application. [Clark, 1991]

So far, however, there is little sign of action to match these words. Here is an example of where, if the new OPSS is given the means to intervene, it could attempt to draw together some existing research and policy-making networks in a bid to develop areas of technology that could serve both defence and civil purposes.

As a final conclusion, it is worth adding that a key need for future research is to develop the fragments of international comparison that were given above into a more sustained analysis. The concept of multistability suggests that different countries will seek different solutions to the same environmental stimuli. We have given some hints of these in national responses to defence cutbacks. Turning these hints into a full analysis would be a worthwhile task for the future.

References

Abernathy, W.J. and Utterback, J.M. (1975) 'A Dynamic Model of Process and Product Innovation', *Omega*, 3, no. 6, 639–56.

Abernathy, W.J. and Utterback, J.M. (1978) 'Patterns of industrial innovation', *Technology Review*, (June/July), 41–7.

ACOST (Advisory Council of Science and Technology) (1989), *Defence R&D: A National Resource*, London, HMSO.

Alic, J. *et al.* (1992) *Beyond Spinoff: Military and Commercial Technologies in a Changing World*, Boston, Harvard Business School Press.

Allen, P.M. (1982) 'The genesis of structure in social systems: the paradigm of self organisation', *Theory and Explanation in Archeology*, New York, Academic Press.

Arthur, W.B. (1983) 'Competing technologies and lock-in by historical events: the dynamics of allocation under increasing returns', International Institute for Applied Systems Analysis, Paper WP-83-90, Luxenburg, Austria.

Arthur, W.B. (1988) 'Competing technologies: an overview' in G. Dosi, *et al.* (eds), *Technical Change and Economic Theory*, London, Pinter.

Arthur, W.B. (1989) 'Competing technologies, increasing returns, and lock-in by historical events', *The Economic Journal*, 99, 116–31.

Ashby, W.R. (1956) *Introduction to Cybernetics*, New York, Wiley.

Betts, P. (1991) 'EC urged to back aerospace industry', *Financial Times*, 7 June.

Burt, R.S., Christman, K.P. and Kilburn, H.C. (1983) *Applied Network Analysis*, Beverly Hills, Sage.

Cabinet Office (1991) *Annual Review of Government Funded Research and Development 1991*, London, HMSO.

Callon, M. (1989) *La Science et ses Reseaux: Genese et Circulation des Faits Scientifiques*, Paris, La Decouverte.

Callon, M. (1992) 'The dynamics of techno-economic networks' in Coombs, R., Saviotti, P. and Walsh, V. (eds), *Technical Change and Company Strategies*, London, Academic Press.

Callon, M., Laredo, P. and Rabeharisoa, V. (1990) *The Management and Evaluation of Technological Programmes and the Dynamics of Techno-economic Networks: the Case of AFME*, Paris, Centre de Sociologie de l'Innovation, Ecole des Mines.

Carlsson, B. and Stankiewicz, R. (1991) 'On the nature, function and composition of technological systems', *Journal of Evolutionary Economics*, 1, 93–118.

Carlsson, B. (1992) *Technological Systems and Economic Development Potential: Four Swedish Case Studies*, presented at the International Joseph A. Schumpeter Conference, Kyoto, 19–22 August.

Chesnais, F. and Serfati, C. (1992) *L'armement en France: genèse, ampleur et coût d'une industrie*, Paris, Nathan.

Clark, A. (1991) Speech on 'Defence and the high technology industries', London, World Economic Forum, 4 September. Available from Ministry of Defence as News Release 106/91.

Commission of the European Communities (1990) 'A Competitive European Aeronautical Industry' (Communication from the Commission), Brussels, SEC(90) 1456 final, July.

Commission of the European Communities (1992) 'The European Aircraft Industry: First Assessment and Possible Community Actions' (Communication from the Commission to the Council), Brussels, COM(92) 164 final, April.

Coombs, R., Saviotti, P.P. and Walsh, V. (1987) *Economics and Technological Change*, London, Macmillan.

CSS (Council on Science and Society) (1986) *UK Military R&D*, Oxford, Oxford University Press.

David, P.A. (1975) *Technical Choice, Innovation and Economic Growth*, Cambridge, Cambridge University Press.

Dickson, K. (1983) 'The influence of Ministry of Defence funding on semiconductor research and development in the UK', *Research Policy*, 12, 113–120.

Dosi, G. (1982) 'Technological Paradigms and Technological Trajectories: a Suggested Interpretation of the Determinants and Directions of Technical Change', *Research Policy*, 11.

Dosi, G., Freeman, C., Nelson, R., Soete, L. and Silverberg, G. (eds) (1988) *Technical Change and Economic Theory*, London, Pinter.

Dosi, G., Pavitt, K., Soete, L. (1990) *The Economics of Technical Change and International Trade*, Hemel Hempstead, Harvester Wheatsheaf.

Duckworth, W.E. (1991) 'Science and technology by independent institutes' in Nicholson *et al.*

Edgerton, D. and Hughes, K. (1989) 'The Poverty of Science: a Critical Analysis of Scientific and Industrial Policy Under Mrs. Thatcher', *Public Administration*, 67, 419–33.

Edmonds, M., Hayhurst, G. and Uttley, M. (1990) 'Defence-critical technology, dependence and civil conversion: the challenge to the UK technological base', University of Lancaster, mimeo, p. 9.

Ergas, H. (1986) *Does Technology Policy Matter?*, Paris, OECD.

Findlay, G. (1991) 'International collaboration' in Nicholson *et al.*

Freeman, C. (1982) *The Economics of Industrial Innovation*, London, Pinter.

Freeman, C. (1987) *Technology Policy and Economic Performance*, London, Pinter.

Freeman, C. (1988) 'Japan: a new national system of innovation?' in Dosi *et al.*

Freeman, C. and Lundvall, B.A. (1990) (eds), *Small Countries Facing the Technological Revolution*, London, Pinter.

Friedman, D. and Samuels, R. (1992) 'How to succeed without really flying: the Japanese aircraft industry and Japan's technology ideology', paper presented at National Bureau of Economic Research conference on 'Japan and the US in Pacific Asia', San Diego, April, Massachusetts Institute of Technology, mimeo.

Gummett, P. (1980) *Scientists in Whitehall*, Manchester University Press.

Gummett, P. and Reppy, J. (eds) (1988) *The Relations between Defence and Civil Technologies*, Dordrecht, Kluwer.

Gummett, P. and Walker, W. (1990) 'The industrial and technological consequences of the peace', *RUSI Journal*, 135, Spring 46–52.

Gummett, P. (1991a) 'The evolution of science and technology policy: a UK perspective', *Science and Public Policy*, 18, 31–7.

Gummett, P. (ed.) (1991b) *Future Relations Between Defence and Civil Science and Technology*, A Report for the (UK) Parliamentary Office of Science and Technology, London, Science Policy Support Group, Review Paper No. 2.

Hébert, J.P. (1991) *Stratégie Française et Industrie d'Armement*, Paris, Fondation pour les études de défense nationale.

Imai, K.J. and Baba, Y. (1991) 'Systemic innovations and cross border networks: Transcending markets and hierarchies to create a new techni-economic system', in OECD, *Technology and Productivity: the Challenges for Economic Policy*, Paris.

Laredo P. (1991) 'State intervention in innovation. The role of technological programmes in the emergence of a new composite economic agent: the techno-economic network', presented at the second international workshop, 'Policies and Strategies for Technology in Industrialised Countries', Moscow, May.

Leadbeater, C. (1990) 'Industry urged to speed up R&D', Financial Times, 24 May.

L'Armement: Revue de la Délégation Générale pour l'Armement (1991) No. 29, October, Paris.

Lundvall, B.A. (1985) *Product Innovation and User Producer Interaction*, Aalborg, Aalborg University Press.

Lundvall, B.A. (1986) 'Long Waves and the Uneven Development of Capitalism', paper presented at the International Workshop in Long Term Fluctuations, Sienna.

Lundvall, B.A. (1988) 'Innovation as an interactive process: from user–producer interaction to the national system of innovation' in Dosi *et al.*

Ministry of Defence (1992) *Statement on the Defence Estimates*, London, HMSO, Cm 1981.

36 Pier Paolo Saviotti and Philip Gummett

Monopolies and Mergers Commission, (1986), *The General Electric Company PLC and the Plessey Company PLC: a report on the proposed merger*, London, HMSO.

Mowery, D. and Rosenberg, N. (1979) 'Market demand and innovation', *Research Policy*, 8, 103–53.

National Audit Office (1991) *Classification of Defence Research and Development Expenditure*, London, HMSO, HC 105.

Nelson, R. and Winter, S. (1977) 'In Search of Useful Theory of Innovation', *Research Policy*, 6, 36–76.

Nelson, R. and Winter, S. (1982) *An Evolutionary Theory of Economic Change*, Cambridge, Mass, Harvard University Press.

Nelson, R. (1988) 'Institutions supporting technical change in the US' in Dosi *et al.*

Nelson, R. (1990) 'Capitalism as an engine of progress', *Research Policy*, 19, 193–214.

Nicholson, Sir R., Cunningham, C. and Gummett, P. (eds) (1991) *Science and Technology in the United Kingdom*, Harlow, Longman.

OECD (1989) *OECD Science and Technology Indicators Report, No. 3, R&D, Production and Diffusion of Technology*, Paris.

OECD (1992) F. Chesnais (ed.) *Technology and the Economy: the Key Relationships*, Paris.

Office of Technology Assessment (1989) *Holding the Edge: Maintaining the Defense Technology Base*, Washington DC, USGPO.

Pasinetti, L.L. (1981) *Structural Change and Economic Growth*, Cambridge University Press.

Porter, M. (1990) *The Competitive Advantage of Nations*, London, Macmillan.

POST Report: *see* Gummett (1991b).

Prigogine, I. and Stengers, I. (1984) *Order out of Chaos*, London, Fontana.

Reed, C. (1991) 'EC awards to meet fair trade rules', *Jane's Defence Weekly*, 9 November, p. 914.

Rosenberg, N. (1982) *Inside the Black Box: Technology and Economics*, Cambridge, Cambridge University Press.

Sahal, D. (1981a) 'Alternative conceptions of technology', *Research Policy*, 10, 2–24.

Sahal, D. (1981b) *Patterns of Technological Innovation*, Reading, Mass, Addison Wesley.

Sahal, D. (1985) 'Technology guide posts and innovation avenues', *Research Policy*, 14.

Saviotti, P.P. (1988) 'Information, entropy and variety in technoeconomic development', *Research Policy*, 17, 89–103.

Saviotti, P.P. (1991) 'The role of variety in economic and technological development' in P.P. Saviotti and J.S. Metcalfe (eds).

Saviotti, P.P. (1992) 'Variety, Economic and Technological Development', paper presented at the International Schumpeter Society Conference, Kyoto, 19–22 August.

Saviotti, P.P. and Metcalfe, J.S. (1984) 'A Theoretical Approach to the Construction of Technological Output Indictors', *Research Policy*, 13, 141–51.

Saviotti, P.P. and Metcalfe, J.S. (eds) (1991) *Evolutionary Theories of Economic and Technological Change: Present Status and Future Prospects*, London, Harwood Publishers.

Schumpeter, J. (1934, original edition 1912) *The Theory of Economic Development*, Cambridge, Mass, Harvard University Press.

Schumpeter, J. (1943, 5th Edition 1976) *Capitalism, Socialism and Democracy*, George Allen and Unwin.

Teece, D. (1981) 'The market for know-how and the efficient international transfer of technology', *Annals of the American Academy of Political and Social Science*, 458, 81–96.

Von Bertalanffy, L. (1950) 'The theory of open systems in physics and biology', *Science*, 111, 23–9.

Walker, W. (1989) 'Thatcherism and Technical Advance: Reform Without Progress?', paper presented at the Columbia University/MERIT project on national systems supporting technical advance, September.

Walker, W. and Gummett, P. (1989) 'Britain and the European Armaments Market', *International Affairs*, 65, 419–42.

Walker, W. (1991) *Britain's Dwindling Technological Aspirations*, Review Paper No. 1, London, Science Policy Support Group.

Williams, R. (1991) 'Overview of the UK economy, society and politics, and the role of S&T', in Nicholson *et al.*

Williams, R. (1992) 'R&D Statistics: A Contribution from the House of Lords', *Science and Public Policy*, 19, 291–5.

Wilks, S. and Wright, M. (eds) (1987) *Comparative Government–Industry Relations*, Oxford, Oxford University Press.

Wright, M. (1988) 'Policy community, policy network and comparative industrial policies', *Political Studies*, 36, 593–612.

2 Science and technology policy in the United States: trading-in the 1950 model

Michael M. Crow

2.1. Introduction

Historically, we in the United States have taken great pride in our technological achievements. We have savored the heady experience of being in the
vanguard of scientific progress and participating in many of the most
significant advances of our time. For the most part, morale remains high.
Yet, in ever-increasing numbers, thoughtful individuals from many quarters
of American life are expressing doubts about the future. There is concern
that America may fall behind in science and technology – that we may miss
out on opportunities to put science to work for the benefit of Americans and
all mankind. Many informed citizens, are asking: 'Do we Americans still
have the right stuff?'

Clearly, if the United States is to prosper, the nation must creatively
expand and exploit its strengths in science and technology. This will require
the efforts not only of our universities and private industries but of the
government as well. Unfortunately, the present policies and institutional
designs of the United States' government concerning science and technology
are inadequate for the challenges that lie ahead. To a large extent the
continued economic vitality of the United States depends on how effectively
we revise this obsolete policy.

In this chapter, I will examine how we got to where we are. Then I will
offer several recommendations for developing a powerful new policy for
science and technology.

We Americans are engaged in a vigorous debate about the role that our
government should play in protecting and advancing our economic well-
being. Of course, that's not news. From our nation's earliest days, we have
wrestled with the difficult question of how far our government should go in
regulating or influencing individual and commercial behavior. On the one
hand, we week a government that is not intrusive – a government that does
not meddle unduly in private affairs. On the other hand, we recognize and
respect the unique ability of government to marshall resources and to
influence events in a positive way. Thus, our government today is a massive
enterprise of agencies and programs. Significantly, however, these agencies
and programs are confined primarily to the areas of national defense, foreign
affairs and social welfare. Little attention has been paid to how the

government can help our nation to extract the maximum economic benefits from our enviable competence in science and technology.

Sometimes our national government will debate issues endlessly; when that occurs, the process of making policy becomes sluggish, even moribund. Other times, when the will to act is present, our government moves decisively. Consider, for instance, that the United States Congress debated for over four years, 1946 through 1950, regarding the design of the National Science Foundation. Congress then took ten more years before fully establishing and funding the Foundation. In contrast, the Office of Naval Research was established almost without debate in 1946 and was generously funded from the very beginning. Similarly, the Atomic Energy Commission was up and running in 1947 within months of the closeout of the Manhattan District Project by the United States Army.[1] More recently, the Strategic Defense Initiative of the early 1980s was funded and underway in less than eighteen months after being proposed by key scientists. Yet, when it came to establishing technology-transfer centers for the manufacturing sector of our economy, Congress resisted taking action for more than three budget cycles.

The message is clear: science and technology issues involving the *military* have not been subjected to prolonged debate over what role the government should take. Hence, these issues have historically been resolved quickly and with minimal political exchange. By contrast, civilian science and technology policies, particularly those related to manufacturing and commerce, have always been hotly contested political issues. For instance, in the 1970s when the Carter administration was trying to expand the coal-related research programs, the coal industry itself was skeptical. The industry felt that any government intervention, including R&D, was negative – even if it was designed to assist the industry.

Today, however, we may be moving toward a national consensus on the benefits of using technology to enhance economic growth. Since the early 1980s, economists and others have recognized the evolutionary way in which an economy advances and the extent to which technology influences that evolution. The time has come to put those insights to work.

Until now, the government has dealt ineffectively with technology development that promises commercial benefit. For the most part, it has adopted only limited and temporary policies – policies tied largely to the national defense. Before 1980, there were no long-term policies for technology advancement on a national scale. Happily, some national leaders are beginning to recognize that the government can do more to encourage science and technology in a way that advances our economic interests and allows us to compete effectively on the international scene.

At last the United States may be moving toward recognition of the existence of what I will call our National System of Innovation, or NSI for short.[2] Our government may finally adopt science and technology policies aimed at turning our nation's R&D capability into a competitive advantage. Unfortunately, many policy makers still seem to feel that the best way for the United States to succeed in the international technology arena is for the government to get out of the way. These policy makers believe that we should let industry do what it can do and needs to do – that the government should simply re-focus its existing R&D institutions to address international competition. Then, they think, all will be well. In my view, this is a simplistic approach to policy making. It ignores the fact that the policy environment for American science and technology needs serious evaluation and re-design.

2.2. The major historical periods[3]

To understand what needs to be done, it is helpful to look at how our science and technology policy has evolved. There have been several distinct periods in this evolution. The first was the *Laissez-Faire* Period which lasted from approximately 1790 to 1940. Then came the War and Post-War Period which lasted through the 1940s. The third period, spanning the twenty-five years between 1950 and 1975, saw a federalizing of the National System of Innovation. The fourth period, which I call the Revisionist Period, lasted from 1975 through the 1980s.

Now, in the 1990s, we are entering a new period in which we are striving for a unified national policy concerning science and technology. Let us consider in some detail the four major historical periods, beginning with the *Laissez-Faire* Period.

2.2.1. The Laissez-Faire *Period (1790–1940)*

Starting in 1790 and for the next 150 years, science and technology in America were driven first by inventors and then by corporations. These inventors and companies were responding to what was to become the largest and fastest-growing domestic market in the world. Government R&D policy, as well as direct research funding, was slow in coming during this period. The government focused almost entirely on the development of agriculture, national resources, military hardware and aircraft. There was no national investment in R&D and no national plan for either science or technology. The dominant government policy affecting innovation was the enactment of strict anti-trust laws.[4] This legislation and its implementation by the executive branch and the courts tended to limit the technological breadth of American industry.

During the *Laissez-Faire* Period, no national agency or program in the United States was charged with stimulating cooperation or competition in the technology field. In those few areas where national investment was made, it was almost always small in character and never at the heart of American industry. One exception was the government's investment in the aviation industry. This investment program started in 1915 as a result of aviation development in World War I. It is interesting to note that the government's efforts to assist the fledgling aviation industry were viewed skeptically by most industrial leaders. What lay behind the government's decision to invest in aviation? Essentially, the government's interest in developing military technology happened to overlap with the desire of the private sector to apply aviation technology to civilian ends. Government, universities and industry worked together for forty-three years (1915 to 1958), planning and directing the evolution of America's aviation and aerospace industry. Today this is one of America's most successful industrial sectors.

The 150 years of *Laissez-Faire* policy resulted in an economy second to none. Independent industrial R&D laboratories became the key institutions in the innovation process. Supplementing these private-sector labs, the government established its own R&D laboratories to support weak industries such as the mining industry. Among other things, the government established the Bureau of Mines and the Bureau of Standards which provided such aid as industrial research and industry infra-technology in the form of weights, measures and standards. In addition, the government provided for natural-resource assessments. In addition to government R&D labs, university R&D established as the home of basic science and advanced training – a role that several universities developed to a fine art between 1880 and 1930. All in all, these roles were defined and in place before the outbreak of World War II in late 1939.

In many ways, the *Laissez-Faire* Period was a pre-policy environment, a period in which the government had no distinct policy or mission behind the investment that it made in research and development. This pre-policy period is best characterized by its lack of central planning, a focus on the industrial R&D lab and a general lack of federal investment. It was truly an American design. Basically, government stayed out of the way of the private sector with the exception of such areas as agriculture, aviation and mineral extractions.

2.2.2. The War and Post-War Period (1940–50)

Major changes in our national policy were to take place during World War II and the years immediately following. During World War II, the United States developed a productive base equal to more than 50 per cent of the world's economy. At that time, the United States' economy was, of course, predominantly military oriented. To support the war effort, the government established many new R&D institutions and a new expanded role for academic science. In addition, it provided the financial means in guaranteed markets by which many private-sector R&D labs could be expanded. These organizations were centrally planned with by the Office of Science Research and Development or by the military services themselves. Large-scale federal investment, federally mandated R&D objectives, targeted funding and industrial and government cooperation were the norm. By the end of the war, hundreds of new R&D labs had been established and the potential of large-scale R&D investment meeting national objectives was demonstrated.

The war was a changing point for American science and technology policy making at many levels. Never before had so much investment and building been undertaken. Never before had the university research community been so totally dominated by national science and technology projects. In fact, never before had universities had the opportunity to show their capability in national research projects. On the industrial side, policy makers learned that the development of new technology could be stimulated through procurement and through direct R&D financing. Policy makers also learned that virtually anything they could imagine in a scientific sense could be done.

Because of the massive economic growth resulting from the war and the vulnerability of the economy to a post-war economic downturn, the government developed a number of strategies for harnessing the economic potential of science and technology. Prominent among these was a recommendation by Vannevar Bush, the Director of the Office of Science and Research Department. He urged the government to continue to invest in science as a key step in maintaining American pre-eminence.[5] His plan called for establishing a national program for basic research and graduate education – programs that would keep the nation ready to meet future military or economic threats. This plan, combined with plans by the military to maintain their R&D enterprise, made possible the establishment by the late 1940s of a new American *science* policy – a policy separate and distinct from any commercial technology policy and separate and distinct from a science and technology policy dominated by national defense. The Bush plan assumed erroneously that investment in science would result in technological and economic success. It assumed that all that was needed was basic research that could be fed to industry for development. While well intentioned, the Bush strategy was not based on sound economic or policy assessment but rather on the naïve assumption that science investment would lead directly to technological performance.

During the 1940s, in addition to increasing its investment and basic science, the nation also began developing a technology policy for civilian uses of nuclear power. Congress established the Joint Committee on Atomic Energy to oversee nuclear policy and also established the Atomic Energy Commission to implement that policy. With these actions, the United States developed a *de facto* science and technology policy in this one area of future industrial activity. Here were the beginnings of a national science policy with strong ties to national defense. Outside of the defense–industrial complex, there was – with one exception – essentially no change in the role of the government in technology development. That exception was the development of a policy designed to keep university researchers active in basic science through the National Science Foundation.

Thus, by 1946 the United States was at the very early stages of what, in hindsight, can be viewed as a critical policy error. Our science policy was aimed predominantly at undirected basic research. This policy was set in the context of an unconnected national defense science and technology policy and a national technology project in atomic power. Between 1946 and 1950, essentially all of the elements of this policy path were in place. America was about to embark on the largest science and technology investment in world history.

2.2.3. The Federalization Period (1950–75)

The next period was to last for twenty-five years (1950–75) and saw the federalizing of the United States' National System of Innovation. Previously, between 1870 and 1925, a National System of Innovation had begun to emerge. It was dominated by a few large industrial research labs, a few university labs and a handful of government labs. During that formative period, the national system was not so much a system as a grouping of research organizations, each operating in its own environment. Between 1925 and 1939, this 'system' of R&D laboratories experienced some limited growth but remained dominated by the independent corporate R&D lab. These R&D organizations were later to become the building materials for a new system, a system that emerged after the potential of 'big science' was discovered during World War II.

At the beginning of World War II, the National System of Innovation was shaped largely by the industrial research laboratories and the notion of corporate competition. By 1950, the National System of Innovation had been federalized. During this ten-year period, the United States moved into the position of world economic dominance – not by plan or by design but as a result of a total military and economic victory in the war.[6] It was assumed that basic research carried out by universities, applied research conducted by industry and specialized research performed by government would be sufficient to maintain the economic position of the nation. The result was that, except for national projects in atomic power, space technology and a few failed efforts in energy technology, the National System of Innovation was designed to avoid government involvement in the development of commercial technology.

Thus, in the twenty-five-year period that began in 1950, five types of institutions evolved to play a role in the National System of Innovation:

(1) Hundreds of large, stand-alone industrial research laboratories became involved in developing technology for the corporation itself or in support of a government mission in defense or space technology.
(2) Dozens of large federal research laboratories supported the development of weapons systems, atomic power and related areas of science and technology.
(3) Thousands of small technology-oriented laboratories or companies attempted to develop a new niche technology or a new break-through technology.
(4) Hundreds of unconnected and unplanned federal laboratories performed applied research tasks in mining, agricultural and other areas where market forces failed or government was the dominant client in a technology area.
(5) Thousands of individual research projects at a hundred leading research universities focused on the research objectives of individual researchers or on disciplinary objectives in basic fields of science, engineering and medicine.

During this twenty-five-year period, thousands of new research organizations were established throughout the United States. Tens of thousands of new scientists and engineers were acculturated into a national system of innovation that, outside of defense, space technology and atomic energy, had no stated objectives other than to do good science. Investments in building the system were measured in billions of dollars. The return was measured in military dominance, space technology dominance, a new atomic power industry and perceived economic dominance.[7]

From the perspective of federal investment, 50–60 per cent of the available resources were used for defense purposes, another 10–15 per cent for space technology and about 5–10 per cent for atomic power development. The remaining 15–20 per cent of federal R&D investment – a substantial sum in total dollars – was divided among undirected basic science, agriculture and health.[8] As a result of this pattern of spending and institutional investment, the United States never developed the national means to sustain commercial technology-based economic change on a national scale.

Consider the large stand-alone industrial research laboratory of the period between 1950 and 1975. A good example was the David Sarnoff Laboratory of what was then RCA. Such an organization, while a national asset, was limited to either pursuing research for the parent company or serving the government through contract research. Furthermore, and to reiterate an earlier point, the serious threat of antitrust litigation limited the areas that such a laboratory could investigate. The result was that while the labs' research capabilities were certainly in the national interest, the future of the lab was determined by the whims of the market place. The system relied on the strength of the individual companies and their managements to maintain a national asset in the international R&D game. As a result of relying on the private R&D sector, R&D assets would come and go, based on short-term market shifts as opposed to long-term national objectives. In fact, the David Sarnoff Laboratory was given away by RCA in the 1980s after the corporate bottom-line could no longer justify the expense of such a large research center.

During the period between 1950 and 1975, the basic roles and structures for the National System of Innovation were set. They were built around the missions of various agencies acting independently, companies acting independently and universities driven by the individual search for basic knowledge.

2.2.4. *The Revisionist Period (1975–90)*

In the 1970s and 1980s, the basic premises of the National System of Innovation began to come under serious attack. Precipitating factors included the oil shocks of 1973–4 and 1979, the economic down-turn of the late 1970s and the defense-led economic boom of the 1980s. Furthermore, people began to recognize that Japan and Europe were true rivals to United States' economic dominance. Informed citizens began to ask perceptive questions: 'Why can't the United States maintain economic dominance with a basic science system that's unrivaled in the world?' 'Why can't we develop a technology fix for energy problems and for our environmental concerns?' 'What's missing in our national R&D capability?' These and other questions led to a period of science-policy revision. Congress considered numerous *ad hoc* technology policies.

While the cold war raged on, toward its final days United States investment in defense science and technology increased dramatically. The demand for new policies aimed at increasing economic competitiveness also increased. With increased funding for defense technology and with a continued assumption that investment and basic science was the best way for a government to contribute to commercial science and technology, by 1988 US science and technology policy was under serious revision.

Consider the following. Between 1980 and 1988, defense R&D spending had increased (in constant dollars) more than 83 per cent while non-defense

R&D spending had decreased 24 per cent. The decrease in non-defense R&D spending is particularly large when one takes into account that there was a 40 per cent increase in spending in the same period for basic science research, primarily in academic centers, unrelated to defense.[9] This was at a time when the economic and technological position of the United States was beginning to slip noticeably in a number of critical areas.

Clearly, the old National System of Innovation prevailed, dominated by defense goals and focused only on basic science. The policy process was not really addressing the need for civilian technology. None the less, Congress, pushed by local political demands, began establishing new programs and agencies dealing with technology policy. Between 1980 and 1988 Congress enacted several major technology policies. Each was designed to make the United States more competitive and to improve the policy model that dated back to the 1950s. Many saw that earlier policy model as a key limiting feature of the National System of Innovation.

The efforts by Congress in the 1980s to change our technology policy included at least nine major statutes. One of them was the Stevenson–Wydler Technology Innovation Act of 1980. This law was designed to put the research-performing organization in charge of developing government-financed intellectual property. The intent here was to enhance the commercial potential of government-financed inventions. This potential had not been realized in the previous forty years of government finance of R&D.

Another statute passed by Congress was the National Productivity and Innovation Act of 1983. This law sought to help American companies work together in joint projects without violating antitrust laws.

Still another new law was the Federal Technology Transfer Act of 1986. This law provided a basis for federal research laboratories to become active entities in technology transfer. It also provided financial incentives for both the labs and the scientist in carrying out technology transfer.

Through these and other legislative initiatives, Congress began to redesign the National System of Innovation to enhance our competitiveness position. The redesign process was, however, limited by the focus on defense technology and by an institutional design that had not been updated in forty years.

While the drive to establish an *ad hoc* technology was developed by Congress and resisted by the administration, the rationale for a science and technology policy based on defense was beginning to change. With the collapse of the Soviet Union and its Eastern European empire, the justification for large-scale investment in the defense sector began to weaken. It became increasingly possible to envision a new policy for science and technology, a policy that was unified and not dominated by defense considerations carrying a predisposition toward only undirected basic science in the academic sector.

2.2.5. The emergence of a Unified Policy (1990–)

In the 1980s, Eric Bloch was Director of the National Science Foundation. He convinced the Office of Management and Budget and the Office of

Science and Technology Policy at the White House that it was in the national interest to double the basic science budget of the National Science Foundation. To sell such an increase to Congress, Bloch had to change some of the basic premises of the Foundation's design. He proposed three basic changes: the first was expanded funding for focused research centers; the second was the establishment of industrial affiliate programs; the third was closer participation in national research and technology initiatives by individual investigators. Congress and the administration agreed with these proposals. The National Science Foundation became a mission agency within the National System of Innovation. This was the first serious advance in science policy since 1950.

The role of the new National Science Foundation is to support the national science and technology enterprise by conducting directed basic research in areas of national need – no more science for the sake of science. As a result of this policy shift, the budget of the National Science Foundation has grown dramatically and its status in the executive and legislative branches of government has been greatly enhanced.

In 1990–1, Congress established the Critical Technologies Institute to map out areas in which strategic investment and policy action might be useful. When first established, the Institute was opposed by the administration. In 1992, the administration endorsed the institute and requested modest funding for its operations. In addition, the administration established or endorsed other congressional initiatives of the 1980s and early 1990s including:

(1)   Renewal of the small business innovation research program;
(2)   Authorizing key national laboratories to enter into agreements for cooperative research and development; and
(3)   Development of a National Competitiveness Council.

Clearly, a change in national policy was in progress. The congressional tempo for new legislation creating new authority, new programs and new coordinating groups dramatically increased. Most notable is the Technology Pre-eminence Act of 1992. This act continued the process of establishing a national technology policy. It did this in several ways. First, it expanded the Technology Administration in the Department of Commerce. Second, the act greatly expanded the spending authority for the National Institute for Standards and Technology (NIST). Third, it created several national commissions aimed at stimulating new technology. Fourth, it established a focus on investing in and creating policies for critical technologies.

Another significant act was the American Technology and Competitiveness Act of 1992. This act has far reaching implications. It will be a major step in unifying science and technology policy in the United States. The act does a number of things. It establishes a nation-wide network of manufacturing outreach and technology transfer centers which will aid in transferring new technology into the workplace. The law expands the advanced technology program dealing with areas of critical technology. This expansion effort includes the development of two new industry and government consortiums and provides for a government-backed pool of venture capital. The act also enhances programs to promote exports and expand investment in worker training, particularly the creation of apprenticeships in key technical areas and science training in elementary and secondary schools.

Passage of this act and others that are developing in Congress or were proposed during the Presidential campaign point to a new era in science and technological policy in the United States. For the first time, the United States will move into a second phase of science policy making, the phase in which a nation begins to devote its science and technology assets towards its economic future.

2.3. The three phases of policy evolution

In his comments on the twenty-fifth anniversary of the science policy research unit at the University of Sussex, Christopher Freeman outlined three phases that industrialized nations have gone through since the 1940s in developing their science and technology policies.[10] In Freeman's view, in Phase I, science policy is directed towards military purposes and is influenced most significantly by physicists and chemists. Phase II goes beyond weapons systems to include economic growth. Finally, Phase III moves science to an even broader focus that includes making life better for people through, for example, the development of job-saving technologies and environmentally neutral technologies. Phase III also focuses on technologies that provide for long-term economic vigor.

Modestly modifying Freeman's system of classification, I will label Phase I as Military Science and Technology Policy; Phase II as Commercial Science and Technology Policy; and Phase III as Comprehensive Science and Technology Policy.

2.3.1. Phase I – Military Science and Technology Policy

This phase focuses on national scientific assets and the building of weapons and weapons systems. Scientific assets are applied to the dominant weapons systems of the era – in our case, the atomic/missile era. The policy promotes the development of new weapons systems for global superiority and the modification of existing technology for local or regional application. The majority of national scientific assets and resources are deployed for military purposes. On a global basis, the vast majority of scientific effort, at least since the mid-1930s, has been directed toward military purposes. This continues to be true in the United States, the United Kingdom, the Russian Republic and other major industrial nations. In addition, countries such as India, Iraq, North Korea, South Africa, China, Israel, Argentina and Pakistan are devoting the vast majority of their national scientific talent to weapons development.

In Japan and Germany, this phase of science policy was eliminated at the end of World War II. In the case of the United States and the former Soviet Union, the end of the cold war provided an opportunity to move beyond Phase I. Other industrialized nations – most notably South Korea, the

Republic of China, Canada, Switzerland, the Scandinavian nations and France – have kept their military R&D expenditures low as a result of either alliances, a general defensive policy or neutrality.

For the most part, nations with an active science and technology policy and with accompanying national investments began their national programs under the auspices of national defense. As noted earlier, the federalization of the National System of Innovation in the United States after 1940 was driven by national defense objectives. It has been driven by these objectives for the last fifty years. A civilian-oriented national policy for science and technology has not developed in the United States to the same extent. One can speculate about the reasons. Perhaps it has been a combination of atomic power development, advanced industrial organization and World War II. But whatever the reasons, the United States is still in Phase I.

In Japan and Germany, movement from Phase I to Phase II was completed with elimination of military research in those nations. Thus, in the mid-1950s for Germany and the early 1960s for Japan, commercial considerations became dominant in those nations' science and technology policies.

2.3.2. *Phase II – Commercial Science and Technology Policy*

In Phase II, a nation devotes its science and technology assets to developing and maintaining the national economy. There is a national strategy that targets specific industries for either direct or indirect technology development or technology protection. Protection of specified industrial sectors or companies is accomplished through trade and financial policies or the development of government-financed research institutes to assist in technology development. The focus is on key technology industries.

Nations such as Germany, Japan and, to some extent France, have had thirty or forty years of experience in developing programs, institutions and policies that enhance development of new commercial activity through national science and technology investment. In the case of Japan, it can be argued that the Ministry of International Trade and Industry has performed several of these functions since at least 1925.[11]

Generally these efforts include applied research centers on a national level that have a commercial orientation; coordinated planning and joint research in key areas of technology; national technology goals and objectives; large multi-year national technology projects; coordinated technology and economic/trade policy; and national legislative committees focused on national technology planning and funding. In addition, in Germany there is a national system of basic science centers that underpin the National System of Innovation and address particularly difficult basic science questions that are important to technology development.

In younger economic powers such as South Korea and the Republic of China, efforts are underway to build quickly all of the elements found in the Japanese and European systems. In Taiwan, the Industrial Technology Research Institute, fledgling in 1980, had grown to more than 8,500 personnel by 1991 and had more than forty-five industrial-focus research labs or centers. This facility, with its numerous new programs and science efforts, is aimed at economic competitiveness.[12] This is all from a nation of fewer than 20 million people.

In the United States, the development of a commercial science and technology policy has only occurred in the agriculture sector, although it may be beginning in the semi-conductor sector. Agriculture is one of America's most successful economic sectors; this is the result of several factors:

(1) National science and technology centers are directed towards problem-solving in key areas of agriculture. Recently, these centers have focused on developing new industrial products from agricultural feedstocks.

(2) Federal and state cooperative research centers are directed towards problem-solving and research service in particular regions or particular industrial sub-sectors.

(3) There are federal and state cooperative extension services which include an R&D component. They also include a mechanism for solving technical problems in the field for both farms and agricultural businesses.

(4) There is a national program for basic science grants. These involve awards based on peer review in selected areas of science.

Other elements of agricultural policy include: price controls and production quotas; export controls and assistance; marketing assistance and standard-setting; and power to regulate technology in such areas as biotechnology and advanced food-processing.

Within the agricultural sector, the clear pattern is to plan and coordinate the national enterprise. Historically, the units of production in agriculture have been small and dispersed, but this is becoming less common. In this area, the United States has a unified policy for science and technology – a policy that is driven by commercial and, increasingly, by environmental objectives. And, although the agricultural subsystem for research is far from perfect, it does represent a valuable working model. Technological advances by producers and processing companies work well in both domestic and export markets.

The characteristics of Phase II policy making are clear whether in the United States or elsewhere. The policy making is focused on planned economic development. In the case of large corporations, Phase II policy making focuses on four elements:

• A cooperative environment for science and technology planning;
• Supportive trade and financial policies;
• National and regional R&D centers that offer support; and
• General guidance from government in selecting technology projects on a national level.

How is a Phase II policy viewed by corporations in nations that have adopted such a policy? Most corporations operating in such an environment maintain that they remain autonomous from government – which is correct. Still, they recognize the government's strong guiding hand in establishing a general direction for technology development.

2.3.3. Phase III – Comprehensive Science and Technology Policy

In Phase III, the national objective is to use science and technology for sustainable growth, environmental quality and general quality of life. Sustainable growth is defined as economic and social advancement that provides for long-term economic well-being, with the highest possible standard of living. It promotes environmental quality and the general quality of life. Policies dealing with science and technology require a focus on the development of non-intrusive technologies. Policies also focus on technologies for social enhancement, as well as zero-tolerance technology systems and environmental controls leading to zero effluent. To be successful, such policy efforts must be fully integrated at the national level and not isolated in environmental or nuclear power regulatory agencies.

Phase III planning requires careful integration of multiple goals and the coordinated use of procurement and regulatory policies, including techniques to stimulate innovation. For example, the government could mandate that all future federal construction projects or leased facilities must utilize environmentally sound materials and energy technologies. This would promote significant advances in various industries such as those involved in heating ventilation and air-conditioning, building materials and construction. The use of procurement policies by the government has been very useful in stimulating innovation. Also, environmental regulations tend to force innovation in the market place.

At present, no nation has fully entered Phase III. Those nations that are closest include Sweden, Japan and Denmark. Furthermore, no nation has yet revised its environmental policy to bring quality of life, sustainability and environmental control forward as more important than economic development.

2.4. Moving toward a new policy

The United States is the world's dominant center for science and technology. It invests heavily in some non-defense R&D areas. None the less, we remain, for the most part, a Phase I science policy nation. Our nation's science policy remains dominated overwhelmingly by defense and is only marginally connected to national economic objectives. The United States has experienced a string of failed national technology products including SST, synthetic fuels, the space shuttle and the breeder reactor.[13] Its rag-tag technology policies cannot be called significant. On an evolutionary scale, the United States has a science and technology policy roughly equivalent to those of regional military powers such as Pakistan or South Africa. Clearly we haven't evolved very far. This is not to say that our efforts in basic science funding or our unified science and technology policies in the area of agriculture are not successful; they obviously are. But science and technology policy, as measured by political attention, the allocation of resources, national economic performance and the distribution of R&D institutions is so heavily dominated by defense issues that our science profile mimics that of smaller, regional military powers.

Consider, for instance, how Congress has organized itself. In defense matters, Congress has essentially created one authorization committee and one appropriations committee to provide policy guidance and resources for the defense establishment. By contrast, in science and technology there are at least five authorizing committees with significant jurisdiction and as many appropriation committees responsible for funding the nation's science enterprises outside of the defense area. In the case of defense appropriations, the relevant committee has no other legislative concerns, while in civilian science and technology programs, the jurisdictions of sub-committees are broad and result in significant conflicts between social programs and science programs.

Moreover, our efforts in basic science are not well coordinated with efforts to develop our national economy. This lack of coordination greatly weakens the extensive basic science investment made through the National Science Foundation and other agencies.

It is likely that, in the next decade, the United States will advance into Phase II – the commercial science and technology phase – but this will require a careful redeployment of US assets and the development of new policy mechanisms. This does not mean that we must completely eliminate all features of Phase I. It is clear that for some time, the United States will maintain a dominant military presence in the world, a presence that will continue to require policies and programs that direct some of our science and technology capability toward military efforts.

As the United States moves into Phase II, numerous shortcomings will have to be addressed. When the United States science policy was designed in the 1940s, our nation was dominant in world science and there was no international network to gather and analyze scientific information. Such networks have been established in Japan, South Korea and other nations that have yet to evolve indigenous large-scale capabilities in basic science. The science world has changed and will continue to change. The super-conductivity breakthroughs in Japan in the late 1980s and the new science institute being established in the People's Republic of China since 1985 clearly demonstrate that the United States is now but one of many scientifically endowed nations. An awareness of world scientific developments will be necessary for any successful National System of Innovation in the United States.

In 1950, it was generally assumed that the development of science and technology was a linear process – a process that started with basic science, progressed through applied science and ultimately moved to technology development and commercialization. At that time, this may have seemed an appropriate model for new technology. The process was similar to that used in the Manhattan Project, the radar development effort and other war-time projects. But it over-simplified the science and technology efforts that went into these projects. Furthermore, it was an inaccurate model of the process by which commercial technology is developed. We now know – but have not implemented in public policy – that technology development involves both a science and a technology development process. Although these processes are separate, they are often linked together for purposes of knowledge exchange. The science process, however, need not be linked to the technology process;

conversely, technology can advance to commercial stages without science investment. There are hundreds of examples of technology advancement that were not based on scientific breakthroughs. There are also several examples of successful commercial technology developments that are not underpinned by a large-scale basic-science policy. Examples of such commercial developments include much of the software industry, advanced steel production and most of the American construction industry.

Historically, our policy makers have emphasized the development of products over the development of manufacturing processes. Also, they have assumed the time it takes to get to market is not a critical factor in commercial success. These and other biases and assumptions are built into the 1950 model of United States' science policy. Such assumptions limit the potential of any Phase II policy and can also limit the ability of the United States to take full advantage of its existing strengths.

2.5. Ten recommendations

Movement from a Phase I policy to a Phase II policy will take time, maybe as much as ten years. Several actions need to be considered if the government is successfully to redesign the National System of Innovation. Because these policy changes may help reverse the present economic decline in high technology, they should be attractive to the private sector.

Here, then, are ten recommended actions for moving the United States into Phase II:

2.5.1. Establish a new Office of Science and Technology Planning and Development

The present Office of Science and Technology Policy is a weak planning and advisory agency on the outer boundary of the White House policy-making process. To succeed as a planning and coordination agency with a focus on economic development and scientific excellence, this Office needs coordination authority similar to that of the Office of Management and Budget. Coordination authority would include budget review and approval of all science and technology programs, long-range program review and inter-agency program management. In addition, the Office would be responsible for identifying strategic technology areas and for coordinating multi-sector planning groups in strategic areas.

The Office would be advised by the existing National Science Board and a new National Technology Board. Both of these groups would be charged with planning for the national interest in areas of science and technology. The Office of Science and Technology Planning and Development would be staffed with technical personnel, R&D evaluation personnel, an economic analysis staff and appropriate personnel for national program coordination.

2.5.2. *Convert selected national laboratories into national technology centers*

In space technology and agriculture, the nation sets its scientific, technological and economic goals and then turns to research organizations and R&D contractor networks. This allows for rapid and efficient implementation of R&D objectives. In the area of commercial technology, the government – if it set national goals or defined national technology projects – would turn to an unorganized set of labs presently operated by or for the Department of Energy or the Department of Defense or to the small facilities owned and operated by the National Institute of Standards and Technology. Together, these labs represent a formidable scientific capability. Alone and programmed as they are toward narrow-mission research problems these labs are poorly positioned for Phase II science and technology efforts.

Converting such labs to support roles in the development of national commercial science and technology would start with a careful inventory of the assets available. Then labs would be reassigned to Phase II objectives. While conversion will not be easy or simple, the nation needs a set of research facilities focused on the development of pre-competitive technology and on directed basic research.

Such laboratories do not need to be owned and operated by the government. We already have research labs owned by the government but operated by private contractors. Such labs successfully match talent with science and technology needs and avoid some barriers to science that are prevalent in a government-operated facility.

2.5.3. *Redesign and recharter the National Science Foundation*

The National Science Foundation, designed as an addendum to the national defense science and technology policy of the late 1940s, is in serious need of re-design and re-positioning. The new NSF should remain at its core the agency of the government charged with funding curiosity-driven science. Beyond its core, need-driven science programs (directed basic research) would be developed and funded in academia that support the national science and technology plan of the government as a whole. These directed basic-science programs would work with industry so as to enhance knowledge transfer and to assist in problem identification and focus.

The new National Science Foundation would also develop a limited number of technology support programs designed to enhance or improve academic science and engineering input to critical national technologies. In addition the NSF would take on a planning and funding role for academic science equipment and facilities investment.

This new NSF would be an expanded enterprise from the present effort and would seek to devise program designs that permit pure basic science to continue its search for new knowledge in an unencumbered way while providing for heavy inter-organizational connectivity in all other areas. Such a design will require new funding routines and proposal review systems.

2.5.4. Establish national science centers under the National Science
Foundation in areas of future industrial activity

Within the next century, new materials and biotech knowledge are likely to
be base technology areas for significant new economic activity. We know that
certain areas of science, such as photosynthesis and oceanography, offer
significant economic potential. In areas of science and technology that
promise a basis for future industries, national science and technology centers
should be established and operated by the new NSF. Such centers should be
large in scale, larger than the present and quite successful National Science
Foundation centers which are funded at the $4–$5 million per year range.
These centers should involve a critical mass of national experts in a given
area or set of areas. By design, such national science and technology centers
would focus on selected basic science questions. Investments of $50–$75
million per year might be appropriate, with one or two institutions serving in
the lead role for each center.

The key here is to focus science assets on a targeted area and to solve
problems associated with those areas alone on a scale large enough that the
problems can be addressed without concern for investment levels.

2.5.5. Expand the National Institute for Standards and Technology into a
National Institute for Industrial Science and Technology

The National Institute for Standards and Technology (NIST) is the only
federal research facility focused on the industrial science and technology
future of the United States, at least in the commercial sense. As such, NIST
must play a critical role in a Phase II science and technology policy. To be
even more useful, NIST should be greatly expanded and become a national
center for technology standards, technology development, the testing,
development and demonstration of manufacturing systems, and as a national
showcase for new technologies. In addition, NIST should develop economic
and planning staff to assist states with their own science and technology
programs. Finally, the NIST program for transferring manufacturing
technology should be greatly expanded to include at least one center in each
manufacturing region, a sort of industrial extension service.

2.5.6. Establish dual-purpose (civilian and military) R&D agendas for
selected defense research laboratories

We should adopt a policy that encourages defense R&D organizations to
develop technologies for both military and commercial purposes. For
instance, if the army and the marines required disposable, yet high-power,
photo-voltaic material, then government R&D labs as well as contractors
could be required to develop a research agenda that produces two versions of
the product.

2.5.7. *Establish regional technology development and transfer centers*

Most research universities have a stockpile of inventions and discoveries that could be useful to small high-tech businesses. To aid in moving basic discoveries to the market-place, the federal government should co-fund (with the states) centers designed to develop technology that can be transferred to industry. Right now, with the emphasis basic science funding, university researchers have little opportunity to turn over promising technology to small businesses that might have a better chance of advancing the technologies.

2.5.8. *Create a national network to support advanced research*

Researchers in all environments need scientific and technical information. A network would help circulate information regarding science and technology efforts in the United States and international settings. The network would develop information systems appropriate to researchers, small businesses, large corporations and policy makers. Science and technology information would be treated as a freely available public asset.

2.5.9. *Establish the American Technology Corporation*

This government-sponsored enterprise (along with private industry) would identify high-risk or economically uncertain technologies that are important to the future national economy. Initially, the government would invest funds in these technologies for research, development and demonstration. Later, industry would also invest. Two or three projects on a large scale and with commercial possibilities would be pursued during any given ten-year period. Initial technologies might include maglev trains, battery technology, super producting generators and desalination or advanced building techniques that are friendly to the environment.

The Corporation would build the necessary coalitions for commercialization that would support critical technologies until successfully deployed.

2.5.10. *Establish a joint committee on science and technology*

Within Congress there is a need to reorganize around this critical area of national policy. For fifty years the Armed Services Committees in the House and Senate have served as the Phase I science policy committees of the United States government. As we move to a Phase II science policy, Congress needs to establish more effective policy-making and policy-oversight mechanisms in the area of science and technology. Similarly, the appropriations committee should reorganize its sub-committee structure to monitor more carefully science and technology investments made at the federal level. During the Phase I policy period, the defense appropriations committee provided complete oversight for the funding of most major science and technology ventures.

2.6. Conclusion

In the 1990s, the United States is discovering that in the decades ahead economic competition will involve technological grappling on a scale equal to the military struggles of the mid-twentieth century. We have two fundamental choices. On the one hand, our National System of Innovation can follow our present policy, which places heavy emphasis on isolated basic science, little emphasis on the development of commercial technology and very heavy emphasis on defense technologies. We are, however, beginning to see the outcome of this course: a continued weakening of our competitive position.

The second path involves a systematic evolution into Phase II of science and technology policy, a unified policy focused on commercial rather than military technology. Other nations have successfully moved into this phase of science policy and have thereby enhanced their economic potential.

To move into this next level of science policy, the United States faces a difficult task. We need to redirect our defense R&D establishment away from its current patterns of research and development – something that has never been successfully done in a nation that maintains its military as a large and active international force. Second, we need carefully to analyze how we should re-organize our innovation system to be more productive. In 1941–2, we quickly organized a national science and technology venture that was centrally planned and highly focused. That effort successfully involved industry, universities and the government. But successful as that system was, we need to remember that fifty years have elapsed. The world obviously is very different today. It is time to update our system.

The beginnings of change in the United States policy have been incubating for the last ten years. The critical mass of support for the transition to Phase II of national science policy is nearly in place. If the transition does occur, we will learn what the largest science and technology research enterprise in the world can do when devoted to the development of commercial technology.

Science and technology development in the United States must evolve from its military beginnings. The American public wants to move beyond the notion of science for the sake of science, as well as a science preoccupied with building better laser-guided missiles. The American public is ready to support a science that enhances the quality of life and makes the nation more internationally competitive. To move in this direction, we must continue the changes that we have initiated during the last ten years; we must dramatically re-configure our science and technology policy system into a new National System of Innovation.

Notes

1. For historical reviews of the evolution of American science and technology policy see: Bruce Smith, *American Science Policy Since World War II*, Washington, Brookings Institution Press, 1990 and A. Hunter Dupree, *Science in the Federal Government*, Baltimore, The Johns Hopkins University Press, 1986.

2. For review of the concept of National Systems of Innovation see David Mowery, 'The U.S. National Innovation System: Origins and Prospects for Change', *Research Policy*, 21, no. 2, 1992, pp. 124–44 and J. Niosi, B. Bellon, P. Saviotti and M. Crow, 1993, 'National Systems of Innovation: A Framework for Analysis', *Technology and Society*, 15, pp. 207–27.

3. This historical interpretation draws from the insights of Lewis Branscomb, 'Americas Emerging Technology Policy', Harvard University Working Paper, 1991; Lewis Branscomb, 'Toward a U.S. Technology Policy', *Issues in Science and Technology Policy*, 7, no. 4, Summer, 1991, pp. 50–5 and Bruce Smith (Note 1).

4. See David Mowery (Note 2) for an excellent summary.

5. It is instructive for all science-policy scholars to look carefully at Vannevar Bush, *Science, the Endless Frontier*, Washington, DC, National Science Foundation, July 1945, reprinted in 1960, 1983 and 1990.

6. See Paul Kennedy, *The Rise and Fall of the Great Powers*, New York, Vintage Books, 1987.

7. R&D Laboratories in the United States: Structure, Capacity and context', *Science and Public Policy*, 11, no. 5, June 1991.

8. See Bruce Smith (Note 1) and David Mowery (Note 2).

9. See Bruce Smith (Note 1).

10. Christopher Freeman, 'Technology, Progress and the Quality of Life', *Science and Public Policy*, 18, no. 6, December 1991, pp. 407–18.

11. See Daniel Okinoto, *Between MIT I and the Market*, Stanford, Stanford University Press, 1989; *German Technology Policy*, Occasional paper, Washington, DC, Council on Competitiveness, 1991.

12. Personal visit by author in April 1991.

13. See Linda Cohen and Roger Noll, *The Technology Pork Barrel*, Washington, DC, Brookings Institution, 1991.

3 Technical alliances in Canada: a transaction cost analysis of national and provincial policy interventions

Réjean Landry

This chapter proposes a transaction cost analysis of the national and provincial policy interventions concerning the promotion of technical alliances in Canada. Contrary to most public policy studies on technological policy, which focus on the content of public policies, my study places the emphasis on the policy instruments employed and the criteria used, for example, in the promotion of competition and redistribution by the various policy instruments. In a more general context, Linder and Peters (1984), Brandl (1988), Moe (1988) and Bryson and Smith-Ring (1990) have noted that the vehicles for the delivery of governmental interventions, or the policy instruments, have received insufficient attention from the students of public policy.

I suggest that in a market economy, the analysis of policy interventions should retain the following characteristics: (1) instead of mainly looking at the general characteristics of the content of policies, we should focus on the specific policy instruments used for targeted interventions; (2) the analysis should pay attention to the market failures at which the intervention is aimed as well as those failures to which the intervention is prone (Bryson and Smith-Ring, 1990: 206); (3) the analytical perspective should take into account a broad range of policy instruments, not just subsidies and tax incentives for R&D; (4) finally, the analytical perspective should include the consideration of explicit criteria of evaluation such as, at a minimum, efficiency and redistribution.

A transaction cost approach to policy interventions, based on the transaction cost theory (Williamson, 1975, 1985) and the principal-agent theory, is helpful in meeting these four guidelines. Conceptual elements of economic theory of transaction costs are increasingly used as a conceptual framework in the study of public policy (Maser, 1988; Calista, 1987a, 1987b, 1988; Bryson and Smith-Ring, 1990). Similarly, they are employed increasingly to address issues concerning technological policies (Watkins, 1991; Landry, 1992). Furthermore, specialists of industrial economics have come to consider the transaction cost approach as the dominant paradigm

* The author wishes to thank the Social Sciences and Humanities Research Council of Canada for its financial support and Chantal Blouin for her assistance in the analysis of the policy interventions.

employed to study the strategies of technical alliances between firms (Gates, 1989; Delapierre, 1991). Finally, the fact that conceptual elements of transaction cost theory are employed by industrial economists whose interests reside in the organizational strategies of the firms, and by students of public policies whose interests reside in the examination of governmental strategies fostering the stimulation of technical alliances between firms, is an indication that transaction cost theory might provide conceptual elements for constructing bridges among specialists that scarcely come in contact.

This chapter has four main sections. First, there is a brief discussion of the significance of technical alliances between firms with respect to transactions failures. In the second section, I argue that transaction cost theory offers a theoretical justification for government stimulation of technical alliances. This approach is then applied to the governmental interventions implemented by the national government of Canada and the provincial governments of Ontario and Quebec. Finally, several conclusions will be drawn about the strategies of these governments.

3.1. Between markets and hierarchies: technical alliances

Over the last decade the business press and academic researchers have been paying an increasing attention to technical alliances. This surge of interest is not due to the novelty of technical cooperation between firms; it is rooted in the fact that technical alliances might denote a significant shift in the strategies of firms.

This shift of strategies can be attributed to various changes increasingly affecting the incentives of firms to forge technical alliances. The studies concerning specifically technical alliances between firms indicate that they can be interpreted as a response to the following pressures;

- Increasing globalization of markets;
- Decreasing technological self-sufficiency of firms;
- Increasing intensity of international competition in high-tech industries;
- Increasing need for rapid access to technological and scientific advances in high-tech industries.

Technical alliances generate a type of inter-firm cooperation that lies between the market and the organization. Relations occurring on the market-place constitute exchanges governed by price mechanisms, whereas relations encountered within an organization are governed through hierarchical principles.

A technical alliance is a contract involving at least two firms. Compared to transactions made on the market, a technical alliance exhibits three distinctive features. It is a formal agreement generating special organizational features, not an implicit collusion between firms. Contrary to instantaneous contracts governing market transactions that liberate participants when the delivered product has been fully paid, technical alliances set up the organization of iterative relations over some period of time. In contrast to the anarchy generated by a myriad of competitors on demand and supply sides, technical alliances substitute a concerted organization of the relations between a limited number of firms. The intermediate status of technical alliances means that a significant fraction of the exchanges made between firms are not governed through price mechanisms but through hierarchical decisions made by the main officers of the firms involved in the alliances.

From the standpoint of the participating firms, technical alliances provide many types of potential benefits: (1) through joint investments, technical alliances facilitate the reach of minimal thresholds of investments that generate economies of scale (Jacquemin, 1987, 1988); (2) technical alliances generate a learning process that, in accelerating invention and innovation, creates dynamic economies (Jacquemin, 1987: 14; Fusfeld and Haklish, 1985: 65); (3) technical alliances generate a lead time allowing participants to try to capture the opportunities generated by technical advances before obtaining patents created by R&D results (Peck, 1986: 230); (4) technical alliances facilitate the distribution of risk on R&D projects through risk-spreading, the distribution of costs and benefits of a project between many firms, and through risk-pooling, the distribution of the resources of one firm among many projects that have an independent probability of success; (5) forging technical alliances may lead to the establishment of technical norms insuring some stability to the technologies developed by the participating firms and thus, generating a body of knowledge that creates new barriers to entry for non-participating firms; (6) forging technical alliances helps to avoid the organizational costs resulting from internalization of R&D, which in turn presents the risk of closure *vis-à-vis* technologies external to the firm. Finally, according to Mowery and Rosenberg (1989: 22), technical alliances reduce the transaction costs of licensing:

Many of the contractual limitations and transactions costs of licensing for exploitation of technological capabilities can be avoided within a collaborative venture. The problem of determining the value of partner's contributions can be reduced through collaboration. Partner firms make financial commitments to a collaborative venture that back their claims for the value of the assets they contribute; such financial commitments can substitute for the complete revelation of the value and characteristics of the asset that would be necessary to complete a licensing agreement.

On the other hand, technical alliances embody many potential difficulties that might induce firms to consider them as a solution of the last resort. If one takes for granted the difficulties created by differences of corporate culture between firms, losses of autonomy of the participating firms and asymmetries in rhythms and types of learning, technical alliances raise three basic difficulties. The first concerns appropriation. Cooperation between firms is not an end in itself. According to Nelson (1989: 239), 'the advantages that can be gained by participating firms will not be gained unless they individually build something proprietary from what they have learned cooperatively'. In this context, private appropriation of results is difficult to organize because the results of cooperation embody some of the characteristics found in public goods.

The second difficulty concerns transaction costs. One would agree that contracting costs involved in an exchange of technical information between firms are trivial. Thus, Mariti and Smiley (1983: 441) have conducted an

		Firm B	
		cooperation	defection
	cooperation	10,10	3,12
Firm A	defection	12,3	5,5

Figure 3.1   Technical alliances as a prisoner's dilemma game

empirical study indicating that if transaction costs are defined as all the costs of negotiating contracts, such costs are not considered an issue in deciding to undertake a technical alliance. More recently, Watkins (1991) has suggested that one should consider a second type that takes into account costs associated with the communication of technical knowledge. According to Watkins (ibid.: 91), technical knowledge 'includes the science base, but also embodies the experience, skill and artisanery of the work force, as well as the manufacturing processes and the management skills which make up the whole infrastructure of the technological community'. The costs associated with the communication of technical knowledge would be, according to Watkins, far more important than contracting costs in the decision-making of firms engaged in technical alliances.

The third kind of difficulty which should be addressed is associated with the instability of technical alliances. Competing firms engaged in a technical alliance are actually submitting to contradictory pressures: on the one hand, they are induced to cooperate with their competitors by contributing their tacit technical knowledge in order to derive the benefits expected from participating in the alliance; on the other hand, they are induced to defect by limiting their input of tacit knowledge to minimize the costs from potential opportunistic exploitative behaviour by their competitors. This system of contradictory incentives creates a situation that is referred to as the 'prisoner's dilemma' by the specialists of game theory. This game is characterized by a strongly stable but deficient equilibrium. Figure 3.1 portrays this situation in assuming that firms A and B each have two strategies at their disposal: either to cooperate in providing tacit knowledge or to defect in limiting or stopping their input of tacit knowledge. The first element of each payoff in Figure 3.1 refers to the share obtained by firm A, while the second element identifies the share obtained by firm B.

In such a game, the dominant strategy is to defect. Each firm is induced to stick to its dominant strategy because if one firm adopts a cooperative behaviour whereas the other continues to defect, the first obtains, say, three million dollars and the second, say, twelve million. Yet, each firm would obtain a better payoff if both simultaneously decided to cooperate because they would each receive a payoff of 10 million (10,10) instead of 5 million if both defect. The equilibrium of this game is strongly stable but deficient because: (1) each firm will prefer not to cooperate if the other cooperates and (2) each firm prefers not to cooperate even if the other does not cooperate. The shift from the strongly stable but deficient equilibrium of joint defection (5,5) to joint cooperation (10,10) would generate a Pareto optimal solution. This difference of payoff is very difficult to capture because the incentive to cooperate goes against the dominant incentive to defect. However, studies on iterative games (Axelrod, 1980a, 1980b, 1981, 1984) indicate that a firm may be induced to cooperate if it expects its probability of additional interactions with another firm to be high and it attributes a high value to the gains produced by the interactions that will occur.

These three kinds of difficulties refer to transactions costs that can generate market failures which, in turn, serve as justifications for government intervention.

3.2. Transaction costs: the rationale for government stimulation of technical alliances

Government interventions aim to induce individuals to do what they would not otherwise do. In this perspective, government interventions concerning technical alliances aim to induce firms to arrange technical transactions that would not otherwise occur. A transaction occurs when goods or information are transferred across separate structural entities.

Transactions are governed through governance instruments. With respect to technical transactions, the preferred governance instruments are private, market institutional arrangements because it is usually assumed that such arrangements produce efficient outcomes. However, these arrangements may lead to transaction failures. These failures can be mitigated, either through internalization of the transactions and their costs or through compensation of transaction costs by governmental interventions.

In this perspective, governments can justify their interventions for two different reasons: on the one hand, government interventions are justified if it can be demonstrated that purely private transactions fail. On the other hand, government interventions are also justified, even if the market does not fail, because governments can also aim to increase the number of transactions associated with merit goods.

To understand why transactions occurring between firms involved in technical alliances can fail, and how government can help, one has to identify the critical dimensions of transactions. In the discussion that follows, I shall focus on these dimensions identified by Williamson (1975, 1985) that are most relevant to transaction failures in technical alliances: opportunism, uncertainty, asset specificity, information asymmetry and small numbers.

Opportunistic behaviours of participants in technical alliances can be explained partly by uncertainty. Following Williamson, I shall distinguish general from behavioural uncertainty. In a technical alliance, general uncertainty is generated by the lack of perfect information on which to base decisions. As such uncertainty increases, transactions are more likely to fail. Thus, the more complex the technical transactions, the greater the likelihood of transaction failures. This type of failure is most commonly cited to justify government interventions.

In the context of technical alliances, behavioural uncertainty arises when one or more of the participants in an alliance are not sure they can fully trust the other(s). As behavioural uncertainty between actual or potential participants in technical alliances increases, transactions are more likely to fail since, as we have indicated previously, each participant is induced to stick to his dominant strategy of defection. Failures caused by behavioural uncertainty are the most difficult to correct with incentives embodied in the instruments of governmental interventions.

Asset specificity may induce participants in technical alliances to adopt opportunistic behaviours. In the case of technical alliances, it is useful to distinguish two types of asset specificity: human asset specificity in which technical knowledge is specialized; and dedicated asset specificity embodying technical knowledge codified in licences and patents. The higher the human asset specificity, the higher the cost of exchanging technical knowledge between participants. Furthermore as asset specificity increases, the greater are the incentives for actual or potential participants in technical alliances to act opportunistically. This potential failure is used as another strong argument in support of government interventions.

In most technical alliances, one participant has more information regarding the assets to be exchanged, the potential benefits of technical knowledge to be developed and so forth than the other participants. According to Williamson, information asymmetries caused by uncertainty and incentives to act opportunistically create information impactedness. This is another actual and potential source of transaction failure that is used to justify government intervention.

Finally, opportunistic behaviour will be inefficient if there is rivalry among a myriad of potential alternative participants in a technical alliance. However, in most actual cases, there are frequently a small number of potential participants capable of exchanging highly specific dedicated assets. Furthermore, once a highly specific asset has been dedicated to one technical alliance, the number of alternative firms with whom the same transaction can be reached tends to be very small. This small numbers condition induces actual and potential participants in technical alliances to act opportunistically and thus, is yet another potential source of transaction failures justifying governmental intervention.

With respect to governmental interventions, the basic question posed by the Williamson tradition of transaction cost analysis is: which governmental instruments of intervention can best remedy transaction failures? This question raises two difficulties: first, transaction costs theory constitutes an appropriate tool to underline actual and potential failures of market transactions, but it does not offer a theory of governmental interventions providing policy instruments to correct the sources of transactions failures associated with the various transactions' dimensions discussed earlier. Second, literature concerning transaction costs analysis of public policy lays the stress on taxonomies of policy instruments (see for instance Bryson and Smith-Ring, 1990: 216–17) at the expense of the specific transactions failures remedied by specific policy instruments. I shall come back to this point in the empirical section of the chapter.

Finally, actual and potential policy instruments must be judged according to the diversity of opinion on evaluation criteria that are commonly used in the public debates that surround technological policies. With respect to the government stimulation of technical alliances, the sets of evaluation criteria boil down to a choice between efficiency and redistribution. These criteria encompass two very different views concerning the role of government. On the one hand, the proponents of efficiency assume that the main role of government is to encourage competition by developing policies that will prevent severe transactions failures. On the other hand, the proponents of redistribution assume that some transactions, such as those made in technical alliances, must be increased because they carry inherent merits. In this perspective, the outcomes of technical alliances can be considered as merit goods that should be stimulated by government interventions because they generate desirable outcomes.

3.3. A case study

Applying the conceptual elements of transaction-cost theory to policy interventions developed to stimulate technical alliances involves three main steps: (1) determining the transactions involved in various organizational structures of technical alliances along critical dimensions of the transactions; (2) determining the set of government instruments used to avoid transaction failures or to stimulate merit transactions; (3) determining which evaluation criteria have been used for each policy instrument developed.

3.3.1. Technique of data collection

The data used in this study were generated by a technique of content analysis based on the explication of a questionnaire to descriptions of governmental interventions. The unit of analysis used is the measure of governmental intervention. Such a measure is made up of five basic components: (1) the governmental unit that supplies the measure; (2) the connecting verb indicating if the purpose of a measure is to increase, maintain or decrease a specific activity within a firm; (3) the activity of the firm targeted by the policy measure, for instance, R&D; (4) the policy instrument used to implement the measure: for instance, subsidies, loans; (5) the characteristics of the beneficiaries of the measure: for instance, industrial sectors, small and medium firms.

A measure of governmental intervention does not necessarily correspond to a syntaxic unit. Many sentences and many paragraphs do not contain any measure. On the other hand, what is usually referred to as a governmental programme may contain more than one measure of intervention. To be specific, here is an example:

Ministry of Industry, Science and Technology	Supports	R&D	By subsidies	Alliances between firms

The questionnaire applied to each measure of policy intervention includes questions about the activities of the firms targeted by the measures, characteristics of beneficiaries of the measures, characteristics concerning the policy instruments employed to implement the measures, and eligibility criteria.

This type of content analysis is actually equivalent to simulating interviews, except that, instead of interrogating a person with a questionnaire, documents are 'interviewed'. The documents used in this research in order to generate the data for the years 1981, 1984 and 1987 are the guides on grants and subsidies produced by the Federal Business Development Bank. The data for the year 1991 have been obtained from *The Handbook of Grants and Subsidies* produced by the Canadian Research and Publication Center. The content analysis of these documents was made by a research assistant working in close contact with those responsible for the project. Tests made by the latter on a sample of questionnaires indicate a degree of reliability above 95 per cent.

3.3.2. Results

The application of this technique of content analysis indicates that the government of Canada has developed seventy measures targeting the stimulation of technical alliances over the last decade, whereas the provincial government of Quebec has implemented thirty-five measures. We have found that the government of Ontario developed only nine measures over the same period. Just as empirical studies concerning technical alliances underline their very rapid rate of augmentation, Table 3.1 indicates that the number of governmental measures specifically targeting the stimulation of technical alliances has doubled every three years in the cases of Canada and Quebec. The fact that Ontario has developed only a quarter of the policy measures as compared to Quebec raises some questions. Are federal policy measures more appropriate for Ontario than for Quebec? Is government stimulation of technical alliances less necessary in more industrialized regions?

The two types of alliances stimulated most frequently by the federal policy measures are technical alliances between universities and firms (50 per cent of the time) and alliances between firms (24 per cent of the time, see Table 3.2). Unlike the federal measures, the Quebec provincial measures more often stress technical alliances between firms (62 per cent of the time) than those between universities and firms (12 per cent). The Quebec government stresses twice as frequently technical alliances between government laboratories, universities and firms (26 per cent of the time) than the two other governments. Contrary to expectations, the most industrialized province, Ontario, more often stresses alliances between government laboratories and firms than technical alliances between firms. Is this latter strategy of intervention due to the presence of a larger number of big government labs in Ontario?

The policy instruments employed to stimulate technical alliances do not correspond to our expectations (Table 3.3). Counter to recent trends

Table 3.1 Policy measures targeting the stimulation of technical alliances

Year	Canada		Ontario		Quebec	
	n	%	n	%	n	%
1981	10	(14.3)	—	(—)	—	(—)
1984	13	(18.6)	1	(11.2)	4	(11.4)
1987	13	(18.6)	4	(44.4)	10	(28.6)
1990	3	(4.2)	4	(44.4)	6	(17.1)
1991	31	(44.3)	—	(—)	15	(42.9)
Total	70	100	9	100	35	100

Table 3.2 Distribution of policy measures by types of technical alliances targeted

Technical alliances between:	Canada		Ontario		Quebec	
	n	%	n	%	n	%
Firms–firms	17	(24.3)	2	(22.2)	21	(61.8)
Universities–firms	35	(50.0)	1	(11.1)	4	(11.8)
Government labs–firms	6	(8.6)	3	(33.4)	—	—
Govt. labs–universities–firms	7	(10.0)	1	(11.1)	9	(26.4)
Unspecified	5	(7.1)	2	(22.2)	1	—
Total	70	100	9	100	35	100

Table 3.1 Instruments used to implement policy measures

	Canada		Ontario		Quebec	
Instruments	n	%	n	%	n	%
Subsidies	57	81.4	3	33.3	21	60.0
Loans	2	2.8	2	22.2	—	—
Fiscal incentives	3	4.3	—	—	5	14.3
Technical assistance	24	34.3	4	44.4	16	45.7
Technical information	5	7.1	1	11.1	8	22.8
Contracts	4	5.7	—	—	—	—
Other	—	—	1	11.1	—	—
% computed on n =	70		9		35	

N.B. Some policies involve several instruments

indicating that government incentives to firms are shifting from subsidies to tax incentives, one is here forced to notice that subsidies are the most frequently employed financial instrument. The emphasis laid on subsidies might indicate that governments aim to prevent transaction failures caused by general uncertainty. In the same vein, one is astonished to observe the great importance assigned by the three governments to technical assistance and technical information. I have indicated earlier that the transaction costs associated with technical information are usually so trivial that they are not

Table 3.4 Activities of firms targeted by policy measures

Activities	Canada n	Canada %	Ontario n	Ontario %	Quebec n	Quebec %
R&D	20	28.6	1	11.1	8	22.8
Product innovations	4	5.7	—	—	4	11.4
Product adaptations	—	—	—	—	2	5.7
Adoption of technology	2	2.8	—	—	1	2.8
Acquisition of machinery	2	2.8	—	—	—	—
Adaptation of technology	3	4.3	1	11.1	—	—
Feasibility studies	3	4.3	—	—	2	5.7
Qualified manpower (Hiring and training)	12	17.1	—	—	—	—
Technical information	4	5.7	—	—	—	—
% computed on n =	70		9		35	

likely to lead to transaction failures in technical alliances. One could apply the same argument with respect to technical assistance.

In principle, government intervention is not pursued to augment the number of technical alliances. Policy measures aim to induce the participating firms to increase special activities. In the same manner as empirical studies on technical alliances indicate that R&D is the most frequent successful activity of partners in technical alliances, one finds that R&D is the most frequent targeted activity of policy measures (Table 3.4). Hiring and training of qualified manpower is the second-most frequent activity (17 per cent) encouraged by the measures developed by the federal government. The stimulation of product innovations ranks in the third position. The other activities targeted by the Canadian measures are not flamboyant. They concern adaptation of technology (4 per cent), feasibility studies (4 per cent), adoption of technology (3 per cent), acquisition of machinery (3 per cent) and, finally, acquisition of technical information (6 per cent). The policy measures of the two provincial governments are much less focused on the stimulation of special activities of firms. In addition to the stimulation of R&D, the Province of Quebec attempts to stimulate product innovations, product adaptations, adoptions of technology and feasibility studies. With respect to Ontario, the only activity of firms that the policy measures aim to foster, in addition to R&D, concerns adaptations of technology. Leaving aside the issue of behavioural uncertainty, one can notice that many of the activities target by the governmental measures do not have a high degree of uncertainty. The degree of general uncertainty associated with the activities of R&D and product innovation might carry a high or a very high degree of uncertainty, but all the other activities targeted by the policy measures involve little or very little uncertainty. Thus, it can be argued that the degree of general uncertainty associated with the innovative activities of firms does not explain the strategies of governmental interventions with respect to promotion of technical alliances.

This point can be elucidated further by paying attention to the criteria of

Table 3.5 Eligibility criteria for assistance provided by policy measures

	Canada		Ontario		Quebec	
Criteria of Eligibility	n	%	n	%	n	%
Minimal contribution from firms	18	25.7	2	22.2	11	31.4
Potential for economic growth	14	20.0	2	22.2	4	11.4
Financial risk	12	17.1	—	—	4	11.4
Potential for exports	9	12.8	2	22.2	3	8.6
Hiring of manpower	9	12.8	3	33.3	—	—
Compatibility with govt. policies	8	11.4	—	—	6	17.1
Involvement in R&D	7	10.0	1	11.1	4	11.4
Quality of management	7	10.0	—	—	1	2.8
Potential for technological opportunities	7	10.0	—	—	—	—
Potential for sectoral growth	7	10.0	—	—	2	5.7
Potential for technological diffusion	8	11.4	3	33.3	3	8.6
Locality of activities	2	2.8	1	11.1	14	40.0
Potential for regional development	1	1.4	—	—	—	—
Number of other criteria	22	31.4	8	88.9	19	54.3
Unspecified criteria	14	20.0	1	11.1	14	40.0
% computed on n =	70		9		35	

eligibility developed for the implementation of the policy measures of governmental assistance. Eligibility criteria embodied in the policy measures of the federal government amounts to thirty-five, whereas they add up to fifteen for Ontario and to twenty-nine for Quebec (Table 3.5). A single measure may be regulated by many criteria whereas, as indicated in Table 3.5, from 20 to 40 per cent of all the measures rest on unspecified criteria of eligibility. The list of criteria that has been identified in Table 3.5 is not unidimensional. I will here highlight three points. The criteria of eligibility to assistance that is most frequently used concerns the requirement of a minimal contribution from participating firms. It can be used by governmental officers as an indicator of willingness by firms to undertake innovative activities associated with some degree of uncertainty. The requirement concerning current involvement in R&D can be used by governmental officers as an indicator of the technical capabilities of firms as well as an indicator of willingness to undertake innovative activities involving uncertainty. These two criteria are usually employed in conjunction with a third criteria concerning the financial risks associated with the project to be undertaken by the participants in technical alliances. This pattern of most frequently used eligibility criteria means that governmental interventions implemented to stimulate technical alliances take into account general uncertainty as well as willingness of applicants to undertake activities associated with general uncertainty. To that extent, one can deduce that government interventions aim to reduce transactions failures. The rest of the criteria could be subdivided into two subsets, one concerning efficiency and the other redistribution. The list of the criteria associated with efficiency includes potential for economic growth, potential for export, quality of management, potential for technological opportunities, potential for technological diffusion and potential for sectoral growth. Although less employed than the first three, these evaluation criteria of efficiency are widely used by the governments of Canada and Quebec.

The set of evaluation criteria that one could associate with redistribution is much shorter. It includes requirements concerning hiring of manpower, geographical location and potential for regional development. Except for hiring of manpower, these criteria are very rarely employed as eligibility criteria.

This survey of eligibility criteria indicates that the governmental policy measures aim to compensate for the costs associated with general uncertainty that would lead to market failures and that the evaluation of the applications for governmental assistance are much more frequently based on criteria involving economic efficiency rather than criteria involving (political) redistribution.

The distribution of the industries targeted by the policy measures surveyed indicates that more than half of the measures do not target special industrial sectors and that industries not associated with generic technologies are more frequently targeted than those are (Table 3.6). These figures indicate that all three governments lay more stress on the promotion of technical alliances *per se* than on stimulation of technical alliances in the new industries of generic technologies.

Finally, Table 3.7 indicates that the policy measures are not tailored for one single group of firms or organizations. Very few are reserved exclusively for large firms or small and medium enterprises. Universities and non-profit organizations are very frequent targets of policy measures for the three governments. The fact that about one-third of all the measures targets non-profit organizations is puzzling. Does it mean that policy measures provide governmental assistance to organizations primarily associated with the provision of technical services?

3.4. Conclusion: incentives versus governmental strategies

Technical alliances constitute a response to pressures especially concerning increasing the globalization of markets and increasing the intensity of competition in high-tech industries. This type of inter-firm cooperation lies between the exchanges governed by price mechanisms of the private market and the relations encountered within organizations governed through hierarchical rules. In addition to the usual general uncertainty associated with technical innovation, technical alliances are submitted to transaction costs resulting from the exchanges of technical knowledge and the high degree of behavioural uncertainty. These difficulties can generate market failures that serve as justification for government intervention. The purpose of policy interventions is to stimulate technical alliances that improve economic efficiency or redistribution within society.

Table 3.6   Industries targeted by policy measures

Industry	Canada		Ontario		Quebec	
	n	%	n	%	n	%
Unspecified	54	77.1	5	55.5	20	57.1
Non-generic industries:						
Manufacturing	1	1.4	1	11.1	9	25.7
Printing, editing	—	—	—	—	2	5.7
Services	2	2.8	1	11.1	1	2.8
Foods	—	—	—	—	2	5.7
Transports	3	4.3	1	11.1	1	2.8
Construction	—	—	—	—	1	2.8
Environment	2	2.8	—	—	2	5.7
Energy	3	4.3	—	—	2	5.7
Forests	1	1.4	—	—	—	—
Fisheries	—	—	—	—	1	2.8
Electrical products	1	1.4	—	—	5	14.3
Chemical products	—	—	—	—	2	5.7
Sub-total	13		3		28	
Generic technologies:						
Information tech.	5	7.1	—	—	6	17.1
Biotechnology	3	4.3	—	—	2	5.7
Advanced materials	3	4.3	—	—	—	—
Sub-total	11		—		8	
% computed on n =	70		9		35	

Table 3.7   Beneficiaries targeted by policy measures

	Canada		Ontario		Quebec	
Beneficiaries	n	%	n	%	n	%
Firms: size not specified	62	88.6	4	44.4	27	77.1
SME	7	10.0	1	11.1	8	22.8
Large firms	3	4.3	4	44.4	2	5.7
Universities	30	42.8	—	—	6	17.1
Non-profit organizations	22	31.4	4	44.4	11	31.4
Profit-making organizations	2	2.8	3	33.3	2	5.7
% computed on n =	70		9		35	

An empirical study of the policy measures developed by the governments of Canada, Ontario and Quebec over the last decade indicates that:

- Policy measures concerning technical alliances almost double every three years;
- Ontario is much less interventionist in this area than Canada and Quebec;
- Quebec lays more stress on alliances between firms than on other forms of partnership;
- The three governments base most of their assistance on subsidies, not on tax incentives;

- The innovative activities of firms targeted by the policy measures of all governments are very often not associated with high or very high degrees of general uncertainty;
- The policy measures of all governments target R&D more frequently than any other innovative activity;
- The three governments base their measures on evaluation criteria fostering economic efficiency, not political redistribution;
- The industrial sectors that are most frequently targeted by policy measures do not concern industries associated with the development of generic technologies.

What does the study reveal about the strategies developed by the three governments? First of all, let us consider the strategy developed by Ontario. The fact that it is very much less interventionist indicates either that the federal measures are judged appropriate for the Ontario economy or that a more industrialized province is less obliged to stimulate technical alliances since they emerge at a lower cost in dense industrialized areas. The fact that Ontario frequently lays more stress than Quebec on alliances between government laboratories and firms might also indicate that the policies regarding the geographical location of federal laboratories have better served Ontario, which can now attempt to capture some benefits from them.

In a context where subsidies tend to give way to tax incentives as an instrument of industrial policy, one is astonished to see that policy measures concerning technical alliances use subsidies as their most frequent policy instrument of intervention. Does this mean that general uncertainty associated with technical innovation in a single firm can be accommodated through tax incentives, whereas behavioural uncertainty associated with technical alliances have to be accommodated through subsidies?

One assumes that the concept of technical alliances signals the idea that partners are involved in technical transactions associated with high or very high degrees of uncertainty. Yet, the governmental measures developed to stimulate technical alliances very frequently concern the promotion of technical activities that are not associated with high or very high degrees of uncertainty. Does this mean that a technical activity associated with a degree of uncertainty that is too high for firms is also too high for government? If so, what is the role of government with respect to avoidance of market failures?

In sum, our study indicates that policy measures aim to increase *per se* the number of technical alliances, but not to induce firms or other organizations to undertake more radical innovative activities. The transaction costs theory illuminates a simple reality of life: innovative activities associated with degrees of uncertainty that are too high for firms are also associated with degrees of uncertainty that can also be too high for governments.

References

Axelrod, R. (1980a) 'Effective Choice in the Prisoner's Dilemma', *Journal of Conflict Resolution*, 24, 3–25.

Axelrod, R. (1980b) 'More effective Choice in the Prisoner's Dilemma', *Journal of Conflict Resolution*, 24, 379–403.

Axelrod, R. (1981) 'The Emergence of Cooperation among Egoists', *American Political Science Review*, 75, 2, 306–18.

Axelrod, R. (1984) *The Evolution of Cooperation*, New York, Basic Books.

Brandl, J. (1988) 'On Politics and Policy Analysis as the Design and Assessment of Institutions', *Journal of Policy Analysis and Management*, 7, 419–24.

Bryson, J.M. and Smith-Ring, P. (1990) 'A Transaction-Based Approach to Policy Intervention', *Policy Sciences*, 23, 205–29.

Calista, D.J. (1987a) 'Transaction Costs Analysis as a Theory of Public Sector Implementation', *Policy Studies Journal*, 15, 4, 461–80.

Calista, D.J. (1987b) 'Resolving Public Sector Implementation Paradoxes Through Transaction Cost Analysis: Theory and Application', *Policy Studies Review*, 7, 1, 232–45.

Calista, D.J. (1988) 'The Relationship between Bounded Rationality and Opportunism in Transaction Cost Economics: A Challenge to Public Policy'. A paper prepared for delivery at the Annual Meeting of the American Political Science Association, Washington, DC, September.

Delapierre, M. (1991) 'Les accords interentreprises, Partage ou Partenariat', *Revue d'économie industrielle*, 55, 135–61.

Fusfeld, H.E. and Haklish, C.S. (1985) 'Cooperative R&D for Competitors', *Harvard Business Review*, 63, 6, 60–76.

Gates, S. (1989) 'Semiconductor Firm Strategies and Technological Cooperation: A Perceived Transaction Cost Approach', *Journal of Engineering and Technology Management*, 6, 117–44.

Jacquemin, A. (1987) 'Comportement collusif et accords en R&D', *Revue d'économie politique*, 97, 1, 1–23.

Jacquemin, A. (1988) 'Cooperative Agreements in R&D and European Antitrust Policy', *European Economic Review*, 32, 2, 3, 551–60.

Landry, R. (1993) 'L'économie politique des instruments de politiques technologiques' in R. Dalpe and R. Landry (eds), *La politique technologique au Québec*, Montreal, University of Montreal Press.

Linder, S.H. and Peters, B.G. (1984) 'From Social Theory to Policy Design', *Journal of Public Policy*, 4, 3, 237–59.

Mariti, P. and Smiley, R.H. (1983) 'Co-operative Agreements and the Organization of Industry', *The Journal of Industrial Economica*, 21, 4, 437–51.

Maser, S.M. (1988) 'Transaction Costs in Public Administration' in D. Calista (ed.), *Bureaucratic and Governmental Reform*, Greenwich, JAI Press.

Moe, T. (1988) 'The Politics of Structural Choice: Toward a Theory of Public Bureaucracy', a paper prepared for delivery at the Annual Meeting of the American Political Science Association, Washington, DC, September.

Mowery, D.C. and Rosenberg, N. (1989) 'New Developments in the U.S. Technology Policy: Implications for Competitiveness and International Trade Policy', *California Management Review*, 32, 1, 107–24.

Nelson, R.R. (1989) 'What is Private and What is Public About Technology?', *Science Technology and Human Values*, 14, 3, 229–41.

Peck, M.J. (1986) 'Joint R&D: The Case of Microelectronics and Computer Technology Corporation', *Research Policy*, 15, 219–31.

Watkins, T.A. (1991) 'A Technological Communication Costs Model of R&D Consortia as Public Policy', *Research Policy*, 20, 87–107.

Williamson, O.E. (1975) *Markets and Hierarchies*, New York, The Free Press.

Williamson, O.E. (1981) 'The Modern Corporation: Origins, Evolution, Attributes', *Journal of Economic Literature*, 19, 1537–68.

Williamson, O.E. (1985) *The Economic Institutions of Capitalism*, New York, The Free Press.

Part II:
Technological alliances of industrial firms

4 Technological alliances in Canadian industry

Jorge Niosi

4.1. Theories on alliances

Technological alliances are a phenomenon in search of a theory. No received analytical framework can explain the existence and rapid development of either inter-firm cooperation in research and development or technological cooperation between industry and university, public laboratories or other government agencies. This chapter recalls some of the themes that the theoretical literature, from different currents of economics and management, has developed about technological cooperation and alliances.

Technological alliances are a particular case of inter-firm cooperation. In a spectrum ranging from informal knowledge-sharing (Von Hippel, 1987) to mergers and acquisitions (and thus to a total consolidation of the firms' technological assets), alliances stand somewhere in the middle. They constitute a median solution between soft and hard technological interaction among business enterprises. More precisely, technological alliances[1] are defined here as long-term contractual agreements between two or more enterprises, aiming at the development of new or improved product or process technologies. Sometimes, research universities and government laboratories are associated with these partnerships. During these alliances, each of the cooperative firms contributes various kinds of resources (technological, financial, capital equipment, laboratories or other) to the achievement of the common goal, and then share the intellectual property results (Mariti and Smiley, 1983; Fusfeld and Haklisch, 1985). Techno-logical alliances may be organized either through joint ventures or, more often, through written agreements between the partners. This definition of technological alliances, insisting in their long-term character, puts them into the realm of strategy; our analysis is, thus, on strategic technological alliances.

This definition of alliances excludes technology transfer, i.e. the sale of a given technology from one economic agent to another, without major alteration. Again, technological alliances are intermediate forms of organiz-ation between hierarchies and markets, and as such they are difficult to classify in received theory. They may or may not include financial considerations, like the acquisition of a minority, non-controlling share-holding position by one partner over another.

Two major types of alliances appear in the literature: *horizontal*, made up of competing firms, operating in the same industry; and *vertical*, composed of a set of firms, the output of some being the input for others. However, complementary assets may be neither horizontally nor vertically linked, since technology is anything but homogeneous, perfectly codified and well defined.

Also, alliances can be classified between those with *national* scope, and the *international* ones, whose members belong to different countries. These two types of alliances present rather opposite characteristics in terms of goals, scope and management.

Part one of this chapter is a reminder of where received theory (neo-classical, industrial and other economic and managerial currents) stands in the area of technological cooperation. Part two proposes a theory of alliances based on evolutionary economics, ecology of organizations, and other unorthodox approaches. It concludes that evolutionary economics and managerial concepts can help to understand the existence of alliances and technological cooperation among firms as well as some of their problems and difficulties. Part three consists of the results of an empirical Canadian study on technical cooperation and compares them with theory.

4.1.1. Technological cooperation in economics and management

The goal of this section is to analyse some major dimensions and contributions of economics and management theories to the understanding of technological cooperation. The review is far from being exhaustive and aims only to localize major themes and topics in economic and managerial theory that can help in the construction of a theory of alliances.

4.1.1.1. Neo-classicism

Technological cooperation among firms, or between firms and universities or public laboratories, is not easily understandable within the framework of received, neo-classical thought. The orthodox paradigm is based on a certain number of assumptions that preclude the very analysis of technological cooperation. These assumptions include the following:

1. Firms are profit maximizers, excluding all other types of motives and behaviours;
2. Firms choose technology within a specific set of options, that constitute well-defined production functions;
3. Technical knowledge is explicit, codified, public, perfectly divisible and free;
4. Technical and scientific change, at the macro level, is a non-economic phenomenon;
5. Flows of information about firms are reduced to price and output knowledge;
6. Competition, and particularly perfect competition, is the main type of relationship among firms, and it is essentially limited to price, as products are homogeneous. (Few neo-classical economists like Hayek, argued that perfect competition was suitable for technological development and innovation (Hayek, 1978));
7. Economic agents are perfectly rational and possess all existing information, whether technical, commercial or other.

Neo-classical literature recognizes special cases of technological collaboration in order to understand cooperative organizations started by small and medium-sized enterprises (SMEs) and for personal consumption. Marshall (1890) saw their usefulness in organizing collective purchases and sales in agriculture and public utilities. In the area of R&D, Norris and Vaizey (1973) saw research associations as useful instruments for the promotion of SMEs' innovation but noted that they were 'not suited for industries where one or two firms have a dominant position' (ibid.: 109).

Against these assumptions a recent, but growing, empirical literature has shown that they are excessively unreasonable as a basis for the understanding of technological change (Nelson and Winter, 1982; Rosenberg, 1982; Elster, 1983; Dosi *et al.*, 1988). More specifically:

1. Firms do not optimize either profits or sales or any other variable but choose the best option available among the specific set of capabilities, rules and routines they possess and master.
2. Technological choice is uncertain, risky and costly. These characteristics stem from the imperfect knowledge firms possess about the existing technological options that can be purchased within their environment and about the eventual costs of internally produced technology.
3. Technological knowledge is only partially codified, free, generic and public, and partially tacit, uncodified, industry- and firm-specific and contains important elements of personal and non-verbalized expertise. Besides, enterprises keep secret a good part of their internally produced knowledge, whether codified or not, thus increasing the opaqueness of this particular market.
4. Technological change at the macro level, is often the result of the firms' efforts to modify their technological routines, mainly through investments in research and development (R&D); technological change is, thus, internal to the economic system and key to the understanding of its dynamics.
5. Technological flows among firms, and between firms and other areas of their environment (universities, public laboratories, government), are frequent and indeed vital to the enterprises' R&D activities. These flows take many forms, including the assistance to technological conferences and the subscription to publications organized by industry associations, the contracting out of research projects to universities and public laboratories, the adoption of public technical standards.
6. Competition is only one frequent type of relationship among business enterprises. Competition may be pure and perfect, or imperfect and monopolistic. Other types of non-competitive relationship include imitation (technical, organizational or other), cooperation (legal or collusive for technical, commercial, political or other purposes) and litigation.
7. Bounded rationality is a much more realistic assumption than perfect rationality for the analysis of technology transactions: economic agents are rational, but their knowledge is limited. Thus, we can explain their search for new, complementary knowledge.

4.1.1.2. *Industrial economics*
Industrial economics is more useful than neo-classicism for the study of technological alliances. Joseph Schumpeter (1911, 1942) definitely linked technology to the basic themes of industrial economics when he proposed, mainly in his later writings, that innovation was the result of the R&D activity of the research laboratories of large firms operating in oligopolistic markets. While basically cast in the neo-classical paradigm, some of the

stringent assumptions of orthodox analysis were abandoned. The novelties included:

1. The assumption of increasing returns to scale. Efficiency increases with the size of the economic units, including R&D units (Scherer, 1970). This allows for R&D economies of scale as one explanation for technological cooperation. If large corporations possess the resources necessary for the development of a large portfolio of research projects, for the purchase of expensive specialized equipment and the hiring of highly qualified specialists, the same holds true for a group of independent firms organized for the conduct of R&D projects. However, industrial economics has dealt exclusively with R&D economies of scale attained *within* the firm and not with efficiencies achieved *by the cooperation of independent firms*.

2. The imperfect character of markets, and particularly of information markets. If information markets are imperfect, they are thus risky, uncertain and costly. It may be deduced that alliances can reduce the risks, uncertainties and costs of collecting opaque and expensive technical information from different sources. Industrial economics, however, has not gone that far.

The reasons that industrial economics has not explored the area of technological cooperation are twofold: first, its roots in neo-classical thought. Information flows between firms are seen as concerning prices and outputs, not technology. Thus, technical cooperation could not appear as a central issue under this current. Second, industrial economics sees imperfect competition as widespread, and considers it the main source of inefficiencies and unfair practices like predatory behaviour, price discrimination and output restriction (Blair, 1982). Antitrust, the normative goal of industrial economics, thus precluded even the most empirical industrial economists from taking any interest in the analysis of inter-firm technological cooperation. In fact, a large share of the industrial economics technology literature has been centred on Schumpeter's themes: the impact of firm size and market concentration of R&D, patenting and innovation (Bonin and Desranleau, 1992).

4.1.1.3. Transaction costs

An important economic current of thought within the management tradition, transaction cost theory, identifies two major types of economic organization: markets and hierarchies (Coase, 1937; Williamson, 1975). Firms use the market when transaction costs are lower than the organizational costs of hierarchies. Transaction costs are defined as the costs of planning, adapting and monitoring task completion under independent governance structures (Williamson, 1985). Uncertainty, appropriability risks and market imperfections cause firms to prefer hierarchies rather than markets, especially in technology markets.

This approach has mostly been used for the analysis of production (Pisano, 1990). Few applications were made to the study of R&D, mainly because the main authors in this current argued that R&D was better organized by hierarchies (or internal markets) than by independent units through arms' length transactions (Williamson, 1975 and 1985; Teece, 1988).

Lundvall has challenged the relevance of transaction cost theory to the analysis of present-day behaviour of firms (Lundvall, 1990). When R&D alliances can be counted by the thousands, when their benefits seem to overwhelm transaction costs, one may wonder about the utility of the approach for R&D management. In the late 1908s and early 1990s, firms' strategies preferred intermediate forms of organization, like alliances, to hierarchies. Thus, in a major departure from his previous work, Teece (1989: 3) admitted that 'cooperation is usually necessary to promote competition, particularly when industries are fragmented. Very few firms "can go it" alone any more. Cooperation in turn requires inter-firm agreements and alliances', and 'the boundaries of the firm can no longer be assessed independently of the cooperative relationships which particular innovating firms may have forged' (ibid: 4). In biotechnology, however, Pisano (1990) found transaction costs responsible for the absorption of small biotechnology firms by large pharmaceutical corporations.

4.1.2. Technological alliances in management theory

In the management of technology literature, cooperative research traditionally received little attention. Cooperative R&D was supposed to be of interest solely for small industrial firms (Hawthorne, 1978). Only in the late 1970s and 1980s, a more empirical literature on technological alliances was developed within the management departments, without a clearly defined link to any specific current of thought. The following section recalls some of the more general findings within this literature.

4.1.2.1. Why do alliances exist?
Many factors have been mentioned in the managerial literature to explain technological alliances and cooperation among independent firms (Chesnais, 1988; Dussauge *et al.*, 1988; Hagedoorn, 1990; Jorde and Teece, 1989). The following are the most frequent:

1. *R&D economies of scale* In the pursuit of a common technological goal, companies and other research units may cooperate either to reduce the R&D costs for each partner or to attain critical masses of resources permitting them to conduct large-scale projects that would be beyond the reach of any particular firm. Mergers and acquisition of competitors may be too costly compared with horizontal R&D agreements. Also, with increasing technological complexity and interconnection, the costs of R&D have been escalating. This hypothesis would predict a larger cooperative effort from smaller firms than from larger ones.
2. *Accelerate innovation* The organization of companies possessing complementary technological assets (such as product versus process technology or design skills versus manufacturing experience) may permit them to achieve faster results than through individual search and learning by each company.
3. *Capturing the knowledge of users* The acquisition and accumulation of technical assets traditionally takes place internally within the firms, either through R&D (learning by searching) or through manufacturing (learning by doing). However, an increasing number of authors has underlined that users also acquire technical knowledge about products through their long-term, repetitive use of them, a

knowledge that is different from the one acquired in the laboratory or the plant (Von Hippel, 1977; Rosenberg, 1982; Lundvall, 1988). This explanation predicts that alliances will occur between users and producers.

4. *Reducing risk and uncertainty* In an economic world characterized by technological turbulence, opening markets and increased competition, the association of several independent firms for R&D projects increases the chances of each partner attaining successful results and remaining in the market.

5. *Shortening life cycles of products* Some of the new technologies, particularly electronics, have very short life cycles. In-house R&D may not be sufficient to keep up with the competition when the product or process is not expected to last more than a few years. It may then be worthless to do long-term in-house R&D, as the companies' technical assets suffer rapid depreciation.

6. *Capturing other complementary assets* Alliances may take place between companies some of which own large or critical technical assets but small distribution networks and access to funds, while others have the opposite range of specialized assets.

7. *Standards* In electronics, the search for common standards is increasing, as compatibility with complementary products may determine the success or the failure of computers, telecommunications equipment, software, numerically controlled machines or consumer products.

8. *New methods of management* Traditional American methods of management emphasized arm's length transactions between assemblers and suppliers. According to Porter (1980), large assemblers would be better served by organizing competition among their many suppliers. The Japanese method of managing assembler/supplier relations is just the opposite: assemblers organize long-term relationships (including R&D cooperation) with their suppliers in order to ensure total quality, reliability and high performance of parts and components.

9. *Government incentives* Governments have been sharing the costs of collaborative R&D in order to increase the competitiveness of domestic companies, accelerate technological diffusion, nurture the development of new industries, reduce duplication of efforts and foster interactive learning.

4.1.2.2. *The management of technological alliances*

The management of external cooperation is something completely different from the management of innovation within the firm. In this latter case, the key issues are the choice between one central or several specialized R&D laboratories, the interfaces between the R&D department and the other functions (manufacturing, marketing, finance and the like), the hiring of the appropriate research personnel, the choice between technical out-sourcing, like technology transfer or subcontracting, and the internal production of the different technical components of the expected product or process.

In technological cooperation, the themes at stake are different. They concern more the quantity and quality of the resources (technical and non-technical) that each partner will bring to the alliance and the ownership of the future results of the collective project. These two issues are dealt with through complicated negotiations. These technical transactions between partners typically culminate in written agreements. Memorandums of understanding (MOUs) are the most frequent way of institutionalizing the new routines within the cooperating firms and the other partners of the alliance. In a few cases, R&D joint ventures are created as semi-independent corporations.

At the beginning, the design of these MOUs is a difficult and painstaking task that can take months and even years. As most of the resources and the results are intangibles (skills, patented and non-patented knowledge on product and process technology), the precise evaluation of these research assets and results is particularly difficult; the negotiations can collapse before arriving at a written agreement. The same risks affect the course of the collaboration, as often totally unexpected results are achieved. However, *firms learn to cooperate*, in a process similar to productive learning (learning by doing), and the marginal transaction cost of each MOU and each alliance decreases through time.

Technological alliances do not abolish the need for internal R&D. In the end, all firms prefer to own some exclusive proprietary knowledge. Thus, typically, cooperative projects conducted with external units are developed parallel to purely in-house projects. New routines are added to the existing ones; they do not replace them. The R&D organization becomes more complex; the strategy used for protecting intellectual property becomes manifold, as some research results are co-patented, or protected by secrecy as common property of all cooperating partners, while others are incorporated into the traditional ways the firm used previously.

4.1.2.3. Horizontal versus vertical alliances

Technological cooperation between vertically linked firms has been observed in a non-systematic way for many years. Electrical utilities and process industries, for instance, have organized technological collaboration for decades with their contractors and suppliers.[2] User–producer innovation appeared in a more systematic way in the managerial literature of the late 1970s and 1980s, mainly in the works of Von Hippel (1977) and Lundvall (1988).

Technological interaction and cooperation between rival firms operating in the same industry was also occasionally observed by business historians (Hounshell and Smith, 1988), but went unnoticed, up to recent days, even by leading management theorists (Porter, 1980, 1985). Both themes arrived in the business administration literature in the early 1980s with Fusfeld and Haklisch (1985), then with Von Hippel and others. Technological cooperation among firms operating in the same industry was harder to admit because of the stringent antitrust regulations prevailing in the United States; in 1984, however, the American government modified the antitrust legislation in order to facilitate technological cooperation among rivals; this legislation attracted some attention from academia. In fact, technological cooperation was already widespread in the USA, as well as in Canada, either through industry associations or through industry–university research consortia (Fusfeld and Haklisch, 1987).

4.1.2.4. National versus international alliances

Purely domestic alliances are different from international technological cooperation. Domestic alliances involve a larger proportion of universities and public laboratories among their partners. These alliances involve also a large number of members and a larger proportion of small and medium-sized enterprises. Their goals are more likely to be either fundamental or basic research than development. Public funding and, sometimes, public initiative of alliances, is widespread. Budgets are smaller than in the case of international partnerships. Typical of these alliances are industry–university research consortia.[3]

International alliances are something different. They are typically initiated by private firms, usually large or at least medium-sized, with little university or public laboratory involvement. Public funding is scanty. Development of new or improved products and processes, not pre-competitive research, is the most usual goal of international coalitions. Development being more costly than research, partnership budgets are, accordingly, much more important. As commercial products or processes are the result of the collaboration, agreements often include production, application and/or commercial clauses regarding the manufacture use and marketing of the R&D end result. Most large multinational corporations, including Canadian-owned and -controlled ones, are involved in international alliances with foreign-based firms (Perlmutter and Heenan, 1986; Mowery and Rosenberg, 1989; Niosi and Bergeron, 1992; Gugler, 1992).

4.2. Towards a theory of technological cooperation

While no existing theory today provides a complete framework for the understanding of technological cooperation, the building blocks for such a framework already exist. They are the increasingly important current of evolutionary theories in economics and management, the concept of technology as quasi-public knowledge, the analysis of flexible production, the concept of techno-economic paradigm, and a few others.

4.2.1. Evolutionary economics

Evolutionary economics provides key elements to the understanding of alliances and technological cooperation. In the course of their life, firms acquire a specific set of operating practices or routines. These routines change slowly, under the influence of changes in the economic environment (Nelson and Winter, 1982). Technological alliances can thus be understood as routines, adopted by firms under internal and external constraints, and changing under the influence of a dynamic environment.

Also, evolutionary economics is based on the assumption of bounded rationality, a condition vital to the understanding of technological transactions of all sorts, including technological alliances. Technology and organization change in a structured way; their state at a given time is a function, among other factors, of their state at previous moments of time; technological and organizational trajectories matter.

Most important, the evolutionary perspective maintains that economics must be, like all present-day natural sciences, an *historical* science, that trajectories – including organizational and technological – matter. In other words, that the nineteenth-century neo-classical paradigm deriving from Newtonian physics has to be exchanged for the new scientific approach based not on an immutable universe but on a world of perpetual change, where equilibrium is only a dimension of dynamic systems. At the end of the twentieth century, big bangs, drifting continents and biological mutations carry the day in natural sciences; economics should adapt itself to the development of general scientific knowledge.

4.2.2. *Organizational ecology*

This current of thought, founded by M.T. Hannah and J. Freeman (1977), puts the accent on the relationships between the firm and its environment – usually formed by other firms – in complex linkages of mutual adaptation, competition and change.

Organizational ecology also brought other fresh elements into the analysis of technological cooperation: organizational forms (like technological alliances) are developed by trial and error, with variation, selection and competition as major factors explaining their change patterns (McKelvey and Aldrich, 1983). The convergence of evolutionism and organizational ecology is currently under way (Singh, 1980).

4.2.3. *Techno-economic paradigms*

Technological development arrives in long-term waves. This seminal idea from J. Schumpeter is at the basis of the concept of the techno-economic paradigm (Freeman and Perez, 1988). Each phase of technological development is accompanied by organizational changes. The chemical and electrical revolution of the late nineteenth and early twentieth centuries brought in its wake the R&D department in the large industrial firms as well as taylorism and the assembly line in manufacturing. The present wave of technological change in the post-war period is based on the micro-electronic revolution. It brings with it new organizational institutions for technological development such as concurrent engineering, just-in-time, lean and flexible manufacturing systems in process technology. Technological alliances and the unprecedented rise of technological cooperation should also be linked to the same phenomenon.

4.2.4. *Technology as a quasi-public good*

Technology is better conceptualized as a quasi-public than as a pure public good. It is quasi-public because a large part of it is tacit knowledge, which can be acquired not by reading articles, books, manuals or blueprints but through a process of localized learning, through the interaction between producers or between users and producers. This characteristic of knowledge has been underlined by several authors (Rosenberg and Frischtak, 1985; Stiglitz, 1987). Technological alliances are R&D processes that constitute interactive learning processes through which innovative units create knowledge which is mostly specific to and useful for their own firms.

4.2.5. *National systems of innovation*

The understanding of the innovative process has evolved from the individual to the firm (in the work of J. Schumpeter), and the slowly incorporated different elements of the environment. The demand was included by J. Schmookler, the role of the science base by N. Rosenberg and the key role of government support by R. Nelson and R. Rothwell. Finally, the total network of institutions within the national economy was incorporated by B.-A. Lundvall (1988, 1992), C. Freeman (1987, 1988) and R. Nelson (1988). The concept of 'national systems of innovation' includes all the innovating units (firms, government laboratories and university research centres) with their environment of financial institutions, technical and scientific education establishments. These units are linked by a whole network of informational, human, financial and commercial relationships of cooperation and competition. Technological alliances are part of these 'national systems of innovation, that enjoy all the characteristics of evolutionary systems, with their own trajectories, time-specific and historical patterns' (Niosi *et al.*, 1992).

4.2.6. *Conclusion*

There is no established theory, either in management (at the firm level) or industrial and evolutionary economics (at the industry level), to explain the present wave of technological alliances. However, it is possible to draw from the present literature a set of concepts and explanations for firms' R&D behaviour in the area of technological cooperation. According to industrial economics literature, R&D economies of scale is the most important factor that explains the development of strategic partnerships; whereas according to management science, the most important explanations are the need to capture and accumulate intangible assets from users and other firms with complementary knowledge, the introduction of new management schemes and the need to reduce risk and uncertainty associated with accelerated technological change and a more open competitive environment. The transaction cost theory, however, has tended to predict that either inter-firm arrangements are marginal or that they are transitional forms evolving towards more classical hierarchical forms of organizing the R&D function.

These elements can be synthetized in an evolutionary theory of cooperation. Evolutionary economics brings to the forefront the concept of organizational routine, a notion that can be fruitfully applied to the understanding of technological alliances. Other useful concepts from evolutionary economics are those of technological trajectories, variation and selection through competition. But above all, this current of thought understands technological change as a dynamic process, involving firms strongly embedded in their environment, an environment that provides them with fresh knowledge, new routines and other key elements they need for survival, adaptation and change. The frontiers of the firm thus appear to be relatively porous, as technological and organizational information, not simply price and output knowledge, flows between the enterprise and its

Table 4.1   Technological cooperation

General description	Informal inter-firm cooperation	Technological alliances	Mergers
Specific forms	Exchange of information; Industrial technical conferences & journals	MOUs; Industry–university consortia R&D joint ventures	Total or partial coordination of all R&D activities

environment. Also, related concepts of the techno-economic paradigm, national systems of innovation, localized learning and technology as a quasi-public good can easily integrate with a framework in which alliances appear as new institutions for R&D in the context of the turbulent environment of the triple generic revolution of micro-electronics, biotechnology and advanced materials.

Technological alliances are situated in a middle ground between informal inter-firm cooperation and outright merger and consolidation of technological assets. Table 4.1 illustrates the place of technological alliances in inter-firm cooperation. The rapid and widespread development of technological alliances in manufacturing industry raises new questions about the sources of innovation, the appropriability and protection of the R&D results, the organization of the R&D activities within a firm and between the enterprise and external units – questions to which no present theory can completely respond. Our goal in this empirical research is to clarify these questions and, provide some new answers.

4.3. Empirical evidence

The different hypotheses inherited from the previous theoretical currents were put to empirical test. They are:

- The R&D economies-of-scale argument;
- Transaction cost theory;
- Adoption of new routines from evolutionary economics theory;
- Other, less structured concepts and ideas coming from more empirical research.

4.3.1. The population and the sample

The study was conducted on Canadian corporations active in R&D in the three new generic technologies (electronics, biotechnology and advanced materials), and the manufacture of transportation equipment. A preliminary survey had shown that these four had the largest number of alliances in Canadian industry. Appropriate samples were designed for each sector: since almost all firms in the four areas conduct partnerships of some sort, the

Table 4.2 Canadian corporations doing R&D in four selected sectors

Industry	Number of Firms conducting R&D	Sample
Electronics	238	36
Advanced materials	100	36
Biotechnology	250	36
Transportation equipment*	37	20

* not automobiles

Source: Statistics Canada: Industrial R&D Statistics 1989, Ottawa, 1991.

conclusions of the research are thus valid for the entire universe from which the samples were extracted. The relationship between population and samples are shown in Table 4.2. A detailed questionnaire was designed, and company representatives were interviewed personally by the principal investigator or by a research assistant. The following are some of the most important results related to the previous theoretical discussion.

4.3.2. R&D economies of scale

This appears as one of the most important reasons invoked by the companies for the organization of technological alliances (Table 4.3), following the search for open windows on new technologies and other complementarities. Other important advantages sought from alliances are new markets or new products on the market; another reason for organizing alliances was in response to demands from users or suppliers.

Nevertheless, R&D economies of scale disappear as an important factor when 'advantages actually drawn' from past alliances are requested. Expectations and results only partially coincide. The capturing of complementarities (knowledge, and others) is the main advantage obtained, followed by new products on the market, accelerated innovation and R&D diversification (Table 4.4).

Two main conclusions seem to follow from the preceding findings. One is that corporations forge technological alliances with limited knowledge of the precise results they can effectively draw from them; alliances confirm Simon's bounded rationality argument. In these opaque markets, corporations do not always obtain what they are looking for. Second, there is an indirect argument supporting the idea that transaction costs were in the end more important than forecasted at the beginning of the alliance; R&D economies of scale were not important advantages drawn in the last resort. R&D cost reductions were probably not achieved, even if other valuable results were obtained.

Alliances thus seem to emerge from a need to capture complementary assets, and they achieve positive results in the same area. Other beneficial results were accelerated innovation and new products on the market. Proprietary knowledge appropriated through patents was only important in

Table 4.3 Why technical alliances were organized

	Electronics	Advanced materials	Biotechnology	Transport equipment	Total
Open windows on new technologies	18	18	13	12	61
Complementarities	16	21	9	8	54
R&D economies of scale	11	21	9	15	49
New markets/new products on market	15	5	17	10	47
Answer to demand from users, suppliers	9	—	11	12	32
Other	9	2	9	8	28
Total valid responses	35	36	33	20	124

Note: Multiple-choice question

Table 4.4 Advantages actually drawn from alliances

	Electronics	Advanced materials	Biotechnology	Transport equipment	Total
Complementarities	21	20	24	17	82
New Products on the market	22	13	21	10	66
Accelerated innovation	17	16	18	6	57
R&D diversification	16	9	16	4	45
Financing	5	14	10	5	34
New customers	11	6	—	6	23
Patents	3	4	14	2	23
Other	7	9	6	4	25
Valid responses	35	36	34	20	125

Note: Multiple-choice question

Table 4.5 Electronics: size of firms and R&D collaborations as a percentage of R&D expenditures

		SMEs	Large companies
Collaborations as a	<10%	5	9
% of R&D expenditure	≥10%	16	3
Total		21	12

Frequency missing: 3. Fisher's Exact Test (2 tail) prob. = 0.006

Table 4.6 Advanced materials: size of firms and R&D collaborations as a percentage of R&D expenditures

		SMEs	Large companies
Collaborations as a	<25%	5	11
% of R&D expenditure	≥25%	11	2
Total		16	13

Frequency missing: 7. Fisher's Exact Test (2 tail) prob. = 0.008

the area of biotechnology, thus confirming Winter's finding of the industry-specific value of patents to protect innovation (Winter, 1989). Financing was of secondary importance, except in advanced materials and biotechnology.

Some indirect evidence appears in favour of the R&D economies-of-scale argument. Smaller firms conduct a larger percentage of their R&D effort (measured by total R&D cooperative expenditures in total R&D expenditures) in collaboration with other, external units. Large companies conduct a larger share of their R&D strictly in-house. While figures are not available for all samples, in electronics and advanced materials the trend is clear: the larger the size, the smaller the collaborative effort (Tables 4.5 and 4.6).

To recapitulate, the industrial economics' argument for alliances in terms of R&D economies of scale receives some support, particularly for small and medium-sized companies. Comments from SMEs included the need to get access to specialized laboratory equipment that partners possessed, to acquire specific skills, and to capture manufacturing and marketing knowledge from larger companies. All these responses point to complementarities, but they also point to the economies that partners possessing them bring to the alliances. However, it may be the case that the economies sought were only partially achieved and that transaction costs partially cancelled the expected R&D cost reductions.

4.3.3. Transaction costs

Transaction costs may constitute absolute barriers to the creation of alliances, as they appeared in the original formulation of the theory; or they

may only constitute relative obstacles, a specific category of costs that cooperative firms have to incur in order to achieve efficient alliances. Our findings show that they may affect costs in specific areas, mainly the intellectual property division and government transactions.

As most companies in the selected sectors do conduct R&D collaborations, one may conclude that transaction costs do not constitute absolute barriers to the formation of alliances. Specific difficulties in the negotiation of the agreements point to the existence of several 'costs of planning, adapting and monitoring task completion under independent governance structures'. The division of the intellectual property resulting from the project is the most important kind of difficulty that the companies met in all sectors. Deciding the financial contribution of members is the second-most important problem. This is probably due to the fact that some of the contributions are 'in kind' technical assets (product and/or process technology) and, as such, difficult to evaluate. 'Other' difficulties included long negotiations about management structures, government red tape and time lags in the approval of the funds, issues concerning confidential knowledge and strategies for the appropriation of the results (patents, secrets, and others).

These transaction problems, nevertheless, were addressed and solved through different intellectual property division and management schemes. Table 4.7 summarizes the intellectual property solutions. The collective property solution is by far the most popular, as it is the easiest to implement: partners invest the same amount of resources and obtain total access to results. Leaders appropriate for themselves the results of the collective project when they bring to it most (typically more than 50 per cent) of the resources. This solution is the most popular in advanced materials R&D, where government laboratories and universities are very active, and companies seeking public partners keep the intellectual property stemming from the collaboration. Leader appropriation also appears in large biotechnology alliances (large pharmaceutical firms with small dedicated biotechnology companies) and in vertical research consortia in transportation equipment between large assemblers and their suppliers. 'Other solutions' include cases where all property belongs to the consortium and companies decide on a 'pecking order' to use the results. Some smaller companies mentioned that they had the right to use the technology in areas other than those of the leader.

Different management schemes also addressed the issues of transaction costs. Coordination by a leading member and the nomination of a coordinating committee were the most popular solutions, except in biotechnology, where (because of the more fundamental character of research) each member conducted its own part of the R&D project, very often behind closed doors (Table 4.8).

To conclude, transaction costs usually existed: nearly 50 per cent of the firms experienced some difficulties in the negotiation of the agreements, but they finally arrived at an acceptable solution in the areas of intellectual property division, management schemes, financial contribution of members and other issues.

Table 4.7   Solving the intellectual property difficulty

Solution	Electronics	Advanced materials	Biotechnology	Transport equipment	Total
Collective property of all members	14	5	26	9	54
Results belong to leader	6	15	6	5	32
Each member owner of its R&D results	7	5	2	—	14
Results belong to user, supplier	3	2	—	1	6
Government is owner	2	1	—	—	3
Other and mixed forms	2	7	—	3	12
Valid responses	34	35	34	18	121

Table 4.8   Managing the alliances

Type of management	Electronics	Advanced materials	Biotechnology	Transport equipment	Total
Dominant member	14	15	1	14	44
Coordinating committee	12	13	11	6	42
Independent R&D by each member	6	1	20	—	27
Other and mixed	3	7	1	—	11
Totals	35	36	33	20	124

Table 4.9 Firms doing collaborative R&D before and after 1980

	Electronics	Advanced materials	Biotechnology	Transport equipment	Total
Before 1980	8	13	11	4	36
1980 and after	28	23	25	16	92
Companies existing before 1980	24	28	13	18	83

4.3.4. Evolutionism

Technological alliances are not exactly new as an organizational form. What is new is the extent of their use, mainly in the areas of the three generic technologies, and in transportation equipment, one of the main users of electronic and materials innovations. Thirty-six companies in the sample (out of eighty-three existing before 1980) had conducted R&D collaborations before 1980. Almost all of them were either industry–university collaborations of start-up companies, or industry–public laboratory cooperation by small and medium-sized firms.

At this point it is important to keep in mind that the three new generic technologies studied here were born in the post-war period. Biotechnology was developed after 1975, and most Canadian companies in this sector were founded after 1980. Thus, these collaborative technically intensive firms only appeared in the R&D landscape in the 1980s, with spillover effects on the chemical, food and pharmaceutical industries (see Table 4.9). On the opposite side, in transportation equipment, only large assemblers have conducted cooperative R&D activities before 1980. The spread of more collaborative patterns of R&D in this industry is probably adopted from both their advanced materials and electronics suppliers, and from their Japanese competitors.

4.4. Conclusion

Technological alliances result from a complex set of conditions, mostly external to the firms. These conditions include the present technological revolution forcing firms to obtain complementary knowledge and other key assets from rivals, suppliers and users, the rise of R&D costs, the increase in global competition.

Explanations coming from the industrial economics tradition (R&D economies of scale) receive some confirmation: companies seek this type of economy, but organizational costs may cancel at least some of the advantages of the collaboration. Nevertheless, SMEs tend to conduct a larger share of their R&D in collaboration with external partners, thus bringing some confirmation to the economies-of-scale argument.

Transaction costs do exist and bring some difficulties to the alliances. However, these difficulties are not important enough to constitute absolute barriers to the creation of alliances. Companies have developed solutions to most of the difficult issues raised by the governance of these complex structures formed by independent partners. Management and intellectual property solutions were explored here.

Alliances appear as a new organizational routine, which existed before 1980 but rapidly spread with the diffusion of the new generic technologies that force companies to collaborate with both rivals and users and suppliers in order to accelerate innovation and obtain complementary knowledge. An evolutionary approach can better understand the development and rapid spread of this routine in the context of a turbulent commercial and technological environment with increasing competition, uncertainty and risk.

Technological alliances are flexible forms of organization for technological innovation, compared both to mergers and acquisitions and purely in-house R&D. They allow the companies rapidly to obtain complementary knowledge, and conduct more complex and variegated R&D projects, while getting new products on the market at a faster rate. They constitute a persistent trait of the present techno-economic paradigm based on the swift development of the three generic technologies and their diffusion over all the industrial spectrum.

Notes

1. In this chapter, technical alliances, partnerships and collaborations are used synonymously.
2. For a detailed account of the collaboration between Ontario Hydro, Atomic Energy of Canada, Canadian General Electric and other firms in the design of the Candu reactor see Bothwell (1988).
3. See, for example, the Center for Integrated Systems (CIS), founded in 1980, based at Stanford University, Palo Alto, California, and funded by some 20 industrial partners, aimed at research on semiconductor design and fabrication.

References

Blair, J. (1982) *Economic Concentration*, New York, Harcourt, Brace and Jovanovitch.

Bonin B. and Desranleau, C. (1992) *Industrial Innovation and Economic Analysis*, Montreal, McGill–Queen's University Press.

Bothwell, R. (1988) *Nucleus. The History of Atomic Energy of Canada Ltd*, Toronto, University of Toronto Press.

Chesnais, F. (1988) 'Les accords de coopération technologique entre entreprises indépendantes', *STI Revue*, OECD, Paris.

Coase, R. (1937) 'The Nature of the Firm', *Economica*, IV, 16, Nov., 386–405.

Dosi, G. *et al.* (1988) *Technical Change and Economic Theory*, London, Pinter.

Dussauge, P. *et al.* (1988) 'Strategies relationelles et stratégies d'alliances technologiques', *Revue française de gestion*, March–May, 7–19.

Elster, J. (1983) *Explaining Technical Change*, Cambridge, Cambridge University Press.

Freeman, C. (1987) *Technology Policy and Economic Performance Lessons from Japan*, London, Pinter.

Freeman, C. and Perez, C. (1988) 'Structural Crisis of Adjustment: Business Cycles and Investment Behaviour' in G. Dosi *et al.* (eds), *Technical Change and Economic Theory*, London, Pinter.

Fusfeld, H, and Haklisch, C. (1985) 'Cooperative R&D for Competitors', *Harvard Business Review*, Nov., 60–76.

Fusfeld, H. and Haklisch, C. (1987) 'Collaborative Industrial Research in the U.S.', *Technovation*, 5, 305–15.

Gugler, P. (1992) 'Building Transnational Alliances to Create Competitive Advantage', *Long Range Planning*, 25, February, 90–9.

Hagedoorn, J. (1990) 'Organizational modes of inter-firm cooperation and technology transfer', *Technovation*, 1, 1, 17–30.

Hannah, M.T. and Freeman, J. (1977) 'The Population Ecology of Organization', *American Journal of Sociology*, 82, 929–64.

Hawthorne, E.P. (1978) *The Management of Technology*, London, McGraw-Hill.

Hayek, F. (1978) 'Competition as a Discovery Process' in F. Hayek (ed.) *New Studies in Philosophy, Politics, Economics and the History of Ideas*, Chicago, University of Chicago Press.

Hounshell, D.A. and Smith, J.K. (1988) *Science and Corporate Strategy. Du Pont 1902–1980*, Cambridge, Cambridge University Press.

Jorde, T.M. and Teece, D.M. (1989) 'Competition and Cooperation: Striking the Right Balance', *California Management Review*, 31, 3, Spring.

Lundvall, B.A. (1988) 'From User–Producer Interaction to the National System of Innovation', in G. Dosi *et al.* (eds), *Technical Change and Economic Theory*, London, Pinter.

Lundvall, B.A. (1990) *Explaining Inter-firm Cooperation and Innovation-Limits of the Transaction Cost Approach*. Paper presented to the Workshop on the socio-economics of interfirm cooperation, Berlin, Wissenschafts Zentrum.

Lundvall, B.-A. (ed.) (1992) *National Systems of Innovation*, London, Pinter.

Mariti, P. and Smiley, R.H. (1983) 'Cooperative Agreements and the Organization of Industry', *The Journal of Industrial Economics*, XXXI, 4, 437–51.

Marshall, A. (1890) *Principles of Economics*, London, Macmillan (8th edition, 1986).

McKelvey, B. and Aldrich, H. (1983) 'Populations, natural selection and applied organisational science', *Administrative Science Quarterly*, 28, 101–28.

Mowery, D. and Rosenberg, N. (1989) *Technology and the Pursuit of Economic Growth*, Cambridge, Cambridge University Press.

Nelson, R. (1988) 'Institutions Supporting Economic Change in the United States' in G. Dosi *et al.* (eds) *Technical Change and Economic Theory*, London, Pinter.

Nelson, R. and Winter, S. (1982) *An Evolutionary Theory of Economic Change*, Cambridge, Mass, Belknap/Harvard University Press.

Niosi, J. and Bergeron, M. (1992) 'Technical Alliances in the Canadian Electronics Industry', *Technovation*, 12, 5, 309–22.

Niosi, J., Saviotti, P., Bellon, B. and Crow, M. (1993) 'National Systems of Innovation: In Search of a Workable Concept', *Technology in Society*, 15, 207–27.

Norris, K. and Vaizey, J. (1973) *Economics of Research and Technology*, London, Allen & Unwin.

Perlmutter, H.V. and Heenan, D.A. (1986) 'Cooperate to Compete Globally', *Harvard Business Review*, March–April, 136–42.

Pisano, G. (1990) 'The R&D Boundaries of the Firm: An Empirical Analysis', *Administrative Science Quarterly*, 35, 153–76.

Porter, M. (1980) *Competitive Strategy*, New York, Macmillan.

Porter, M. (1985) *Competitive Advantage*, New York, Macmillan.

Rosenberg, N. (1982) *Inside the Black Box: Technology and Economics*, Cambridge, Cambridge University Press.

Rosenberg, N. and Frischtak, C. (1985) *International Technology Transfer. Concepts, Measures and Comparisons*, New York, Praeger.

Scherer, F.M. (1970) *Industrial Market Structure and Economic Performance*, Chicago, Rand McNally.

Schumpeter, J. (1911) *The Theory of Economic Development*, Cambridge, Mass., Harvard University, 1934.

Schumpeter, J. (1942) *Capitalism, Socialism and Democracy*, London, Allen & Unwin.

Singh, J.V. (ed.) (1980) *Organizational Evolution, New Directions*, Newbury Park, CA, Sage.

Stiglitz, J. (1987) 'Learning to Learn, Localized Learning and Technological Progress' in P. Dasgupta and Stoneman, P. (eds), *Economic Policy and Technological Performance*, Cambridge, Cambridge University Press.

Teece, D. (1988) 'Technological Change and the Nature of the Firm' in G. Dosi *et al.* (eds), *Technical Change and Economic Theory*, London, Pinter.

Teece, D. (1989) *Competition and Cooperation in Technology Strategy*, International Business Worker Paper IB-11, Berkeley, University of California at Berkeley, School of Business.

Von Hippel, E. (1976) 'The Dominant Role of the Users in the Scientific Instrumentation Innovation Process', *Research Policy*, 5, 212–39.

Von Hippel, E. (1987) 'Cooperation between rivals: informal know-how trading', *Research Policy*, 16, 291–302.

Williamson, O. (1975) *Markets and Hierarchies*, London, Free Press.

Williamson, O. (1985) *The Economic Institutions of Capitalism*, New York, Macmillan.

Winter, S. (1989) 'Patents in Complex Contexts: Incentives and Effectiveness', in V. Weil and J. Snappers (eds), *Owning Scientific and Technical Information*, New Brunswick and London, Rutgers University Press.

5 High-tech entrepreneurship and organizational choice

Weijian Shan

Technological changes have long been recognized, from Marx to Schumpeter, as the *primum mobile* of social and economic progress. Arguable, however, it is entrepreneurial activities that provide the crucial linkage between technological changes and the evolution of capitalist institutions. Entrepreneurial institutions distinguish themselves from established incumbents not only by being new but also by being organizationally different. The success of an entrepreneur depends on his ability to find the most effective and efficient way to organize activities for the purposes of (1) translating ill-defined technologies into technically and commercially feasible innovations (Rosenberg, 1976) and (2) capturing the maximum value from those innovations (Teece, 1986). The viability of a new organizational form derives from its compatibility with the new technological regime and market conditions (Hannan and Freeman, 1989). It is in this sense that the Schumpeterian concept of 'creative destruction' may be reinterpreted as destruction of the existing forms, structures and routines, as well as those non-adaptive, established institutions themselves.

The objective of this study is to analyze the factors that determine the choice of organizational forms adopted by high-technology startup firms to commercialize an innovation. The analysis will focus on the choices among independent operation and cooperative relationships. The study is confined to those new, independent firms formed for the specific purpose of commercializing a new technology (in response to an exogenous change of technological regime) which promises large economic potentials. This condition, within the constraints of a macroeconomic system, creates entrepreneurial opportunities, leading to the founding of 'high-technology startups' and to the rise of new industries or industry sectors. It is in this context that the results of this study are generalizable, although the data for empirical analysis are drawn from new biotechnology firms (to be defined later).

A cursory review of the history of high-technology industries reveals a pattern of linkages and interaction among technological changes, entrepreneurial activities and innovations: major technological changes cause a

* Financial support by the Reginald H. Jones Center of the Wharton School is gratefully acknowledged. I also wish to thank K. Visudtibhan for her contribution to the earlier version of this chapter, Amy Glass for research assistance and John E. Rutter for editorial assistance.

surge of entrepreneurial activities (Schumpeter, 1934). Entrepreneurs, with the help of venture capital, start up new firms to undertake intensive applied R&D and to compete with each other to transform the technical knowledge into innovations of commercial value. In the process, they help advance the state of the art of the technology.

To the high-technology entrepreneurial firm, how to organize its activities to commercialize a new technology is as much a strategic issue as an organizational one. While there seems little question that the main objective of an entrepreneurial firm is to appropriate the highest return to its technology (Teece, 1986), it is by no means obvious which of the many competing organizational forms will allow it to do so without a careful analysis of the dynamics of the outcomes and future implications associated with each. Therefore, the selection of an organizational choice depends on the strategic intention of the entrepreneur, resource requirements of the organizational form and its potential outcome.

In addition to the factors conventionally regarded as influencing joint-venture formations, this chapter analyzes variables of competitive and market conditions as well as those that reflect the strategic considerations of the firm. The first section develops theory and hypothesis. This will be followed by a section on data and methods. Then results of statistical analysis will be presented. In the discussion section I analyze the results and their implications.

5.1. Theory and hypotheses

The unit of analysis is the organizational form with which a high-technology startup firm commercializes a new product. The firms in this study are defined as those formed for the specific purpose of commercializing a new technology, such as recombinant DNA and monoclonal antibodies (bio-technology). To motivate the study, this section begins with a brief discussion of the possible causes of technological prowess of 'high-tech' startup firms, and hence the need to study them. Hypotheses are then developed based on the existing literature on the strategic, as well as economic, causes of cooperative relationships formed by these firms. The hypotheses will be tested in the next section.

5.1.1. High-technology entrepreneurship

It should not escape even a casual observer that major technological developments such as those of semiconductors and biotechnology are environmental disturbances preceding the mass entry of startup firms.Yet, it is somewhat bewildering that high-technology firms frequently become leaders of technology in their own industries,[1] in spite of the fact that established firms are likely to enjoy a commercial advantage in scale and scope economies, intangible assets and established marketing networks. What, then, accounts for the failure of established firms to lead in the new technology?

Within a given environmental context,[2] a number of reasons explain the phenomenon of 'high-tech startups'. First, a change in technological regime equalizes, to a large extent, the technical capability between an established and a startup firm, particularly if the technological change occurs in the public domain (Porter, 1985). Second, the established organizational form and methods may no longer fit the changed technical environment. Yet inertia caused by embedded forms, routines, and skills keeps established incumbents from adapting (Hannan and Freeman, 1977; Nelson and Winter, 1982). Third, internal incentive structures of the established firm may not sufficiently reward the taking of large risks (e.g. drastically alter the research agenda). Finally, if the new innovation 'cannibalizes' or replaces existing products, the producer has an added disincentive to innovate, unless pressured by competition (Rumelt, 1987). Therefore, beyond a certain large size, innovative activities decrease as the firm further grows (Kamien and Schwartz, 1982; Hitt *et al.*, 1990).

To understand entrepreneurial activities, it is useful to draw a conceptual distinction between technological change and innovation.[3] While a technological change can be defined as an advance in the state of the art in know-how that may potentially have commercial applications, an innovation is *the application* of a technology (or technologies) which may or may not represent an improvement in technical know-how. Major technological change is frequently exogenous to the firm and closely related to scientific discoveries (Phillips, 1971).[4] In contrast, innovations are almost always endogenous to the firm (Schumpeter, 1939) as part of the commercialization process.

A cursory review of the history of high-technology industries reveals a pattern of linkages and interaction among technological changes, entrepreneurial activities and innovations: major technological changes cause a surge of entrepreneurial activities (Schumpeter, 1934). Entrepreneurs, with the help of venture capital, start up new firms to undertake intensive applied R&D and to compete with each other to transform technical knowledge into innovations of commercial value. In the process, they help advance the state of the art of the technology.

In contrast with established firms, entrepreneurial startups have the freedom to organize their activities to fit the nascent technological environment: there are no embedded norms to fight against. The incentive for success is high-powered (Williamson, 1985) and risks are likely to be borne largely by venture capitalists (Schumpeter, 1939). While they do not have to be concerned with protecting existing market or market share, they have every incentive to strive to establish one.

5.1.2. Cooperation or independent operation?

While these conditions may provide the startup firm with a competitive edge in a new technology, the established incumbents probably enjoy an advantage in commercial, especially downstream, capabilities through their possession of many types of tangible and intangible assets. If the commercialization of a new technology requires the services and support of these assets, there exists a complementarity between startup and incumbent firms. The complementarity arises from the fact that sharing with the owner of certain assets is more cost efficient than building and running an integrated operation before the efficient scale or scope can be achieved.

Under what conditions should a startup firm build an integrated operation to commercialize a new technology? Stigler (1951) postulates that vertical integration characterizes firms in a new industry where the demand is too low to support specialists. As the industry matures, firms disintegrate because it becomes more economical to source from specialists. In this stylized model, vertical integration is inevitable because, as Adam Smith put it, division of labor is limited by the extent of the market, and no alternatives are available (Kogut, *et al.*, 1989).

However, frequently, even a major technological change is commercialized in *existing* industries, where incumbent firms may be able to redeploy their assets to serve the requirements of the startup firm, especially for downstream activities. If so, the startup is presented with a difficult organizational option by the availability, from the incumbent firms, of complementary assets. These are defined as existing assets that must be employed in conjunction with other assets to commercialize a new product (Teece, 1986). Under the circumstances, should the startup build an integrated operation or contract for the services of complementary assets in exchange for monetary payments, as in any market exchange; or form cooperative relationships with incumbent firms, in which they share the usage of one another's assets as well as the profits of the new innovation?

The economics literature of neo-classical tradition has little to offer in explaining alternative organizational forms (Williamson, 1975). One school of thought that has attempted to address this question invokes the framework of transaction cost economics (eg Hennart, 1988; Shan, 1987; Stuckey, 1983). Referred to as 'organizational failures framework' (Williamson, 1975, 1985), it postulates that firms select the organizational form that minimizes costs of transactions. Simple market exchange for the services of assets may subject the transacting parties to higher transaction costs than those for other organizational forms. These 'market hazards' consist of actual, potential and opportunity costs resulting from small-number bargaining conditions, uncertainty, bounded rationality, opportunistic behavior of the transacting party and the necessity of repeatedly negotiating, monitoring and enforcing complex contracts (Williamson, 1975, 1985). The transaction cost approach argues that vertical integration of internalization of transactions within the firm mitigates these costs, and therefore, under certain conditions, is a better alternative to the market.

However, integration may have to be accomplished through acquisition of assets in the market, a scenario which may present similar transactional difficulties (Shan, 1987). Moreover, if markets are imperfect, a startup firm may be constrained by available resources from building an integrated operation, as, for example, when what turn out to be viable projects fail to attract financing from the market. Finally, the costs of an integrated operation may not be justified if the acquired assets cannot be utilized to the efficient scale.

Under these circumstances, a cooperative relationship may provide a better organizational alternative. This intermediate form of organization attenuates market hazards by synchronizing or uniting the economic interests of the parties while avoiding the difficulties and diseconomies of building and running an integrated operation (Hennart, 1988; Shan, 1987, 1990).

The transaction costs theory provides a plausible explanation for cooperative relationships. However, aside from the fact that actual and potential transaction costs are difficult or impossible to measure, its generality suffers from the restrictions of neo-classical assumptions (Robins, 1987). The theory implicitly assumes that (1) profit maximization is the objective of the firm; (2) firms are myopic or non-strategic in their behavior and therefore would not engage in activities that would reduce current income; and (3) the market is competitive, so cost minimization equals profit maximization.

While there is no doubt that firms strive to minimize both transaction and production costs, *ceteris paribus*, alternative organization forms imply very different revenue streams (Kogut, 1988). By definition, the market for new innovations is not of perfect competition. The entrepreneur forgoes present income for the uncertain prospect of entrepreneurial profit. The innovator may also mortgage away its future income by forming a sharing arrangement with a cooperative partner to save the costs of organizing commercial activities. From a strategic point of view, the firm ought to choose the organizational form that maximizes the present value of the innovation over the life of the technology. Motivations for their organizational and managerial behavior are likely to be both short and long term. Therefore, although the transaction costs theory provides a useful point of departure, a complete theory of cooperative relationships must include strategic considerations of the firm as well as economic causes.

5.1.3. Variables of firm attributes

As a firm-dependent variable, the formation of a cooperative relationship necessarily reflects the characteristics of the firm. The vast literature on joint ventures and cooperative relationships (eg Kogut, 1988; Contractor and Lorange, 1988) suggests that the cooperative behavior of an entrepreneurial startup firm is motivated, at least in part, by three economic considerations: (1) economies or 'synergies' arising from the complementarity of assets owned by cooperating parties, (2) the limited scale and scope of operation with at least one of the partnering firms and (3) resource constraints. The implications of these economic considerations vary, of course, among firms. It is imperative to investigate the relationship between key dimensions of a firm's attributes and the organizational strategy of the firm, in order to better understand the motivation for the formation of cooperative relationships.

5.1.3.1. Firm size
The synergistic effects of a cooperative arrangement arise from risk reduction, economies of scale and scope, production rationalization and convergence of technologies, which provide the partners with either cost savings or enhanced revenue, or both, as a result of pooling the resources of cooperating partners (Harrigan, 1985; Contractor and Lorange, 1988). Apparently, the potential of synergy is larger the greater the complementarity

of assets between partnering firms. The need for complementary assets is likely to be great for a startup firm which, by definition, is still in the early growth phase, when the scale of its operation may not be sufficiently large to warrant an integrated operation. Even if the current scale of its operation justifies an integrated operation, the startup firm may still be constrained by the available resources. The resource dependence theory (Pfeffer and Salancik, 1978) suggests that firms may be driven to a partnership by the need for resources and by its dependence on the constraining elements of a task environment (Thompson, 1967).

This analysis indicates that both its internal capabilities and the scale of its operations help explain the cooperative behavior of the startup firm. These capabilities are likely to be positively correlated with firm size, a key dimension of a firm's attributes. Empirical evidence shows that small-sized firms are more liable to fail because they have many disadvantages compared with larger firms (Aldrich and Auster, 1986; Freeman and Hannon, 1983; Singh and Lumsden, 1990). In addition to providing needed resources and access to complementary assets, a cooperative relationship may also lower the costs of capital to the small firm by reducing its risks of failure and by enhancing its market valuation (McConnel and Nantell, 1985).

Empirical evidence, however, is inconclusive about the effect of size on firms' external relationships. Boyle (1968) finds that larger firms account for a higher relationship of joint subsidiaries than smaller ones. His finding is likely to be biased because the sample only represents 500 of the largest US manufacturing firms, whereas, collectively, startup firms are usually much smaller in size. Shan (1990) finds a negative correlation between firm size and cooperation for a sample of biotechnology firms without controlling for firm age which may confound the effect of size. It is possible that the relationship between the two variables is neither linear nor monotonic.

Consider two startup firms which differ by size at founding. Although resource and other constraints may compel both firms to form cooperative relationships, the smaller one may be less attractive as a cooperative partner, therefore, less likely to form a relationship, than a relatively larger one. As the smaller firm grows in size, its likelihood to form cooperative relationships also increases. However, after they both reach a certain size, scale economies, their increased abilities to generate resources and other capabilities will put a negative effect on their need for cooperative relationships.[5] Therefore, the following hypothesis is formulated:

Hypothesis 1: The propensity of the startup firm to engage in cooperative relationships increases with its size and then decreases as it further grows beyond a certain point.

5.1.3.2. Firm age

The age of the firm is recognized as another important dimension correlated with firms' ability to survive (Freeman et al., 1983; Freeman and Hannan, 1983). Although the age of a firm may be related to its size, numerous empirical studies in organizational ecology show that firm sizes vary even at founding. In many ways, the effect of age is a substantive question in its own right (Singh and Lumsden, 1990). The age of the firm may capture the effects of many of the intangible assets such as experiences, name recognition, goodwill, legitimacy, managerial skills and organizational knowledge which constitute an important part of the firm's internal and external capabilities and which must be accumulated over time. Singh and Lumsden suggest that age be seen as 'a surrogate for multiple underlying constructs that vary with age' (1990: 168). Younger firms are more vulnerable to environmental pressures and threats and more prone to failures. The burden of 'the liability of newness' (Stinchcombe, 1965) may force younger firms to cooperate. As firms grow older, the need for cooperation diminishes. Therefore,

Hypothesis 2: The propensity of the firm to engage in cooperative relationships decreases with firm age.

5.1.3.3. Number of products marketed

Many high-technology startup companies are the so-called R&D boutique houses specializing in innovative activities. In the biotech-pharmaceutical industry, for example, many firms have not reached the stage of manufacturing and marketing, and therefore, lack downstream capabilities. As they develop marketable products, the resource constraint may compel them to form cooperative relationships. In addition to access to downstream capabilities, a cooperative relationship allows the new entrant to learn or acquire the 'tacit knowledge' and superior production techniques of a partner (Kogut, 1988). In contrast, a firm which has had a number of products in the market may have either acquired, or otherwise gained access to, downstream capabilities. Their need for a cooperative partner for the commercialization of a new product is likely to be small.

Hypothesis 3: The propensity to cooperate by a high-technology startup firm is negatively correlated with the number of products it has brought to the market.

5.1.4. Entrepreneurial strategy and organizational forms

In contrast to the formalized strategy that reflects the organizational context of an established firm, the entrepreneurial strategy represents, to a large extent, the vision of the entrepreneur, which provides a general direction for the new firm (Mintzberg and Waters, 1985). The entrepreneurial strategy contains two crucial elements: one is the long-range goal or objective which the management of the entrepreneurial firm envisages for the firm; the second is an organizational strategy which delineates the organizational structure that the firm will build to accomplish its long-range objectives. The issue becomes the determination of the appropriate organizational strategy that can help the firm achieve its strategic objectives.

One dimension of an organizational form is the degree to which the firm intends to integrate or specialize its operations. Hannan and Freeman refer to this organizational choice as a 'classic problem' for organization designers: 'should they seek to become jack-of-all-trades (and masters of none), or should they concentrate on developing one or a few capacities?' (1989: 106).

Some entrepreneurial firms may see themselves as specialized firms and opt to concentrate their activities on one link of the value chain, either R&D or manufacturing, for example. Others may intend to build an integrated operation. Different organizational strategies are required to achieve dissimilar objectives.

Although intended strategies do not necessarily coincide with realized strategies (Mintzberg and Waters, 1985), the intended strategic goal of the startup firm is likely to have some predictive power for the emergent organizational form that the firm eventually adopts to commercialize its new products, given its resource and environmental constraints. The firm which wants to build an integrated operation must distribute its resources across several links of the value chain while a specialized firm can concentrate its resources on one of the links. However, 'investment in the capacity to perform one kind of action efficiently and reliably means less investment in other capacities, since resources and the time of members are finite' (Hannan and Freeman, 1989: 105).

Moreover, to build an integrated operation exposes the firm to a larger set of environmental challenges. The new firm must learn to cope with these challenges through a gradual process that involves both organizational learning and adaptation. Cooperative relationships are conducive to the transfer of organizationally embedded knowledge across the boundaries of the firm (Kogut, 1988). The specialized firm may form cooperative relationships horizontal to its operations and its vertical relationships are likely to be confined to the immediate downstream activities. An integrated operation, however, requires the firm to interact through multiple relationships with a larger group of market players at several links of the value chain. Therefore,

Hypothesis 4: A startup firm with an intended strategic objective to build an integrated operation is more likely to form cooperative relationships than a firm which does not intend to do so.

'Integrated operation' is defined as the firm's involvement in both upstream (research and development) and downstream (manufacturing and marketing) activities of the commercialization. In contrast, a specialist firm concentrates on either the upstream or the downstream phases of the operation.

5.1.4.1. Business diversity

Another dimension of the organizational form with which an entrepreneurial firm is founded is the number of business domains in which the startup firm operates. Analogous to the concept of 'generalism' (Freeman and Hannan, 1983), business diversity measures the categories of business in which the firm operates, a concept clearly related to that of diversification.

Both industrial organization and strategic management literatures have extensively examined the performance implications of corporate diversifications (eg Bettis, 1981; Caves, 1981; Miller, 1973; Montgomery, 1979; Montgomery and Singh, 1984; Rumelt, 1974). Diversification is also found to affect innovative activities of the firm (Hitt *et al.*, 1989). However, the literature almost exclusively deals with established, large-firm samples. Much of the realized diversification for established firms represents the cumulative results of a deliberate strategy, achieved through acquisitive or internal growth or joint venturing over time. For this group of firms, the degree of diversification is found to be correlated with joint-venture activities of the firm (Stopford and Wells, 1972). It might be difficult to infer causality, though, because firms may use joint ventures to diversify. In fact, consistent with the findings that related diversification strategies generally perform better than unrelated ones (eg Bettis and Hall, 1982; Montgomery, 1979; Rumelt, 1974), Harrigan (1988) finds evidence that joint ventures that represent related diversification for the parent firms are similarly more successful.

The variances in business diversity have behavior and policy implications for entrepreneurial firms because both their requirements for resources and their tolerance for the same level of environmental variability differ (Hannan and Freeman, 1989). A startup firm with businesses in multiple domains must spread its limited resources. It may therefore be forced to 'engage in a depth-for-breadth tradeoff' (Williamson, 1985: 289). To manage the 'breadth' of its operation, the firm may have to rely on other firms for 'depth'. Therefore, a multiple-business firm may have stronger incentives than a single-business firm to form cooperative relationships in a quest for additional resources (Stopford and Wells, 1972). The need for complementary assets is expected to be larger the more diverse the firm is in its commercialization efforts.

Hypothesis 5: The propensity of the startup firm to cooperate is positively correlated with the degree of diversity of the business domains in which it operates.

5.1.4.2. Number of prior relationships

It might be argued that some firms have an inherent tendency to form cooperative relationships (Kogut *et al.*, 1989). This argument is consistent with Nelson and Winter's (1982) notion of organizational routine and Hannan and Freeman's (1989) concept of inertia. If so, those firms which have more cooperative relationships might have a higher propensity to cooperate. Therefore,

Hypothesis 6: The propensity to cooperate by a high-technology startup firm is positively correlated with the number of its existing cooperative relationships.

5.1.5. Market and competitive conditions

5.1.5.1. Product market breadth

The unit of analysis, the organizational form with which a high-technology startup firm commercializes its new product, is also a product-specific variable. As such, it should be influenced by the market conditions for the product being commercialized. The resource and competence constraints on a firm vary with its task environment or the 'market breadth' for a particular product. For example, one product may be specifically targeted at a government agency, requiring a relatively small sales force or none at all. A pharmaceutical product that must be marketed to general-practice physicians requires a much larger sales force. These differences between products may necessitate dissimilar organizational strategies.

The market breadth can be defined as the minimum efficient scale and scope of operation required to serve a market. The larger the market breadth for a particular product, the greater the need by the innovating firm for downstream capabilities to reach the market. A startup firm may find it more difficult to integrate into a broader market than into a narrow niche market. Even if resource constraint does not prevent a startup firm from building an integrated operation, it may not efficiently utilize its capabilities because of the narrow scope of its operations. For example, it would not be cost effective for a 500-person sales force to handle a sole cosmetic product when it has the capability of handling twenty. This situation can motivate a startup firm to cooperate with a firm that has an established marketing network and experiences.

Hypothesis 7: The propensity of the startup firm for cooperation is positively correlated with the market breadth for the product to be commercialized.

5.1.5.2. Competition position

One important motivation for the formation of cooperative relationships is to pre-empt competition in the commercialization of high-technology innovations. The empirical evidence indicates a significant correlation between competitive positions of entrepreneurial firms in the commercialization of new products and their propensity to form cooperative relationships (Shan, 1990). In industries where the first-mover advantage is significant, the speed at which a product is brought to the market often determines success or failure of the commercialization efforts (Lieberman and Montgomery, 1988). Strategic cooperation may increase the probability of pre-empting competition, and hence, market success. When the life span of the technology is likely to be shortened by competition, cooperation allows the innovating firm to maximize value by expediting the return to the innovation. Therefore, a cooperative arrangement may not only provide a vehicle for the partners to capture synergies, it can also be regarded as a tool of competitive strategy in high-technology competition.

Accordingly, the competitive position of a firm is likely to influence its willingness to form cooperative relationships. A firm that leads the competition should feel less concerned about the threat of market pre-emption by a competitive follower. In contrast, a firm that falls behind in the competition faces the danger of jeopardizing its investment in the commercialization efforts, if it is late in bringing the product to the market. If the formation of a cooperative relationship improves its competitive position, the gain to the innovating firm may outweigh the costs as a result of having to share the monopoly profits with a partner. Therefore,

Hypothesis 8: The propensity to cooperate is negatively correlated with the competitive position of the firm in the product category. A leader is less likely than followers to form cooperative relationships for the commercialization of a new product.

5.1.5.3. Number of competitors
Another variable that is likely to affect a firm's organizational choice is the number of competitors in a given product market. If potential cooperative partners with complementary capabilities represent resources external to the firm, it is likely that a large number of competitors reduces the probability of each finding a suitable partner. However, if Hypothesis 8 is true, then the number of competitors should have little effect on a firm's organizational choice after controlling for its competitive position; and the competitive effect from those lagging in competition should be minimal on a leading firm. It is the relative position in competition that really matters in determining who will be the first to the market.

Hypothesis 9: The number of competitors in a product category is unlikely to influence a firm's propensity to cooperate

5.2. Data and methods

The data for the empirical analysis are drawn from the commercialization of the new biotechnology (the techniques of recombinant DNA and monoclonal antibodies). The unit of analysis is the organizational form chosen by the new biotechnology firm (NBF) in commercializing a particular new biotechnology product. All the organizational forms are product-specific. The population of firms in this research consists of independent, entrepreneurial firms incorporated in the United States for the purpose of commercializing the new biotechnology in the pharmaceutical industry.

5.2.1. Industry background

The pharmaceutical industry is characterized by long and costly commercialization processes. It is estimated that it takes, on the average, fourteen years to commercialize a new drug, at a cost of over $100 million (eg Thomas, 1988: 165). The regulatory process is complicated, costly and time consuming. It is also an industry in which the first-mover advantage is known to be significant and a firm may establish itself with the success of a 'blockbuster' product (Thomas, 1988).[6] The market for patented drugs is dominated by large, integrated, multinational companies. The industry is R&D intensive, spending an average of 8 to 10 per cent of its total sales on R&D (OECD, 1985: 24).

Since around the beginning of the last decade, there has been a mass entry of entrepreneurial firms to exploit the potential of the new biotechnology (US Congress, 1988). NBFs applied the new biotechnology in intensive research to innovate new therapeutic and diagnostic products. Although established pharmaceutical companies have intensified in-house biotechnology programs, most of the major biotechnology drugs approved for marketing by the Food and Drug Administration (FDA) were innovated by NBFs (ibid.).

The competition in new biotechnology commercialization centers on specific product categories. Usually, the basic property and its estimated market potential are known even before a drug has been innovated. These prospects motivate firms with the particular technical competence to compete to commercialize the product. The organizational forms adopted by NBFs are typically product-specific. For example, Genentech cooperated with Eli Lilly to commercialize the biotechnology version of human insulin, but it commercialized TPA (tissue plasminogen activator, a blood-clot dissolving drug) through independent operation.

It should be noted that a few features distinguish the biotech-pharmaceutical industry from another high-technology industry, semiconductors, although both have seen mass entry of entrepreneurial startup firms in the US. The drug industry is retail-oriented, and regulatory approval and retail marketing are crucial to market success. In contrast, the semiconductor merchant market consists of, at the outset, the US government alone, and later, industrial buyers or system producers (Borrus *et al.*, 1982). Therefore, while success for a semiconductor startup hinges on its capability to innovate and mass produce, an NBF faces the additional and much more formidable challenge of multiple phases of mandatory testings, complicated regulatory approval process and retail marketing.

As a result, the downstream commercial advantage of the established firm is substantial in the pharmaceutical industry, in comparison to that in the semiconductor industry, leading to strong vertical complementarity in capabilities between the startup and the integrated pharmaceutical houses. This is probably why, in the semiconductor industry, mostly horizontal and R&D-oriented cooperative venturing is a more recent phenomenon (Steinmueller, 1988), whereas vertical cooperation between the startup and established firms characterize the early history of the biotech-pharmaceutical industry. Therefore, variables of market competitive conditions may take on particular importance in determining organizational strategies biotechnology firms.

5.2.2. Data

Because many of these firms are privately held, data needed for analysis have not usually been available from public sources and were taken from several other sources. The sample has been generated with the help of Prudential-Bache's (PB) Biotechnology Scorecard (*Prudential-Bache Securities*, 1987), which provides a summary of the competitive status of companies in the biotech-pharmaceutical market. It lists all the major therapeutic and diagnostic products at various stages of commercialization, provides their generic names (eg IL-2, Interferon beta and TPA), the names of the companies competing in each product category, the names of their cooperative partners, if any, and the commercialization status of the product by company (eg research, Phase III clinical trials).

To control for variances that may bias results, the following criteria had to be met before a venture was included in the sample: (1) it must involve a new biotechnology firm; and (2) it must not entail a relationship structured either exclusively for financial purposes or between an NBF and a public or non-profit organization, as the interest of this research focuses on for-profit business ventures. There are 228 records of product- and company-specific biotechnology ventures involving thirty new biotechnology firms. After removing records which either did not fit the selection criteria or miss values, the final sample included 110 product-specific ventures, of which forty-six are independently operated and sixty-four are cooperative relationships.

The hypotheses developed in the theory section suggest three sets of explanatory variables: the first set entails firm attributes; the second set includes those variables which reflect firm strategies; the third consists of variables of competitive and other market conditions for the firm in given product categories.

Data were collected from primary as well as archival sources. The major source of data was *Bioscan*, a commercial database (all issues since its inception in 1987), supplemented by surveys with sampled firms and other archival sources specified in the discussion of each of the explanatory variables. The survey was designed to solicit factual data, not the subjective opinions of the respondent. To the extent possible, data are cross-verified to ensure accuracy and quality.

5.2.3. Variables

The variable SIZE is approximated by the number of employees of the firm. The traditional measure of firm size, sales, is not appropriate because many NBFs had yet to realize any sales.[7] Using employees is consistent with the literature on entrepreneurship studies (Low and Macmillan, 1988) where the level of employment was accepted as a better measure of size and growth of entrepreneurial firms. Data were obtained from *Bioscan* and surveys of sampled firms.

AGE of the firm is the number of years between its founding and the formation of the venture. Data were obtained from sources similar to those for SIZE.

The variable PRODUCT is an arithmetic count of the number of products that the firm has brought to the market, as reported in *Bioscan*. This approach has its limitations because products are treated equally. It is conceivable that some products have a larger effect on firms' downstream capabilities than others. In the absence of such information, the potential bias of this approach is controlled, to some extent, by the inclusion in the model of variables of product market breadth which measure the differences in the need for downstream capabilities and the difficulties in marketing various products.

Their overt strategic goals divide startup firms in the biotech-pharmaceutical industry into two camps: those which aspire and strive to become integrated pharmaceutical houses; and those which intend to specialize in the upstream phases of the commercialization chain – research and development (Coleman, *et al.*, 1987). A dummy variable STRATEGY was constructed, designated '1' if the pronounced strategy of the firm is to become an integrated pharmaceutical house and '0' if not. Data obtained from *Bioscan*, provides a brief description of the strategic goals of some of the firms, supplemented and double-checked in some cases with firms' annual reports.

The variable DIVERSITY covers the number of industry sectors in which the sampled firm operates. Commercialization of the new biotechnology is a multi-industry phenomenon. The industrial sectors include therapeutics, diagnostics, energy, food and breweries, veterinary products, agriculture, instrumentation, waste and pollution control, and others. While all the sampled firms operate in the pharmaceutical industry, the extent of their diversity in other business sectors varies. Data have been obtained from *Bioscan*.

RELATION is a variable count of the number of cooperative relationships the sampled firm had. Again, data were obtained from *Bioscan*.

To measure the effect of market breadth on the firm's organizational choice, a variable, BREADTH was constructed, which ranks all products according to the degree of broadness of the product's targeted market. A market is 'broad' if the product is targeted at doctors' offices, requiring a large marketing force to cover a national market. A market is 'narrow' when a product is targeted at special clinics, such as cancer clinics, which can be covered by a small sales force. In addition to the difficulties of covering a broad market such as general hospitals and doctors' offices, a startup firm is unlikely to build its own downstream capabilities before efficient scope and scale in its operation can be reached. Therefore, according to Hypothesis 7, a firm is more likely to cooperate if the targeted market is broader. BREADTH assumes a value of '1' for special clinics, '2' for major medical centers and general hospitals, and '3' for doctors' offices. A larger value in the variable indicates an increased degree of broadness, and hence difficulties when marketing the product. BREADTH is expected to be positively signed. Data were obtained from a study by Arthur D. Little's Decision Resources (1988) which identified the target markets for all the biotech-pharmaceutical products.

Although the values of BREADTH are clearly ordinal, the uniform intervals between the three assigned and discrete values are somewhat arbitrary. To verify the validity of this measure, a parallel set of categorical dummy variables was constructed, which indicate, respectively, whether the product is targeted at major medical centers and general hospitals (CENTERS), doctors' offices (DOCTORS), or special clinics. To compare their results, BREADTH and the dummy variable were estimated in two separate models. The purpose of this testing strategy was to ensure the validity of the BREADTH measure while independently estimating the effect of a particular target market on the organizational choice of the firm. Only two dummy variables, CENTERS and DOCTORS, have been included in the model and were expected to be positively signed.

Shan (1990) tested a variable which measures a firm's position when competing to commercialize a particular product. In biotechnology, it was found that followers are more likely to form cooperative relationships than leading firms. This hypothesis has been tested here using more recent data. PB reports the stages of development for each product for each firm, from which the competitive position of a firm can be identified. The competitive position of the firm in a particular category has been determined by a firm's specific stage of commercialization. These stages are defined by the regulatory process of the FDA, including, for example, research, pre-clinical trials, phases I, II and III clinical trials, and approval for marketing. At each stage of development, an application must be filed with, and granted by, the FDA. Since information then becomes public knowledge, it is possible, therefore, to identify a firm's competitive position in a product category according to their status in this process.

A variable, POSITION, was constructed to measure the relative competitive position of the firm. For the specific product category, the variable was coded '1' if it is a leader, '2' for a follower, or '3' for a distant follower. A leader is defined as the firm leading other firms in the product commercialization process; a follower trails behind a leading firm in the commercialization of the same product; a distant follower is behind two or more competitors.

To verify the validity of this variable, which assumes three discrete values with uniform intervals, dummy variables were constructed for each competitive position. These variables indicate whether the firm is a leader in the product category (LEADER), a follower (FOLLOWER), or a distant follower. The two measures of competitive positions were estimated separately, for the same reasons that were given regarding the measure of the market broadness. Since the dummy variables are mutually exclusive, only two of them, LEADER and FOLLOWER were used in the statistical estimation.

To test Hypothesis 9, a variable, RIVALS, was constructed to count the number of competitors in the same product category. Data were obtained from Prudential-Bache's (PB) Biotechnology Scorecard (*Prudential-Bache Securities*, 1987).

In addition, a variable, STAGE, was included, which measures at which stage the firm was in commercializing a product, or its distance to the market, to control for the possible effect of this variable on a firm's organizational choice. As stated, a pharmaceutical company registers with the FDA at each stage of its commercialization process. Six stages of the regulatory approval process have been identified: (1) research, (2) pre-clinical trials, (3) Phase I clinical trials, (4) Phase II clinical trials, (5) Phase III clinical trials and (6) approval. These stages are ordinal and each stage up is sequentially closer to the market than the one below.

5.2.4. Specification of the models

The empirical analysis entails estimation of a logit regression model. The dependent variable is binary, equal to 1 for a cooperative relationship, and 0 otherwise. The statistical procedure involves estimation of the following model:

$$\text{Prob } (Y=1) = \exp(x'\beta)/[1+\exp(x'\beta)] \tag{1}$$

where Y is the dependent variable and x and β are vectors of explanatory variables and their coefficients, respectively.

The model of the general form in equation (1) is specified with a set of explanatory variables consistent with the hypotheses developed in the theory section. We wish to estimate the vector of regression parameters, β, which corresponds to a vector of explanatory variables where:

$$
\begin{aligned}
x'\beta = {}& \alpha'\beta_1 + \text{SIZE}'\beta_2 + \text{SIZE}^{2\prime}\beta_3 + \text{AGE}'\beta_4 + \text{PRODUCTS}'\beta_5 \\
& + \text{STRATEGY}'\beta_6 + \text{DIVERSITY}'\beta_7 + \text{RELATION}'\beta_8 \\
& + \text{BREADTH}'\beta_9 + \text{POSITION}'\beta_{10} + \text{RIVALS}'\beta_{11} \\
& + \text{STAGE}'\beta_{12}
\end{aligned}
$$

The regression procedure estimates the coefficients β for the independent variables, α is intercept. Note that consistent with Hypothesis 1, a quadratic relationship is specified for the explanatory variable of SIZE by the inclusion of a quadratic term SIZE^2.

Table 5.1 provides a summary of descriptive statistics and correlations between variables.

5.3. Results

The results of statistical analysis are reported in Table 5.2. As expected, Table 5.1 indicates that significant correlation exists between variables of firm attributes, particularly between SIZE and AGE. SIZE and SIZE^2 are highly correlated as expected, since the latter is a monotone function of the former. Since BREADTH and POSITION are not analyzed in the same model as their equivalent dummy variables, the high correlation between them does not present a problem. The existence of a high level of correlation poses a potential problem of multicollinearity. This problem is analyzed first, followed by reports of statistical results.

5.3.1. Multicollinearity[8]

There is no easy solution to the problem of multicollinearity (Kmenta, 1971). The existence of multicollinearity is likely to inflate the standard errors of the estimated coefficients and diminish their statistical significance. In other words, multicollinearity tends to bias the results in a conservative way (Singh *et al.*, 1990).

Because of this conservative tendency of bias, multicollinearity is not a problem as long as significant results are obtained from estimated coefficients. One way to address the problem of multicollinearity is to have the offending variables removed from the model. However, errors of misspecification occur if exclusion of variables significantly worsens the fit of the model (Kmenta, 1971). Another approach is to compare the log-likelihood ratios of the full model and a restricted model with the target variable removed (Maddala, 1977). This differential approximates a chi-squared distribution from which the true significance of the targeted variable can be tested. This analysis was performed for the binomial logit model and

Table 5.1 Correlation among variables

	Means	S.D.	1	2	3	4	5	6	7	8	9	10	11	12	13	14	15
1. Y	.4182	.4955															
2. Size	288.95	268.74	-.1237														
3. Size²	155060	270560	-.1409	.9760***													
4. Age	7.9	2.7292	-.2130*	.6655***	.5738***												
5. Products	3.6182	4.0091	-.3761***	.4202***	.3660***	.4929***											
6. Strategy	.4909	.5022	.0154	.5050***	.4683***	.3307***	.3765										
7. Diversity	3.6091	1.1971	-.0621	.3788***	.2960**	.4878***	.4102***	.1848									
8. Relations	3.3909	2.5127	.2580***	-.0254	-.0464	.0954	-.0625	.0210	.1123								
9. Breadth	1.9455	.6330	.1319	.0236	.0094	.0074	.1002	.0850	-.1374	-.1134							
10. Centers	.60	.4921	-.3612***	.1078	.1369	.0792	.2567**	-.0148	-.1900*	-.3175**	.1060						
11. Doctors	.22727	.4210	.1119	-.0808	-.0871	-.0519	-.2253*	-.0552	.2143*	.2708**	-.8138***	.6642***					
12. Position	2.3364	.8270	-.3240**	-.1083	-.0729	-.1435	.0004	.0627	-.1440	-.2272*	-.0523	-.0045	.0419				
13. Leader	.2273	.4230	.2879**	.1391	.1309	.0918	-.0677	.0316	.1233	.2795**	.0469	-.0886	.0165	-.8803***			
14. Follower	.2091	.4085	.0626	-.0674	-.1220	.1012	.1388	-.1919*	.0374	-.1161	.0090	.1917*	-.1188	-.2101*	-.2788**		
15. Rivals	3.2818	3.0384	-.1034	-.0150	.0089	.0333	-.0137	.0408	.0205	-.1864†	-.1971	-.0650	.1862†	.2029*	-.1796†	-.0405	
16. Stage	3.0545	1.2767	-.0654	.0559	.0178	.0463	.1134	-.0278	.1041	.0448	.1286	.0788	-.1428	-.1479	.1474	-.0045	.3517***

Note: N = 110

† P < .10
* P < .05
** P < .01
*** P < .001

Table 5.2   **Results of binomial logit analysis**

	(1)	(2)	(3)
Intercept	1.25800	1.33343	2.0565
	(2.16037)	(1.98426)	(2.00285)
Size	.01415*	.00005	.01041
	(.00695)	(.00167)	(.007551)
Size^2/100	−.00128*	—	−.00088
	(.00066)		(.00067)
Age	−.49316*	−.29013	−.51513†
	(.24658)	(.19174)	(.27717)
Products	−.32927***	−.309281***	−.32836**
	(.09406)	(.08880)	(.10568)
Strategy	1.11381†	1.14694†	1.59231*
	(.61597)	(.59494)	(.70625)
Diversity	.264530	.38552	.04991
	(.25453)	(.24468)	(.30585)
Relations	.26482*	.23751*	.25544†
	(.12370)	(.11489)	(.14137)
Breadth	1.14214*	1.06392*	
	(.48874)	(.46265)	
Centers			−2.87392**
			(.89111)
Doctors			−2.55026*
			(1.07887)
Position	−1.22462**	−1.18246**	
	(.38052)	(.36693)	
Leader			2.55435**
			(.84431)
Follower			2.99607**
			(.91532)
Rivals	.05477	.02222	.03243
	(.09503)	(.09185)	(.09973)
Stage	−.24339	−.18619	−.24827
	(.21713)	(.21075)	(.23206)
Log-likelihood	−47.455	−49.964	−42.817

† p = .01
* p = .5
** p = .01
*** p = .001

part of it is reported in Table 5.2 (Column 2). The results indicate that the fully specified model improves the fit significantly as compared to the restricted ones, attesting that (1) the model is correctly specified, and (2) multicollinearity does not present a problem in the current analysis.

5.3.2. Results of statistical analysis

Column 1 of Table 5.2 reports the results of the fully specified model. The log-likelihood test shows that the overall model, which converged after six iterations, is significant at $p < 0.001$. Column 2 is the restricted model with the quadratic term for size removed. The restricted model significantly worsens the fit. Column 3 reports the results of using the dummy variables instead of BREADTH and POSITION.

To see if (1) SIZE is a significant variable and (2) if a quadratic term correctly specifies the underlying relationship between SIZE and the dependent variable, one restricted model was run and reported in Column 2. In Column 2, variable $SIZE^2$ is removed. Likelihood ratio calculation shows that the full model (Column 1) provides a significantly better fit than the restricted model in Column 2. Similar exercises (not reported) were performed for each, and for combinations, of explanatory variables that were significantly correlated to calculate the significance of individual coefficients and to ensure that the fit cannot be improved by elimination of variables.

Equally significant, the sign for SIZE is positive and for $SIZE^2$ negative, indicating a concave-shaped quadratic relationship. This suggests that the propensity to cooperate increases as firms grow in size and then decreases after the firm size grows beyond a certain limit. A similar trial with a quadratic term for the variable AGE produces misspecification errors, however. In Column 1, both AGE and PRODUCTS are significant and negatively signed, indicating that younger firms and those with fewer products in the market are more likely to cooperate than older ones and those with more products in the market.

The variable of STRATEGY was significant and positively signed. Consistent with our hypothesis, firms with the professed goal of building an integrated operation were found to have a higher propensity to enter into cooperative relationships. DIVERSITY was not found to be significant, although it assumes the hypothesized sign.

The variable of RELATION was found to be significant and positively correlated with the dependent variable, indicating, not surprisingly, that those firms which had more relationships had a higher propensity to form cooperative relationships.

The variables of market conditions, product market BREADTH and competitive POSITION were both significant. The positive sign with the variable of market BREADTH suggests that firms were more likely to cooperate for products targeted for broader markets than for markets of narrower breadth. However, the sign for POSITION is negative, suggesting that firms which are leaders in competition were more likely than followers to be in a cooperative relationship. As reported in Column 3, using dummy variables for targeted markets and competitive positions (Column 3) produced consistent results, confirming the validity of BREADTH and position as independent variables.

RIVALS is insignificant, confirming Hypothesis 9. The result suggests that a firm is more likely to be concerned with its relative position in a R&D competition, or its real rivals, than with the number of firms trying to develop a similar product.

STAGE is insignificant, confirming that a firm's organizational decision is independent of the stage of development for the biotechnology product. This result is consistent with the observation that firms in the biotechnology industry make an organizational decision very early in a drug's development process (Shan, 1987).

5.4. Discussion

The empirical evidence is fairly strong that firm attributes have significant explanatory powers of organizational choices, thereby providing support to the theory that high-technology startup firms seek cooperative relationships to gain access to complementary assets.

The result confirmed Hypothesis 1, showing a concave-shaped quadratic relationship between firm size and the firm's propensity to cooperate. The signs indicate that this propensity increases with firm size only to a certain degree, after which it declines as the firm continues to grow. Several points may be made in interpreting this result. (1) Although cooperative ventures are formed out of the need for complementary assets, the probability of forming cooperative ventures depends on the startup firm's ability to contribute its own specialized assets, which grow with the firm size; and (2) after a certain critical point (on the quadratic curve) when the firm may become more integrated, the need for complementary assets diminishes, as does the propensity to form cooperative relationships.

It is particularly interesting to note that without proper specification to control for the quadratic effect of the size variable, the significance of both variables of size and age disappears and their coefficients substantially fall in value (Column 2). It is therefore apparent that the correct specification of the size variable allows the model to separate out the age effect, which is undoubtedly confounded by the firm size. It is, of course, not surprising and consistent with the findings in many studies of organizational ecology that startup firms of the same age may very well differ in size. The result indicates that the propensity to cooperate falls as firms age. However, after controlling for the firm age and before a certain size limit, larger firms tend to cooperate more than smaller firms. But the propensity to cooperate falls eventually when firms grow beyond a certain point. Therefore, age captures the effect of those constructs that must grow with age in spite of the firm size, which represents the more tangible capabilities of the firm.

In spite of the fact that PRODUCTS is a crude measure of a firm's success in the market, it turns out to be a strongly significant explanatory variable. The result of PRODUCTS corroborated Hypothesis 3, providing further support to the hypothesis that as the firm accumulates capabilities and experiences in the commercialization process and in the marketplace, it becomes less likely to form cooperative ventures.

However, the significant results of variables other than firm attributes confirm that a complete theory must take into account the market, competitive conditions and the strategic intent of the firm. The variable of STRATEGY is found to be significant with the hypothesized sign (Hypothesis 4). This result supported our theory that startup firms with a strategic objective to build an integrated operation face multiple challenges at several links of the value-added chain in comparison to a specialized firm and, therefore, have a greater propensity to cooperate. It should be noted that, conceptually, an integrated operation here refers to involvements in multiple aspects of the business from R&D to marketing. It does not mean that an integrated firm excludes cooperative relationships. In fact, such integrated semiconductor system producers such as IBM, AT&T, and NEC of Japan all maintain multiple cooperative relationships. Therefore, it is not paradoxical, as it may seem, that firms with the professed goal of building an integrated operation are more likely to form cooperative relationships.

It is plausible, based on our theory, that in order to survive in the intense high-technology competition and in the marketplace, a precondition for building an integrated operation in the future, the firm will cooperate to commercialize its earlier products. The same firm may opt to commercialize its future products independently once it has acquired the commercial capability to do so. Viewed from this perspective, cooperative relationships may be understood as strategic tools through which a long-term objective can be achieved.

Therefore, the finding of the relationship between the strategic objective and the propensity to cooperate for a startup firm enhances our understanding of the motivation of cooperative relationships. It suggests that a theory of cooperative relationships is incomplete without consideration of the strategic or long-term thinking of the firm. The variable STRATEGY is but a rather crude measure of a firm's stated strategic objective. It is, of course, always possible for a firm, especially a startup, to change its strategic objective and strategies during the course of its growth. The realized strategy may be very different from the intended one because a firm may adapt its strategic thinking to reflect the realities of the organization and the environment, which also change over time (Mintzberg and Waters, 1985). Our result, therefore, points to the necessity of studying other aspects of a firm's strategy and the locus of its strategy formulation in future studies of the causes of cooperative relationships.

Although the variable of DIVERSITY assumed the hypothesized sign (Hypothesis 5), the result is not significant. One possible explanation is that the ventures in our sample were structured to commercialize pharmaceutical products, which remain the 'core' business for the sampled firms. The degree of diversity of a firm's business may not significantly influence the organizational strategy of its core business, although the variable may affect the organizational mode for its peripheral business (Stopford and Wells, 1972). It is impossible, however, to obtain conclusive evidence without a firm-level analysis of all its cooperative relationships.

Furthermore, as a simple count of the number of business domains in which the firm operates, the measure of diversity does not discriminate between related and unrelated businesses, a distinction found to be significant in the study of the effects of diversification on a firm's performance (Rumelt, 1974). By the logic of our theory, it remains a possibility that diversity in related business should not have as much effect as diversity in unrelated business. The absence of a measure of relatedness is a limitation that needs to be addressed in future studies of the diversity variable when data become available.

It came as no surprise that RELATION was found to be significant and positively signed. Kogut *et al.* (1989) found similar results with a network analysis of cooperative relationships in the biotechnology industry. One interpretation of this result is that some firms have a natural tendency to form cooperative relationships, and this tendency is captured by the number of relationships that the firm has entered into. Another interpretation focuses on the information effect of cooperative relationships (ibid.). According to this argument, firms accumulate information on potential cooperative partners. Therefore, each of the cooperative relationships that they form can be thought of as a step in the learning process. Those firms with more relationships are likely to be more experienced with potential cooperative partners and with managing these external relationships; therefore, they are more likely to form cooperative relationships than those firms which have fewer relationships. The two interpretations are not necessarily inconsistent, inasmuch as tendency, routine and inertia are results of accumulative actions.

The product market condition was found to be a significant consideration in the formation of cooperative ventures by the sampled firms. The product market BREADTH was significant and positively signed, supporting Hypothesis 7. The two dummy variables, CENTERS and DOCTORS, were both found to be significant and positively signed (Column 3). Therefore, in comparison with the excluded dummy variable indicating special clinics, a firm is more likely to form a cooperative relationship if the target market for the product is either major medical centers and hospitals or doctors' offices. The result indicates that the firm is more likely to commercialize a product independently if the product market is a narrow niche market. A broader market breadth imposes much higher demand for resources and commercial capabilities, which the startup firm generally lacks, and drives the firm to seek cooperative relationships. This result lends support to both synergy (through vertical complementarity) and strategic behavior hypothesis of interfirm cooperation.

The preceding discussion on firm strategies may also shed some light on the result of the variable POSITION. Leading firms were found to be more likely than following firms to be in a cooperative relationship, contradicting Hypothesis 8 and the findings of Shan (1990). The age of the data used in the two studies differs. Further scrutiny reveals that the competitive positions of some firms found in both samples improved their competitive positions *after* the formation of earlier cooperative relationships (eg Amgen, Genetics Institute and Interferon Science). Therefore, the findings may indicate that cooperative strategy has a positive effect on firms' competitive position, although causality cannot be inferred from the current analysis.

On the other hand, this result might also suggest that leaders are more likely to find cooperative partners. It is almost certainly incorrect to assume that a firm can always do what it wants to do. It may have determined that it is in its best interests to form a cooperative relationship, but it may fail to find a suitable partner, a situation analogous to one with which we are familiar in human relationships. From the perspective of a potential cooperative partner, the high price of courting a leader might be compensated for by the potential return associated with the increased probability of success, given the fact that competition is intense.(Every drug in our data is being researched and developed by multiple firms.) One possible argument is that the desire to work with a leader is enhanced as the product is brought closer to the market when the competitive outcome can be better predicted. However, this argument is not confirmed by the insignificant finding with STAGE, which measures the closeness of the product to the market.

A longitudinal study is necessary to ground either of these interpretations on firmer evidence. The empirical results of variables of firm attributes, however, indicate that cooperative strategies are preferred by firms that are likely to be competitive underdogs. Therefore, firms of middle-range size, with fewer experiences and fewer products in the market are more likely to opt for cooperative ventures. If our hypothesis is that cooperative relationships are strategic tools used to improve competitive positions, it should not be surprising that leading firms are found in cooperative relationships. This possible dynamism, unfortunately, cannot be captured within the static design of the current research. Further research of a dynamic nature, from a strategic perspective and with longitudinal data, may help pinpoint the relationship between cooperative strategies and firm performances in high-technology competition.

A caveat is advised in attempting to generalize the results of this research. There are significant differences, as pointed out earlier, between high-technology industries. The biomedical market is characterized by the strong vertical complementarity between startup and established firms because of the prolonged and complicated drug development process and the necessity for marketing capabilities. Such complementarity is largely absent in the semiconductor industry, where cooperative relationships are more likely to be horizontal and motivated by the convergence of technologies in new products (Teece, 1986). Competition in biotechnology concentrates in upstream R&D and downstream marketing, while R&D and manufacturing are likely to matter more in semiconductors. Therefore, further testings of our hypotheses with data from other high-technology industries are needed to generalize our results.

Notes

1. Semiconductors and biotechnology are the more recent examples (eg Borrus *et al.*, 1982; Shan, 1987). Foster (1986) documented similar occurrences in many other industries.
2. It is beyond the scope of this chapter to examine the contextual conditions that surround the phenomenon of high-technology entrepreneurship such as the availability of venture capital, macro-economic and industrial policies, and legal and regulatory frameworks. It suffices to note, however, that environmental conditions are important, to say the least. The commercialization of both semiconductor and genetic engineering technologies has followed very different paths of development in Japan, where, unlike the United States, established firms clearly dominate commercialization efforts.
3. The terms of technological change and innovation are frequently used interchangeably in the literature and are given conflicting definitions. Schumpeter

(1944), noted for his failure to distinguish between the concepts of technical change and innovation (Heertje, 1988), considers innovations as 'changes in production functions which cannot be decomposed into infinitesimal steps'. In contrast, Nelson and Winter (1977: 48) argue that 'almost any nontrivial change in product or process . . . is an innovation', and that 'the sharp distinction between moving along a production function and a shift to a new one' should be abandoned. Sahal (1981: 38) argues for an evolutionary view of technical progress and dismisses the distinction between incremental and radical changes as 'pointless'.

4. Major, qualitative technological changes are the center of attention for both theoretical and empirical researchers, and are referred to as either changes of technological regimes (Nelson and Winter, 1982), paradigms (Dosi, 1982), or guideposts (Sahal, 1981) that destroy the competence of incumbent firms (Tushman and Anderson, 1986). The fact is that a layman's perception of 'innovation' is much more tangible and concrete than the type of technological change that created the Silicon Valley, for example.

5. Contractor's (1985) analysis of licensing agreements indicates that the propensity to form inter-firm relationships may be greater among the smaller and largest firms rather than in the middle group, suggesting the possibility of a U-shaped quadratic relationship between firm size and the propensity toward cooperative relationships.

6. This is due to the fact that, in the pharmaceutical industry, 'market features radically skew the returns to innovation so that a handful of first movers remain highly successful while most products are relative failures' (Thomas, 1988: 167).

7. Total assets is another indicator of firm size. It is not used in this study because (1) the amount of physical assets possessed by an NBF does not necessarily reflect its competitive strength, since its 'human assets' at the early stage of commercialization and (2) data for total physical assets are not available.

8. The author wishes to thank Jitendra V. Singh for helpful suggestions.

References

Aldrich, H.E. and Auster, E.R. (1986) 'Even dwarfs started small: liabilities of age and size and their strategic implications' in B.M. Staw and L.L. Cummings (eds), *Research in Organizational behavior*, 8: 165–98. Greenwich, Conn: JAI.

Arthur D. Little, Decision Resources (1988) *Biotechnology Companies as Pharmaceutical Competitors: Their Marketing Strategies May Hold the Key*, January.

Bettis, R.A. (1981) 'Performance differences in related and unrelated diversified firms', *Strategic Management Journal*, 2, 379–92.

Bettis, R.A. and Hall, W.K. (1982) 'Diversification strategy, accounting determined risk, and accounting determined return', *Academy of Management Journal*, 25, 254–64.

Borrus, Millstein and Zysman (1982) *U.S.-Japan Competition in the Semiconductor Industry*, Berkeley, Institute of International Studies, University of California.

Boyle, S.E. (1968) 'An estimate of the number and size distribution of domestic joint subsidiaries', *Antitrust Law & Economics Review*, 1, 81–92.

Caves, R.E. (1981) 'Diversification and seller concentration: Evidence from change, 1963–1972', *Review of Economics and Statistics*, 63, 289–93.

Coleman, K.D., Keating, R. and Jemison, D.B. (1987) *Note on the Biotechnology Industry*, Palo Alto, Graduate School of Business, Stanford University.

Contractor, F.J. (1985) *Licensing in International Strategy, a Guide for Planning and Negotiations*, Westport, Quorum Books.

Contractor, F.J. and Lorange, P. (1988) 'Why should firms cooperate: The strategy and economic basis for cooperative ventures', in F.J. Contractor and P. Lorange (eds), *Cooperative Strategies in International Business*, Lexington, Mass, Lexington Books, 3–30.

Dosi, G. (1982) 'Technological paradigms and technological trajectories', *Research Policy*, 11, 147–62.

Foster, R. (1986) *Innovation, the Attacker's Advantage*, New York, Summit Books.

Freeman, J., Carroll, G. and Hannan, M. (1983) 'The liability of newness: Age dependence in organizational death rates', *American Sociological Review*, 48, 692–9.

Freeman, J. and Hannan, M. (1983) 'Niche width and the dynamics of organizational populations', *American Journal of Sociology*, 88, 1116–45.

Hannan, M.T. and Freeman, J. (1977) 'The population ecology of organizations', *American Journal of Sociology*, 82, 929–64.

Hannan, M.T. and Freeman, J. (1989) *Organizational Ecology*, Cambridge, Mass, Harvard University Press.

Harrigan, K.R. (1985) *Strategies for Joint Ventures*, Lexington, Mass, Lexington Books.

Harrigan, K.R. (1988) 'Strategic alliances and partner asymmetries' in F.J. Contractor and P. Lorange (eds), *Cooperative Strategies in International Business*, Lexington, Mass, Lexington Books, 205–26.

Heertje, A. (1988) 'Schumpeter and technical change', in H. Hanusch (ed.), *Evolutionary Economics*, New York, Cambridge University Press, 71–89.

Hennart, J.-F. (1988) 'A transaction costs theory of equity joint ventures', *Strategic Management Journal*, 9, 361–74.

Hitt, M.A., Hoskisson, R.E., Ireland, R.D. and Harrison, J. (1989) 'Acquisitive growth strategy and relative R&D intensity: The effects of leverage, diversification and size', *Academy of Management Proceedings*, 22–6.

Hitt, M.A., Hoskisson, R.E., Ireland, R.D. (1990) 'Mergers and acquisitions and managerial commitment to innovation in M-form firms', *Strategic Management Journal*, 11, 29–47.

Kamien, M.I. and Schwartz, N.L. (1982) *Market Structure and Innovation*, New York, Cambridge University Press.

Kmenta, J. (1971) *Elements of Econometrics*, New York, Macmillan.

Kogut, B. (1988) 'Joint ventures: Theoretical and empirical perspectives', *Strategic Management Journal*, 9, 319–32.

Kogut, B., Shan, W. and Walker, G. (1989) *The Structuring of an Industry: Cooperative Agreements in the Biotechnology Industry*, Working paper No. 89-20, Reginald H. Jones Center for Management Policy, Strategy and Organization of the Wharton School.

Lieberman, M.B. and Montgomery, D.B. (1988) 'First-mover advantages', *Strategic Management Journal*, 9, 41–58.

Low, M.B. and MacMillan, I.C. (1988) 'Entrepreneurship: Past research and future challenges', *Journal of Management*, 14, 2, 139–61.

Maddala, G.S. (1977) *Econometrics*, New York, McGraw-Hill.

McConnell, J. and Nantell, J. (1985) 'Common stock returns and corporate combinations: The case of joint ventures', *Journal of Finance*, 40, 519–36.

Miller, R.A. (1973) 'Concentration and marginal concentration, advertising and diversity: Three issues in structure-performance tests', *Industrial Organization Review*, 1, 15–24.

Mintzberg, H. and Waters, J. (1985) 'Of strategies, deliberate and emergent', *Strategic Management Journal*, 6, 257–72.

Montgomery, C.A. (1979) 'Diversification, Market Structure, and Firm Performance: An Extension of Rumelt's work', Ph.D. dissertation, Purdue University.

Montgomery, C.A. and Singh, H. (1984) 'Diversification strategy and systemic risk', *Strategic Management Journal*, 5, 181–91.

Nelson, R. and Winter, S. (1977) 'In search of useful theory of innovation' in *Research Policy*, 6, 36–76.

Nelson, R. and Winter, S. (1982) *An Evolutionary Theory of Economic Change*, Cambridge, Mass, Harvard University Press.

OECD (1985) *The Pharmaceutical Industry, Trade Related Issues*, Paris, OECD.

Pfeffer, J. and Salancik, G. (1978) *The External Control of Organizations: A Resource Dependence Perspective*, New York, Harper and Row.

Phillips, A. (1971) *Technology and Market Structure*, Lexington, Mass, Heath Lexington Books.

Porter, M.E. (1985) *Competitive Advantage*, New York, The Free Press.

Prudential-Bache Securities (1987) *Biotechnology World Review*, November.

Robins, J.A. (1987) 'Organizational economics: Notes on the use of transaction-cost theory in the study of organizations', *Administrative Science Quarterly*, 32, 68–86.

Rosenberg, N. (1976) *Perspectives on Technology*, Cambridge, Cambridge University Press.

Rumelt, R.P. (1974) *Strategy, Structure and Economic Performance*, Cambridge, Mass, Harvard University Press.

Rumelt, R.P. (1987) 'Theory, strategy and entrepreneurship' in D.J. Teece (ed.), *The Competitive Challenge*, Cambridge, Mass, Ballinger, 137–58.

Sahal, D. (1981) *Patterns of Technological Innovation*, Reading, Mass, Addison-Wesley.

Schumpeter, J.A. (1934) *The Theory of Economic Development*, Cambridge, Mass, Harvard University Press.

Schumpeter, J.A. (1939) *Business Cycles*, vols I and II, New York, McGraw-Hill.

Schumpeter, J.A. (1944) 'The analysis of economic change', reprinted in H. Somers (ed.) *Reading in Business Cycle Theory*, Philadelphia, The Blakiston Co.

Shan, W. (1987) 'Technological Change and Strategic Cooperation: Evidence from Commercialization of Biotechnology', unpublished doctoral dissertation, University of California, Berkeley.

Shan, W. (1990) 'An empirical analysis of organizational strategies by entrepreneurial high-technology firms', *Strategic Management Journal*, 11, 2, 129–39.

Singh, J.V. and Lumsden, C.J. (1990) 'Theory and research in organizational ecology', *Annual Review of Sociology*, 16, 161–95.

Singh, J.V., Tucker, D.J. and Meinhard, A.G. (1990) 'Institutional change and ecological dynamics' in W.W. Powell and P.J. DiMaggio (eds) *The New Institutionalism in Organizational Analysis*, Chicago, University of Chicago Press.

Steinmueller, W.E. (1988) 'International joint ventures in the integrated circuit industry' in D.C. Mowery (ed.), *International Collaborative Ventures in U.S. Manufacturing*, Cambridge, Mass, Ballinger, 111–46.

Stigler, G.J. (1951) 'The division of labor is limited by the extent of the market', *Journal of Political Economy*, 59, 185–93.

Stinchcombe, A.L. (1965) 'Social structure and organizations' in J.G. March (ed.), *Handbook of Organizations*, Rand McNally, 153–93.

Stopford, J.M. and Wells, L.T. (1972) *Managing the Multinational Enterprise: Organization of Firm and Ownership of the Subsidiaries*, New York, Basic Books.

Stuckey, J.A. (1983) *Vertical Integration and Joint Ventures in the Aluminium Industry*, Cambridge, Mass, Harvard University Press.

Teece, D.J. (1986) 'Profiting from technological innovation: Implications for integration, collaboration, licensing, and public policy', *Research Policy*, 15, 285–305.

Thomas, L.G. (1988) 'Multifirm strategies in the U.S. pharmaceutical industry' in D.C. Mowery (ed.), *International Collaborative Ventures in U.S. Manufacturing*, Cambridge, Mass, Ballinger, 147–82.

Thompson, J.D. (1967) *Organizations in Action*, New York, McGraw-Hill.

Tushman, M. and Anderson, P. (1986) 'Technological discontinuities and organizational environments', *Administrative Science Quarterly*, 31, 439–65.

US Congress, Office of Technology Assessment (1988) *New Developments in Biotechnology*, Washington, DC, US Government Printing Office.

Williamson, O.E. (1975) *Markets and Hierarchies*, New York, The Free Press.

Williamson, O.E. (1983) 'Credible commitments: Using hostages to support exchange', *American Economic Review*, 73, 519–40.

Williamson, O.E. (1985) *The Economic Institutions of Capitalism*, New York, Macmillan.

6 European alliance strategies in the information-processing industries[1]

Michel Delapierre

Inter-firm agreements have experienced a rapid rate of growth over the last decade. Alliances in themselves are not a new phenomenon and have long been a common feature of firms dealings with their competitive environment. However, whereas in the past such relationships were mainly one-way linkages involving the provision of a given service at a given price, such as licensing or sub-contracting, two modes of interaction are emerging into genuine partnerships in which the two participants contribute through the mobilization of their own specific skills and assets.[2]

The increasing number of two-way agreements between firms raises the question of the transformation of their mode of external growth,[3] from mergers and acquisitions to memorandums of understanding (MOUs). On the one hand it can be argued that contracts are ways to establish a controlling relationship through means other than outright acquisition, that they are quite often asymmetrical and that one partner will reap the benefits at the expense of the others.[4] In that sense, agreements can be analysed as new forms of direct investment[5] or as a kind of hierarchy in opposition to market forms of organization.[6] According to this view, MOUs would act as a substitute for acquisitions.

On the other hand, mergers, acquisitions and contractual agreements have exhibited parallel trends of growth. Therefore they appear complementary rather than as a substitute. Firms combine both modes of growth in their overall strategies. The hypothesis on which our analysis is built is that these two modes fulfil two separate objectives: control and co-ordination.

Control is best implemented through acquisitions and is particularly suited to reach critical mass on world markets in order to benefit from scale and scope advantages.[7] Co-ordination is more like the establishment of networks, where the complementarity of diversified skills and assets, rather than their accumulation, is needed.[8]

The LAREA/CEREM has undertaken a research programme on alliance behaviour by European firms. In order to compare control and co-ordination strategies, a data base has been developed on external relationships involving at least one European corporation and ranging from mergers and acquisitions to MOUs.[9] In that respect, alliances must be understood as any kind of relationship built between two or more corporations – regardless of its purpose, control or co-ordination, and of its type – acquisition, joint venture or MOU.

This chapter will focus on the information-processing industries. It will first present the general picture or the dynamics of European alliances in these domains before addressing the question of the impact of co-ordination strategies as new modes of organization on the structure of firms and industries. Information-processing products cover a wide range of industries, which can be collectively grouped into what is currently called 'the industrial electronics network', made up of a highly diverse range of products and clientele. While at times the different information-processing sectors have been thought to be converging towards a single industry, it has been observed that the basic technological community has not necessarily evolved towards homogeneous product and demand characteristics.

6.1. The dynamics of the European information-processing alliances

6.1.1. *Coverage of this study*

The information-processing industries have the dual characteristics of inter-linking community of technologies and the wide diversity of technological applications which can be found in the compatible and systemic nature of the products. These are in effect specific systems built up through the combination of highly standardized elements. Microprocessors are used for a wide variety of applications in computers, telecommunications, production and consumer electronics. In the same vein, computer terminals can be integrated into computer networking systems as well as telecommunications. System builders are therefore constantly in search of element compatibility between their own system and those of their colleagues while at the same time designing and adopting standards allowing for the inter-connection and inter-operation of their products.

The information-processing industries also display both mature and emerging industry traits. As is the case in mature industries, they have oligopolistic structures dominated by large corporations with significant market share in each market segment. As is common in emerging industries, the rate of innovation is rapid, resulting in short product cycles and the constant entrance of new players.

Finally, the European information-processing industries in a number of sub-sectors – primarily components, followed by computers – demonstrate a clear lack of global competitiveness in spite of industrial policies which have targeted their development. Because of their strong capacity to contribute to productivity gains, the information-processing industries represent a major factor in future European industrial competitiveness as a whole.

The cooperation and restructuring strategies of European firms are therefore of specific interest. This field is particularly ripe for the combination of industrial capacities and technical competencies. In the context of intense international competition, the strategies of the principal European firms towards the building up of European-based global industries or the search for sheltered local positioning behind the mostly non-European shield is a critical issue for analysis.

We have defined the information-processing industries as including computer hardware and software, telecommunications, micro-electronic processors and production technologies dealing with data processing rather than process technologies. Given this definition, the analysis will focus on those industry segments with a significant number of alliances in computers (for which 560 cases were identified during the 1980s), telecommunications (273 cases) and components (109 alliances) which together represent slightly more than 95 per cent of the overall sector total of 990.

External alliance activity among European firms – memorandums of understanding, equity positions, mergers and acquisitions – in the information-processing sector grew considerably during the 1980s. There was, however, a relative levelling off of alliances towards the end of the decade, indicating a possible peaking of alliance activity. Despite the lack of exhaustive coverage of the data bases due to the recording of cases through press clippings, the various data bases built elsewhere, by other research teams, give the same global trends.[10]

Alliances between companies can be divided into three categories. *Memorandums of Understanding (MOUs)* cover all alliances which do not involve a transfer of assets between partners. Alliances involving asset transfer have been divided into *joint ventures* and minority equity participation, and *controlling operations*: entailing equity participation of higher than 30 per cent and acquisition, in so far as the former category assumes the partner's independence and the latter leads to a fusion of the two into one single entity.

The distribution of alliances over time underscores the strong dynamics of MOUs during the period covered in this study despite a precipitous drop in 1989. MOUs in fact stagnated from 1985 on. It should be pointed out that 1985 corresponds with the launching of the ESPRIT programme followed a few years later by Eureka. One can legitimately be led to believe that in the area of collaborative research, alliances subsidized by the European Community and the Eureka member states had a substitution effect on European alliance activity. Alliances in the computer industry, the sector most directly targeted by ESPRIT, dropped off in the year following the launching of the programme's first two phases in 1985 and 1988.

Until at least 1988, joint ventures followed a parallel evolution consistent with cooperative character in which the various partners retained their strategic autonomy outside of those areas covered by the alliance. Conversely, controlling acquisitions show a low level of activity until 1985, followed by an extremely rapid increase in 1989 – even overtaking the level of MOUs.

The number of operations does not in itself indicate the relative significance of this phenomenon. The type of linkage created at a given point in time does not necessarily reflect the same degree of strategic importance. A collaborative agreement for the development of a new technology or product can have a more fundamental strategic implication than an alliance involving the distribution of a minor product in a limited market. Conversely, while certain MOUs may have significant strategic implications for a firm at a given point in time and others may be of only marginal importance to one or another of the partners involved, the acquisition of an enterprise almost always has major strategic implications.

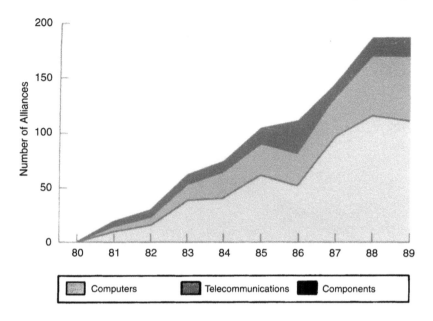

Figure 6.1 Evolution by industrial sub-sector

A second analytical problem involves the imprecise nature of information on MOUs in comparison with operations involving the transfer of assets. At the time of their signature, MOUs clarify the partner's intentions or, more precisely, what the partners wish their competitors to believe are their intentions. The actual impact is not understood at that particular moment and it is therefore difficult to evaluate their relative importance. Moreover, mergers and acquisitions are obliged to be publicized by capital market regulatory institutions. The collection of information from these operations is therefore less complicated than for other forms of alliances.

Regardless of these limitations, analysis of the three forms of alliance operations we have identified and their comparative evolution underscores their complementary rather than their substitutional character. Companies can be involved in takeovers and alliances with independent firms at the same time. Joint ventures and minority equity participations in particular followed the same trajectory as MOUs until 1988 and mergers and acquisitions only demonstrated divergent trends from 1984 to 1986. Therefore, in the light of these data, it cannot be said that a firm defines its external growth strategy by favouring one form of alliance activity over another. Rather firms appear constantly to play out the complete range of possibilities open to them. The high rate of acceleration in mergers and acquisitions which dominates the latter half of the 1980s clearly corresponds with the preparations associated with the competition of the Single European Market in January 1993 through the application of market-share acquisition strategies.

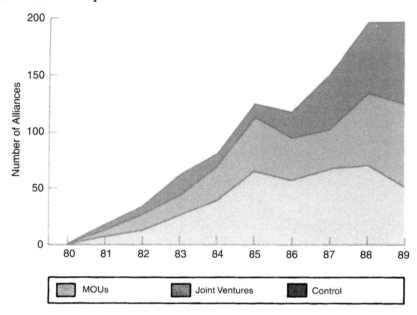

Figure 6.2   Evolution by type of alliance

6.1.2. Types of alliances

The distribution of the inter-firm relations surveyed by the type of alliance (Table 6.1) shows that MOUs represent 41 per cent, followed by joint ventures and minority equity participation with 33 per cent and control operations with 26 per cent, respectively. Partner selection by European firms is characterized primarily by a high propensity towards internationalization: close to three-quarters of the identified linkages involve firms of different nationalities. At the international level, linkages with American firms predominate in 56 per cent of cases, while strictly intra-EC linkages represent less than one-quarter of alliances and Japanese firms are involved in only 11 per cent of cases surveyed.

At the geographic level, as has been generally observed, activities are highly concentrated in the global economic triad comprising Europe, the USA and Japan. Non-triad linkages represent less than 3 per cent of cases surveyed, and even those alliances linking EC firms with other European companies represent less than 4 per cent of cases.

In general, one can nevertheless point to a bi-polarization of linkages: between European firms in favour of North American partners in 41 per cent of the cases surveyed and intra-European alliances in 44 per cent of cases. In the area of information processing, relations with Japanese firms remain relatively undeveloped (Table 6.2).

Table 6.3 shows that, when the US firms are dominant partners, the agreement tends to be a Memorandum of Understanding. Conversely, European firms tend to acquire the control of their partners.

Table 6.1   Linkages by type (%)

	Total
MOUs	41.1
Joint ventures	33.0
Control	26.0

Table 6.2   Linkages by nationality (%)

Rest of the World	6.6
Japan	8.1
USA	41.0
Intra EC	17.5
Domestic	26.7
Total	100.0

Table 6.3   Relationships with US partners, according to type of agreements and nationality of dominant partner (%)

Type of agreement	European Union	United States	No dominant partner
MOUs	35.2	60.3	51.3
Joint ventures	27.3	21.4	48.0
Control	37.5	18.3	0.7
Total	100.0	100.0	100.0

If one considers the type of alliances, from MOUs to acquisitions, a number of trends emerge in relation to the nationality of the partner. Control operations tend to dominate intra-national alliances, in which partners are of the same national origin (45 per cent), while MOUs are only evident in 23 per cent of alliances. In the case of international linkages, partnership through MOUs is the dominant form of alliance; the further away the partner – Europe, USA and finally Japan – the greater the tendency to enter into MOUs rather than other forms of alliances (Table 6.4).

Two strategies, or rather two complementary strategic orientations, appear to be at work here. The first aims to reinforce the original national market position of each firm through the buyout and integration of local firms of the same nationality.[11] This is partially a traditional oligopolistic strategy based on the acquisition of market share but also a strategy aimed at building up a design and production base to support the development of a globalization strategy. The second strategic orientation indicates the globalization policy where it is imperative to develop independent partner relationships based on collaboration rather than control. In the case of EC partners control positions are targeted in one case in four, while with American partners

Table 6.4 Linkages by type of alliance and partner nationality (%)

Partner nationality	MOU	Joint venture	Control
Intra EC	30.0	34.6	36.9
Domestic share	22.9	34.4	45.0
EC share	40.7	34.9	24.4
USA	49.3	33.3	17.5
Japan	69.7	22.4	7.9
Rest of world	27.6	40.0	26.3
Total	40.6	33.1	26.3

control is an issue in one out of six alliances and with Japanese firms in a little more than one out of twelve.

Nevertheless, European firms remain largely polarized on their local markets. In such cases they will trade market share for technological competencies. Two-thirds of alliances involve European markets, while only 15 per cent involve a global market dimension. In other words, a large proportion of collaborative MOUs signed with American and Japanese firms primarily involve the local market of the European firm.

In such cases, European firms will trade market share for technological competencies and for competitive advantage against other European firms rather than against principle world producers. The preference for MOUs rather than mergers and acquisitions by EC corporations can not be said to reduce their dependency on Japanese and American firms. In so far as firms increasingly favour partnership relationships, the increase in the proportion of MOUs does not necessarily indicate an autonomous position for European firms beyond the general decentralizing trends of large multinationals.

6.1.3. Motives

The motives underpinning alliances undertaken by European corporations can be gleaned from the functions that are assigned to them. It is important to remember that these objectives are communicated through the press or by the firms themselves. Given that the information obtained is that which the partners wish to be known inevitably introduces a certain degree of bias.

6.1.3.1. The principle industrial objectives of the alliances

Alliance objectives have been classified in five major categories: research and development (R&D), covering all alliances aimed at producing technical competencies; production, including manufacturing licensing; commercialization; standardization and a comprehensive category covering all the objectives as a whole.

Table 6.5 shows a hierarchy of objectives. The most frequently cited are comprehensive alliances immediately followed by commercialization, far

Table 6.5   Linkages by objectives (%)

Comprehensive	31.1
Standardization	4.9
Commercialization	30.1
Production	15.3
R&D	18.0
Total	100.0

ahead of R&D, production and standardization. Evidently, market strategies predominate. Comprehensive alliances precisely articulate all the industrial activities in a particular area – type of product or solution – and even the complete range of activities of one or the other participant. Partners cooperate in the design, manufacture and commercialization of a product or a product range. In the majority of cases such agreements are highly asymmetrical with one of the partners playing a predominant role, leading eventually to the integration of one partner's activities into the other. The Olivetti–AT&T alliances provides a good example of this trend. The original objective was to allow each of the two partners to enhance its range of activities and market reach. Olivetti would distribute AT&T's private switching systems in Europe, while AT&T would market Olivetti personal computers on the North American continent. The agreement involved the almost complete integration of the two firms, covering the complete range of information-processing activities and world markets, but an equally balanced role between the two partners could not be achieved or maintained.

Indeed, from the start, the difference in size was characterized by a minority equity participation by the larger AT&T in the smaller Olivetti. It became evident soon after that the two firms were unable to set up an effective partner relationship through the undertaking of common tasks rather than a simple division of product ranges and markets. Following the failure of this alliance, AT&T proceeded to complete integration and subsequent subordination of its partner by asking to play out its capital option clause in Olivetti from a minority to a controlling position. Wishing to maintain its autonomy, Olivetti refused and instead accepted a transfer of AT&T's participation to a share in Olivetti's holding company, resulting in a change from industrial partner to financial participant.

Commercialization agreements do not imply the complete integration of firms resulting in one homogeneous entity but tend to be more associated with market-sharing objectives. Imbalances are most often the result of one-way market access, with one partner marketing the other's product without a reciprocal agreement. More than one-third of alliances surveyed (37.2 per cent) were one-way marketing alliances.

One-way alliances also include OEM (Original Equipment Manufacturer) agreements which are highly common in information-processing industries. A firm that manufactures its own products supplies another vendor who in turn markets the product under its own name. Such agreements go beyond sub-contracting or client–supplier relationships in as much as the original

Table 6.6　Principal alliance objectives established by European corporations (%)

R&D		Production		Commercialization	
Pre-competitive	6.6	Co-production	38.2	One-way	37.2
Development	73.9	Sub-contract	5.9	OEM	13.1
Technology acquisition	14.2	Input acquisition	5.9	Complementary product range	19.4
Other	6.6	Secondary source	6.5	Market sharing	6.3
Comprehensive	1.3	Licence	33.3	Other	11.5
		Other	7.0	Comprehensive	18.6
		Comprehensive	3.2		
Total	100.0	Total	100.0	Total	100.0

manufacturer is also a competitor with his client – with each partner commercializing the product under its own name.

Research and development alliances are the third most important objective with close to 23 per cent of all cases surveyed. Given that this survey does not cover agreements made within the EC Framework and Eureka programmes, data on R&D alliances thus underestimates their real significance in linkages among European corporations. Moreover, the level of R&D activities within individual firms is relatively lower than for other in-house activities. Greater weight should be therefore given to R&D alliances than is indicated by the survey data.

Alliances listed in this category deal specifically with the production of technical competencies. Simple transfers, generally undertaken through production licensing agreements are listed under the production objective. R&D alliances are in effect true partnerships. In three-quarters of the cases surveyed, they involve co-development of a product or process. These alliances are therefore shared tasks and not simply the division of completed results or assets.

Production is the fourth most frequently cited objective. Achieving scale economies is a key motive in these alliances, where 38 per cent of production alliances are co-production agreements. Thus each partner can achieve an optimum size and assure a competitive price level for all of the participants. Co-production is more partnership-oriented than OEM alliances because it leads to a sharing of responsibilities between co-producers while OEM is limited to marketing authorization of the original manufacturer's products under the trademark of the final vendor. The majority of co-production alliances include clauses giving each partner the right to sell the complete product range under its own name.

In one-third of the cases surveyed, with the exception of cross-licensing agreements, licence concessions demonstrate the domination of partners controlling intellectual and industrial property rights over the licensee. The limited level of sub-contracting agreements is evidently due to the lack of publicity given to this traditional and common relationship by the partners and the professional press.

Standardization agreements are the least frequent (6 per cent). Their relatively small number should nevertheless not be underestimated. They often bring together a large number of partners and involve almost all the major players in the industry. Cooperation aimed at defining or adopting standards is almost completely absent from other industries covered in the LAREA/CEREM data base. The systemic nature of the information-processing-industry products, a distinct characteristic already noted in this study, is reflected in the number of standardization alliances. Standards are required to allow for the compatibility of new hardware entering the information-processing market. A standard can thus be the result of a complementary agreement between specialized producers. More broadly, standards can allow for market development by guaranteeing the inter-operability of different installed systems. Agreements made between a large number of firms can be seen as a coordinated strategy to ensure overall market viability. The data base contains one alliance involving twenty-three participants and six with six or more partners.

In the first case, standardization allows two firms with complementary activities to combine their products into systems. The second case allows firms competing in final-product markets to cooperate so that cooperation becomes a prerequisite for competition. In the absence of standardization, agreements on inter-system compatibility, products or 'proprietary systems' launched by a producer tend to lock the user into the original choice. Without interconnecting possibilities, information-processing networks are more difficult to build up thus slowing market development possibilities. Cooperation between competitors for standardization is a typical zero-sum game where the best result is achieved through the cooperation of each player.[12]

6.1.3.2. *Alliance objectives by type*
The breakdown of alliance objectives in European corporate alliances by type – control, joint venture and MOUs – is consistent with the two strategic orientations we have highlighted in this study: market domination and collaboration.

Two-thirds of the linkages aimed at producing knowledge are MOUs without asset transfer, while the rest involve joint ventures or minority equity positions. There are virtually no R&D agreements involving controlling positions. Specific production alliances also tend to be cooperative in nature but with an equal distribution between MOUs and joint ventures/minority positions. Production activities require more significant capital support and, more often than not, a non-recoverable investment commitment in specific hardware. Such agreements justify strategies allowing for the appropriation of results through proprietary control.

Somewhat paradoxically, commercial alliances are MOUs in 60 per cent of cases. As pointed out earlier, they tend to deal with client–supplier complementarities. Less than 20 per cent of such alliances involve the control of one partner over the commercial activities of the other.

Comprehensive alliances, which deal with the corporate industrial oper-ations as a whole, quite understandably involve the transfer of assets: joint ventures, minority equity participation, and above all, in close to 60 per cent of cases, takeovers, mergers or acquisitions.

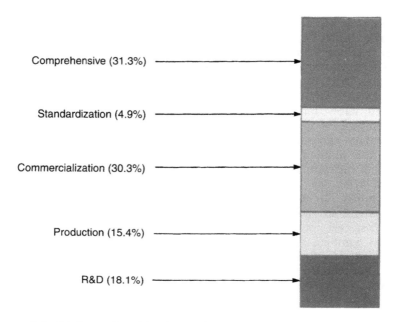

Comprehensive (31.3%)

Standardization (4.9%)

Commercialization (30.3%)

Production (15.4%)

R&D (18.1%)

Figure 6.3   Linkages by objective and type

A breakdown of corporate alliances by type indicates a clear distinction between short-term operations, which are limited in product range, and comprehensive alliances covering a complete spectrum of industrial functions. The former, which results more from the co-ordination of mostly independent firms, involve primarily MOUs or minority participation. The latter cases, involving fuller integration between partners, lead more often to traditional forms of control through capital holdings.

Moreover, it has not been demonstrated that the closer one gets to the market – from R&D to commercialization – the more one tends to get into control situations. While two-thirds of R&D alliances are MOUs, 60 per cent of commercial alliances also involve MOUs. One can detect two strategic orientations in MOUs: partnership with the common objective of achieving a coordinated action and sharing relations through the redistribution of existing assets such as market segments or products.

6.1.3.3.   Objectives by partner nationality

Consideration of the partner's nationality, as illustrated in Figure 6.4, confirms the previous observations made with respect to corporate strategies and different geographic markets. Domestic linkages between firms of the same nationality are comprehensive alliances in 60 per cent of the cases. This is consistent with strategies aimed at controlling local markets. Alliances involving foreign partners from within the EC demonstrate a fairly equal distribution between R&D, commercialization and comprehensive objectives. In the case of American firms, European corporations clearly tend

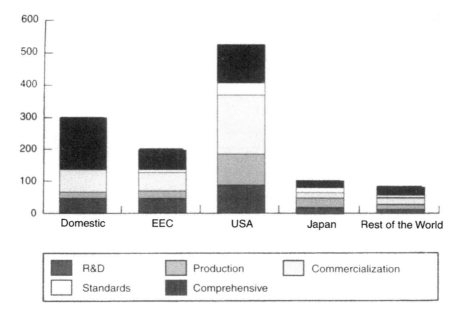

Figure 6.4 Linkages by objective and nationality

to favour commercial over comprehensive objectives. Alliances with Japanese firms almost never involve integration but tend to favour specific alliances with R&D, production and commercialization objectives.

One general observation to be made is that European firms are not being bought out by non-European firms[13] and that they endeavour to reinforce their domestic bases before European ones. Fifty-eight per cent of comprehensive and 42 per cent of R&D alliances are between European firms primarily of the same nationality. The relative importance of intra-European R&D alliances, especially given the exclusion of major EC-sponsored projects in this data base, strongly indicates a desire among EC corporations to promote innovation strategies. One should not, however, lose sight of the fact that while some firms and sectors endeavour to improve their global competitive positioning, others appear highly dependent upon non-European firms; more than half the production and commercialization alliances have been with American companies.

A closer analysis of the various objectives shows that the majority of intra-European R&D alliances, whether domestic or inter-European, involved the development of products or processes which complement the pre-competitive EC-sponsored R&D programmes such as ESPRIT. Technology acquisitions were most often (in 25 per cent of R&D alliances) undertaken with Japanese firms. Co-production activities were clearly more prevalent than licensing in production alliances in 40–50 per cent of cases for intra-EC alliances and with American firms.

Where Japan is concerned the opposite is true. Manufacturing licences (46

Table 6.7 Distribution of linkages by targeted geographic market zone and by objective (%)

Objective	EC	Non-EC	USA	Japan	Rest
R&D	90.0	5.0	40.2	31.5	30.1
Production	88.2	11.8	28.0	19.4	21.0
Commercial	89.0	11.0	26.2	16.6	16.0
Standards	100.0	0	44.6	37.5	35.7
Comprehensive	84.3	15.7	25.3	9.9	11.7
Total	88.3	11.7	28.8	18.1	18.0

per cent) were more frequently cited than co-production activities (29 per cent). While alliances with commercial objectives tended to be complementary between national partners, one-way agreements tended to characterize alliances with other partners and there was a noticeable OEM bias with Japanese firms.[14]

6.1.3.4. Objectives by geographic zone
Information provided by alliance participants makes it possible to identify the regional or global geographic market targeted by the operation. The global market is only mentioned in a small fraction (15.4 per cent) of the alliances surveyed. Alliances tended to be more tightly focused; two-thirds involved the EC market, 8.4 per cent the United States and only 1.3 per cent solely Japan. These figures are consistent with the precise nature of linkages developed by European corporations. However, in a significant number of cases several regions were implicated. For example, the EC alone or with other market zones was targeted in 88.3 per cent of alliances, while the US and Japanese markets were implicated in 28.8 and 18.1 per cent respectively. These alliances are examples of situations where each partner opens its market to its counterpart or penetrates the other's market. The huge European market has been the principal focal point for alliances, as much for intra-European alliances as for alliances between European and non-European firms.

Distribution by objectives confirms a number of previous observations. In 71.2 per cent of cases, comprehensive alliances are concerned exclusively with the immediate EC markets of European firms. Standardization is more globally focused where a good third of alliances have a world-market perspective. In this same vein, R&D alliances have the second largest global market focus (28.8 per cent) but with a strong triad bias; Europe is mentioned in 95 per cent of cases, the USA in 40.2 per cent and Japan in 31.5 per cent. The closer an alliance approaches the final market, the more precise the geographic focus. In particular, the European market is exclusively targeted in R&D (55.7 per cent), production (62.9 per cent) and commercialization (67.7 per cent).

Two remarks can be made at this level of analysis. First, corporate European alliance strategies with other firms have relatively limited objectives. This does not imply that the overall commercial strategies of these companies are limited to market segments, but that their general alliance strategies cover a wide spectrum of relationships with a large number of different firms. Second, European information-processing firms none the less demonstrate a clear lack of global market perspective in their alliance strategies since two-thirds of linkages are focused exclusively on the EC market. This indicates two consequences of the relative weakness of European information-processing corporations. They were confronted with the impact of non-European firms attempting to penetrate the European Single Market; they were then forced into a defensive strategy, concentrating their efforts on conserving or re-establishing their position within their own domestic markets in Europe before moving on to global operations. The dynamism of a limited number of European firms should not, however, be overlooked since 12.5 per cent of comprehensive alliances target the American market.

6.1.3.5. Alliance objectives by type and partner nationality

Cross-analysis of three variables, as illustrated in Table 6.8, provides a recapitulation of the study to this point.

Looking at the most important objectives – R&D, production, commercialization and comprehensive – and initially at their most significant values, one can distinguish a distinct propensity of European corporations towards control-oriented objectives with firms involved in domestic alliances (10 per cent of all cases) and a tendency towards MOUs when there were commercial alliances with American firms (11.6 per cent of all cases). This is indicative of an intermediate strategy for European firms: they have striven to consolidate their market position within the EC through the acquisition of local companies, followed by a strengthening of their competitive positioning in these markets through the acquisition of products and technologies from mostly American world leaders.

A more detailed analysis reveals the emergence of an intra-European strategy for the design of new products and technologies. Twenty-five per cent of R&D alliances were intra-European and predominantly international as compared to 28.8 per cent with American firms. The high intra-European R&D alliance level is even more significant given that this data base does not include EC framework or Eureka programmes. Moreover, MOUs signed with American firms most often focused on product and process development and rarely on pre-competitive research.

As previously noted, linkages between European and Japanese firms were still underdeveloped despite the increase in direct Japanese investment in these industries in Europe during the time frame covered in this study. The highly specific nature of European linkages with Japanese firms can be seen in the relative importance (11.5 per cent) of production agreements of which about half have been manufacturing licences. Co-production agreements were much less common, and the linkages between European and Japanese firms were therefore highly asymmetrical, with the European partner having tended to play a more passive receptor role.

Table 6.8 also underscores the more continental rather than global European corporate strategy orientation in so far as EC firms have not aimed to cover the global market through linkages with partners throughout the

Table 6.8 European corporate linkages by alliance objective, type and partner nationality (% of total for each objective)

	MOU	J. venture	Control	Total
R&D				
EC	26.5	14.2	0.9	41.6
Dom. share	11.1	8.8	0.4	20.4
EC share	15.5	5.3	0.4	21.2
USA	28.8	10.6	1.8	41.2
Japan	8.0	2.7	0	10.6
Other	4.0	2.2	0.9	7.1
Production				
EC	11.5	12.1	0.5	24.2
Dom. share	6.0	4.4	0	10.4
EC share	5.5	7.7	0.5	13.7
USA	23.6	28.0	1.1	52.7
Japan	11.5	3.8	0.5	15.9
Other	1.6	6.0	0	7.7
Commercial				
EC	18.1	9.9	5.5	33.5
Dom. share	9.6	5.8	3.3	18.7
EC share	8.5	4.1	2.2	14.8
USA	31.6	17.3	2.7	51.6
Japan	6.9	2.5	0.3	9.6
Other	2.5	1.9	0.5	4.9
Standard				
EC	16.9	8.5	0	25.4
Dom. share	5.1	1.7	0	6.8
EC share	11.9	6.8	0	18.6
USA	49.2	8.5	3.4	61.0
Japan	6.8	0	0	6.8
Other	3.4	0	0	3.4
Comprehensive				
EC	0.8	20.6	36.0	57.4
Dom. share	0.8	12.7	27.2	40.7
EC share	0	7.9	8.7	16.7
USA	1.1	14.3	15.6	31.0
Japan	0	1.6	1.3	2.9
Other	0	3.2	1.1	4.2

world. This lack of global perspective, the preoccupation with rationalization, the defence of domestic market share, and the dependence on American and Japanese firms at the production and commercialization stages is in contrast to the highly dynamic nature of the R&D alliance strategies which EC firms appeared to be building up in European information processing. One may be tempted, however, to ask if this European-style restructuring is nothing more than a façade masking the penetration of non-European products and technologies in the EC markets without clear reciprocity for European firms in global markets.

Analysis of inter-corporate alliance types – MOUs, joint-ventures, minority equity participations and acquisitions – has indicated their complementary rather than their alternative nature. The question remains as to what extent these alliances lead to the building up of competing blocks of partner linkages or to a more complex entity of firms both competing and collaborating with one another.

6.2. Alliances and the structuring of firms and industries

The principal firms in the information-processing industries are easily identified. The sector covers mostly well-established industries which have reached a relatively high level of maturity in comparison with the biotechnology sector for example. Many of these industrial sub-sectors are characterized by an oligopolistic structure and, by extension, by large corporations with significant market share. Finally, the European Community itself recognized, if not confirmed, this hierarchy by bringing together the twelve largest information-processing firms for the launching and follow-up of the ESPRIT programme in 1980. Today, no more than nine remain – eight if only firms under European control are considered. Nixdorf, Plessey and AEG have disappeared. Nixdorf was absorbed by Siemens, Plessey was divided up between Siemens and GEC and AEG was bought out by Daimler Benz.[15] ICL has survived but is controlled by Fujitsu.

The restructuring of the twelve-largest European information-processing companies is consistent with the findings in the first part of this study which highlighted the consolidation strategies of European corporations via takeovers on their domestic markets.

We have therefore considered the nine major firms (see Table 6.9) from the ESPRIT programme-directing committee, while retaining ICL since it was not under Fujitsu control during the period covered by this study of European alliances.

The alliance classification of the three firms which were absorbed by the other leaders during the 1980–9 period has been consolidated into the nine remaining firms. Hence, the industry leader alliances have been differentiated from those of other firms in Europe. This, however, does not imply a clear differentiation between large- and small-firm alliance strategies. In fact, among the partners surveyed in the data base, several firms of comparable size with the leading information-processing corporations such as Schneider, Fiat and British Aerospace[16] have been identified but their principal activities are only marginally involved in information processing. The purpose of this differentiation is to identify clearly specific behaviour patterns among the principal players in the European information-processing sector. This analysis will be presented in two parts, first by comparing the strategy of the leading nine firms with that of other European corporations and second, through a more detailed analysis of the leaders' behaviour as a group.

Table 6.9 The nine-largest European information-processing corporations (ranked by number of cases identified in data base)

Firm	Number of linkages
CGE	68
Olivetti	60
Bull	59
Thompson	58
Philips	56
Siemens	43
ICL	39
STET	28
GEC	13
Total	351

6.2.1. Comparisons between the nine major European firms and the European information-processing industry

More than one-third of the linkages surveyed in the data base (36 per cent) involve the nine major European firms, indicating that they are also major alliance partners in the European information-processing industries.

Distribution by nationality (Table 6.10) illustrates the highly intra-European orientation of the nine industry leaders. Only 19.1 per cent of their alliances are with firms of the same nationality compared to 31.1 per cent for other European firms. Close to one-quarter (24.8 per cent) of the leading nine firms' alliances were with other EC partners compared to 13.5 per cent for the others. There is little difference (40.5 per cent and 41.1 per cent respectively) between the group of nine firms and the others in non-EC alliances. The only difference is a greater apparent propensity towards Japanese partners (9.7 per cent) among the leading nine firms than for others in the industry (6.7 per cent).

These findings tend to differentiate between the levels of the European information-processing industries. Secondary players attempted to reinforce their local market positions while the majors were establishing a European-wide industrial structure. This cannot, however, be interpreted as an industrial and geographic restructuring through the simple redistribution of alliance activities between the two groups, with the European market being consolidated for the majors and the national markets for the rest. Both categories demonstrated the same degree of activity with respect to American firms, and while the majors had more alliances with Japanese corporations, the others had a relatively more important range of activities with other European and non-European partners elsewhere in the global market. Exposure to the USA may nevertheless cover highly asymmetrical relations: an expansion of the larger firms in the American market and penetration of the European market by American firms via alliances with other European corporations. Analysis of partner dominance by alliance, however, does not

Table 6.10 The leading nine firms compared to other European firms: distribution by partner nationality (%)

Partner	9 majors	Others
EC	43.9	44.6
Domestic share	19.1	31.1
EC share	24.8	13.5
USA	40.5	41.1
Japan	9.7	6.7
Others	4.6	7.8
Total	100.0	100.0

Table 6.11 The leading nine firms compared to other European firms: distribution by dominant partner in alliances with American firms (%)

Dominant partner	9 majors	Others
EC	32.9	30.8
USA	24.5	34.6
Equal	42.7	33.8
Total	100.0	100.0

Table 6.12 The leading nine firms compared to other European firms: distribution by type (%)

Type	9 majors	Others
MOU	47.0	37.8
J. venture	37.0	30.7
Control	16.0	31.5
Total	100.0	100.0

confirm this hypothesis. The European firm was the dominant partner in about one-quarter of the alliances surveyed for both the nine majors and the other firms (see Table 6.11). The only identifiable difference is that the American firm was the dominant partner in one-third of the alliances compared to one-quarter with the nine leaders. Hence, the nine European majors tended to play an equal role with their American counterparts more often than other European firms. Clearly, however, despite the greater offensive capability of the nine European leaders, the European information-processing industry cannot be broken down into a simple geographic market hierarchy.

Analysis of alliances by type provides a more contrasting picture of strategies between the nine majors and the rest of the European industry. Table 6.12 highlights the clear propensity of the nine leaders towards

Table 6.13 The leading nine firms compared to other European firms: distribution by objective (%)

Objective	9 majors	Others
R&D	29.6	19.2
Production	25.6	14.4
Commercial	35.3	37.8
Standards	8.8	4.2
Comprehensive	30.2	42.9
Total	100.0	100.0

MOUs, while the other European firms tended to be more involved in acquisitions. This coincides with the previous finding which indicated the more domestic character of the other group's alliance activities. This finding gives the impression that the major European producers have virtually completed the restructuring and consolidation phase and were moving towards a cooperation–competition alliance strategy within the industry.

The third major variable covering the industrial objectives of alliances (Table 6.13) confirms this impression. One can in fact distinguish the concentration of firms outside the group of nine leaders in alliances with comprehensive industrial objectives (42.9 per cent), followed by commercial alliances (37.8 per cent). Conversely, while not ignoring this strategy, the nine majors were significantly more inclined to be involved in R&D and production alliances.

In general terms, the European information-processing industries taken as a whole tended to focus their alliance strategies on Europe. The secondary firms were primarily involved in restructuring activities within their domestic markets and more specifically in rapidly developing niches such as software service. The nine majors who occupied dominant market positions in the more mature industry sub-sectors were more involved in cooperative alliances which tended to take on the role of industry regulation as opposed to acquisition of market share.

6.2.2. Alliance strategies of the nine majors and information-processing-industry restructuring: emergence of an industry-wide network.

As previously indicated, alliances involving at least one of the nine majors represents over one-third of cases surveyed in the database. In order to provide a more detailed analysis of the alliance strategies of these corporations, their interactions have been broken down into the following categories: alliance between majors; other large firms, including European, with primary activities outside of the information-processing industries as well as non-European firms, primarily American and Japanese; and other relatively smaller firms though not strictly small and medium-sized enterprises (SMEs).

Table 6.14 **Alliances of European majors: distribution by partner (%)**

Firm	Intra 9	9 + large	9 + others
CGE	22.1	23.5	54.4
Olivetti	15.0	35.0	50.0
Bull	25.4	23.7	50.8
Thompson	19.0	41.4	39.7
Philips	25.0	51.8	23.2
Siemens	32.6	51.2	16.3
ICL	20.5	46.2	33.3
STET	17.9	64.3	17.9
GEC	23.1	69.2	7.7
Total	10.2	44.4	45.3

Table 6.15 **Alliances of European majors: distribution by partner nationality (%)**

Partner	Intra 9	9 + large	9 + others
EC	100.0	24.4	50.3
Domestic share	25.0	14.1	22.6
EC share	75.0	10.3	27.7
USA		49.4	40.4
Japan		20.5	1.3
Others		1.9	4.4
Total	100.0	100.0	100.0

Alliances undertaken strictly within the group of nine industry leaders represented 10 per cent of cases, while linkages with other large firms and with smaller firms were 44 per cent and 45 per cent, respectively. Given the limited number of firms within the majors, the level of interactions between them is anything but negligible. Taken individually, the alliance interactions of the nine firms, illustrated in Table 6.14, can be broken down into two sub-groups. The first group made up of CGE, Bull, Philips and Siemens[17] is strongly oriented towards alliances within the group, while the rest tend to be externally focused. Overall, however, close to 55 per cent of the Majors' linkages are with larger firms, either from within or outside the group.

In terms of partner nationality (Table 6.15), the EC polarization observed in the previous table can be seen as a result of alliances from within the group of nine – by definition intra-EC – but which, in three-quarters of cases, were with non-domestic partners and with other smaller European firms.

The linkages established through alliances with other large firms were primarily with American and Japanese corporations – the latter making up 20 per cent of the cases. This is not in any way surprising given that the

Table 6.16   Alliances of European majors: distribution by type (%)

Type	Intra 9	9 + large	9 + others
MOUs	50.0	52.6	40.9
J. ventures	44.4	41.0	31.4
Control	5.6	6.4	27.7
Total	100.0	100.0	100.0

other major firms in the information-processing industries are predominantly American or Japanese.

The significant share (40.9 per cent) of alliances with smaller American firms is also notable. This corresponds to a dual strategy of US technology and market-share acquisition. Conversely, alliances with smaller Japanese firms are almost non-existent, reflecting the different industrial structure in Japan – where there are fewer innovative start-ups – and the different alliance strategies of the nine leaders with respect to Japanese partners. The European majors endeavoured to penetrate the Japanese market via alliances with large local firms rather than through the acquisition of small domestic enterprises.

Quite predictably, interactions by alliance type (Table 6.16) between the nine leading European information-processing corporations with other large firms include almost no takeover operations. The few acquisitions that do appear in the data base are, in part, transactions previously alluded to in this study: the Siemens takeover of Nixdorf and the acquisition of Plessey by GEC and Siemens; and industry rationalization through asset sale or exchange between members within the group. Although control-oriented alliances were few, they often involved major capital transactions. MOUs were clearly most common between the large firms both within and outside the group of European industry leaders. Joint ventures and minority equity participations were also relatively numerous, for the most part aimed at achieving the optimum size required to stabilize and reinforce the oligopolistic structure of the industry in Europe.

While the nine industrial leaders were more frequently involved in takeover transactions with respect to smaller firms, they were somewhat less predatory (27.7 per cent) than other firms (31.5 per cent) in a category which would appear to provide numerous acquisition opportunities. This confirms the more cooperation-oriented strategies of the nine major European firms in comparison to the more control-focused strategies of other European corporations.

One can conclude from this analysis that the major European information-processing firms established relatively specific alliance strategies with respect to firms within the group of majors and other firms. Such a differentiation is consistent with the construction of a two-level industrial network: one corporate and the other sectoral. For the purposes of this study, the term *network* refers to the structuring of industrial activities: first, at the level of the firm, combining traditional forms of industrial integration of activities

Table 6.17 Alliances of European majors: distribution by partner

Firm	Intra 9	9 + large	9 + others
CGE	8	14	43
Olivetti	8	18	41
Bull	8	14	34
Thompson	8	18	25
Philips	8	24	23
Siemens	8	16	13
ICL	8	115	25
STET	8	22	6
GEC	8	15	5

through ownership and more recent collaborative alliances between firms which remained legally autonomous; and second, at the sectoral level which illustrates the development of collaboration between competing firms. Collaborative interactions are thus complements rather than substitutes for integration strategies.

6.2.2.1. The corporate network

The distribution of alliance partners among the nine leading European information-processing corporations (Table 6.17) shows the relatively extensive linkages that were established between the majors and smaller firms. This trend is probably underestimated in the data base given that the primary sources of information tended to have a large-firm bias. These smaller enterprises participated in the constituent network of the larger firms in the industry. Yet in virtually all of the cases surveyed these smaller firms were linked to only one large firm. In more than 95 per cent of the cases, they were involved in two-partner alliances, but it was extremely uncommon to find a firm involved with two different major firms. The few cases where the smaller firm was involved with more than one major firm is either in an OEM situation involving several larger corporations or in multi-partner alliances with common R&D or standardization objectives.

The distribution of alliance objectives by partner category (Table 6.18) underscores the smaller firms' role in the corporate alliance network. While in 41.5 per cent of cases these firms were involved in comprehensive alliances, they were also frequent commercial partners (39 per cent). The smaller firms were also involved in one out of five production agreements either as co-producer or as an exclusive sub-contractor.

The smaller firms in this industry can be referred to as 'network enterprises' because, on the one hand, they have played a subordinate role dictated by the larger firms in all the various alliance objectives from R&D through to commercialization and, on the other hand, they were able to participate in the larger firm network without losing their judicial and industrial autonomy to the larger firms. The major industrial corporations included the smaller firms in their alliance activities and respected their judicial and industrial autonomy in so far as the smaller firm's role was limited to one dimension of the corporation's activity. These are indeed

Table 6.18 Alliances of European majors: distribution by objective (%)

Firm	Intra 9	9 + large	9 + others
R&D	47.2	37.8	17.6
Production	13.9	34.0	20.1
Commercial	11.1	37.2	39.0
Standards	22.2	10.9	3.8
Comprehensive	27.8	19.2	41.5
Total	100.0	100.0	100.0

indications of new forms of corporate definition and structures, made up of specialized divisions, subsidiaries and exclusive partners covering the complete spectrum of industrial functions.

6.2.2.2. *The sector network*

Table 6.19 provides evidence of a parallel dimension to the leading corporate European information-processing alliance network. On the one hand, the nine majors have established individual corporate networks of highly specialized exclusive alliances to coordinate their industrial activities and to bring smaller firms into their sphere of influence. On the other hand, the nine European industry leaders have built up a sector network of collaborative alliances among themselves and with other large corporations.

The first major characteristic which emerges in the sector alliance network is the dense web of interactions between the major industrial players. The growing intensity of linkages between the leaders could indicate a cartelization trend within the industry aimed at carving up the European market among the major producers. While commercial alliances between major firms are the first to be picked up by the professional press, there were relatively few (11.1 per cent) found in this study. Conversely, R&D alliances between the majors were by far the most frequent, representing one out of every two cases, 69.4 per cent, if one includes standardization alliances. Rather than dividing up existing markets, these alliances are targeting the development of future compatible and inter-operable products and technologies. Our data confirm the deepening R&D relationships within the group of majors. Internal R&D alliances were the most numerous for virtually all of the firms within the group, while the share of alliances with partners outside the group was higher for the other objectives. The intense nature of linkages within the group is also apparent in the number of alliances with more than two partners. Close to 28 per cent of alliances within the group involved more than two major corporations.

A similar picture emerges when alliances with other large firms are examined. Again, the share of linkages with three or more partners is significant (23.7 per cent) and it is not uncommon to find more than two of the majors involved in alliances with other larger firms. Table 6.19 shows the numerous cooperative linkages that have been established between the nine European majors and their principle large non-European competitors in the information-processing industry.

Table 6.19 Alliances of European majors: principal non-European partners

Firm	Number of linkages with 9 majors	Number of partners among 9 majors
ATT	11	8
IBM	8	7
Toshiba	7	4
Fujitsu	6	3
CDC	5	3
Sony	5	2

At the level of alliance objectives, the relations with the non-European industry leaders are much more complex than those within the group of majors. Both commercial and production agreements represented more than one-third of alliances, reaching the level of R&D collaborations. The same ambiguity previously noted between European corporations and their Japanese and American counterparts is again apparent here.

6.3. General conclusions

Several general conclusions can be drawn from the analysis of European corporate alliance strategies. They concern the new modes of industrial and corporate organization and the strategy orientation of the European information-processing industries in the context of global competition.

First, the alliances indicate the emergence of new forms of corporate and industrial structures. Firms are increasingly evolving into a network of coordinated activities. The network structure, in contrast with a highly stratified industrial hierarchy, above all facilitates more efficient diffusion of information. It shortens communication channels within the firm, thereby optimizing the decision-making process and improving firm responsiveness. The network structure also increases the range of firm responses to changes in its operating environment. An alliance is a much more rapid mechanism than an acquisition and does not necessarily last longer than the few years required to achieve the specific objective.

Alliances are not necessarily easier forms of industrial activity. On the contrary, many firms stress the difficulties associated with managing alliances with several partners, often in another language and with different corporate cultures in comparison with internal corporate development. The fundamental element in alliances, however, is the complementary of skills and competencies between partners. Hence, many alliances are not a substitute for a market transaction but rather a form of joint value production.[18]

It is nevertheless clear from the data collected on corporations in the European information-processing industries that alliances cover a wide range of inter-enterprise interactions, from integration to partnership. The problem that none the less results from the proliferation of alliances is a confusion between the alliance network and the actual assets controlled by the corporate head office or holding company.

The network structure, partially based on alliances, quickly expands beyond the scope of the firm to the level of the industry structure as a whole. A number of factors come into play at this stage. First, the number of products increases which is particularly evident in the case of the information-processing industries. This variety, as in the corporate network, is obtained through a combination of products, technologies and standards. This, in turn, implies the compatibility of the basic elements which will be eventually combined into final systems but which limits exclusive niche-market possibilities. Standardization alliances are not easily avoided outside of a *de facto* adoption of one set by an industry leader.

As a result of their dual nature, the large information-processing corporations are involved in major industrial activities due to the scale economies associated with the production of electronic components or its related peripheral hardware and the continuous production of new knowledge, on the one hand, and the close linkages between scientific progress and the permanent launching of new products on the other. Competitive industrial positioning, traditionally determined through the control of scale economies and market share has been fundamentally altered. There are two levels of uncertainty resulting from this situation. First, there is no dominant leader to set the standard, the direction and the rate of technological evolution, particularly for the smaller firms. Second, this turbulence also affects the larger firms who are driven into large investments with little hope for short-term payoff. Hence, the industrial corporations are driven to seek out stability through alliance rather than market transaction strategies. The principal firms weave an intricate web of alliances with the goal of regulating technological evolution through diffusion of technologies, collaborative R&D and the co-determination of inter-operability and compatibility standards.

The proliferation of alliances between the industry leaders in Europe has not necessarily led to cartelization; competition still exists within the market sectors. In fact, the findings indicate that the large corporations had created exclusive networks of outsourcing and commercialization alliances with smaller enterprises. At the market stage, where the firm enters into a transaction arrangement with a given client and product, each corporation attempted to establish its own market territory in a general context of conventional oligopolistic competition through differentiation.

The information-processing industry intervenes downstream from the market without an exact overlapping between industries and market segments. This study has shown that the major European corporations entered into knowledge-generating alliances with each other and with non-European firms beyond their principal final market activities. Hence, at a technical level, the telecommunications, computer hardware, consumer electronics and computer-assisted production systems have been relatively homogeneous. Similarly, but to a lesser degree, common basic elements such as micro-electronic components and peripherals have been incorporated into differentiated systems. There has been, therefore, a break between the common technological base, the production capacities and the traditional industry-defined final markets. In the case of the information-processing industries, as well as other sectors which have common generic technological bases, the network structure superimposes levels of activity between industries with different end markets. The technological level is in many ways very close to basic science and covers a wide range of possible applications. This can be seen in the wide variety of skills and knowledge which have been combined in cooperative agreements among the large corporations. Indeed, the study illustrates that these alliances have not been strictly limited to the information-processing industries but extend to other industries outside the sector.

The production stage leads to another level of alliance activities, bringing together the manufacturing capacities of discrete elements and eventually integrated into specific systems. This stage tends to be characterized by the development of joint ventures aimed at attaining optimum scale economies.

The final level of specific applications and final demand is more fragmented and increasingly dominated by the need for customization and problem-solving. Alliances generally tend to be control-oriented at this stage, leading to the direct acquisition of market share.

The industrial firms define their respective roles within the network through the articulation of elements at each of these levels: the common exchange and development of technologies, the production of universally compatible components and the provision of value-added to specific application conditions. Different divisions within the firm at each level of activity are thus led to link their activities, to varying degrees, with the external scientific, manufacturing and client communities, while maintaining internal coherency and efficiency among the other corporate divisions. Partnership alliances are well adapted to the functioning of this type of structure.

The deployment strategies of the European information-processing corporations were designed to operate within this framework. A final issue to be addressed is the industrial structuring on a national level. The globalization trends in the information-processing industries: the intensifying international flow of products and the growth of multinational corporations does not result in homogeneous final products and players. A number of differences remain. Industrial firms have developed specific alliance strategies: few comprehensive and control-oriented alliances by Japanese firms and a preference for MOUs with commercial objectives for American firms. Yet beyond the evident differences illustrated in the data base, there have been more fundamental differences in the industrial structures, in the formation and operation of corporations and in the industrial policies supporting their development. It is at this level that the competitiveness of companies and nations is defined.

In Europe, the competitiveness of the information-processing industries is frequently an issue of concern. Whether the trade balance or the penetration of non-European firms is used as an indicator, the situation is decidedly worrisome.[19] Analysis of European corporate alliances does not lead one to conclude that they have a definite strategy aimed at building up a distinctly European competitive capability. At the technological level, the European firms appear to be intensifying intra-European linkages which is a good indication of a common will to influence the technological trajectory of the global industry. This development is a reflection of the interest and effectiveness of both national and EC technology policies.

At the manufacturing and commercialization stages, however, European corporations have poorly articulated linkages between R&D, production and marketing. Alliances at these levels are more oriented towards non-European firms who supply products previously designed in other user environments through manufacturing licences. The European partner risks becoming dependent on suppliers who are potentially direct competitors on other international markets. Commercialization agreements lead to a market division which could limit the international market potential of European firms. The fact that the major European corporations are simultaneously using forms of alliances to consolidate their domestic market while producing and marketing non-European products indicates the existence of a highly competitive intra-European industry. Dependence on Japanese and American producers has become the price to pay for market share on the European continent.

One of the weaknesses of the European information-processing industries that is revealed through an analysis of their alliance activities is the difficulties they encounter in responding to local demands. A coherent industrial policy should focus on the development of communication channels between users and producers.[20]

A final observation is more of a paradox. One of the primary concerns expressed by non-European industrial leaders was the emergence of the EC as a 'European fortress' which would artificially shut out the penetration of external products. Yet it appears that the systematic sourcing of non-European products by EC firms to protect their local market share is resulting in a retrenchment European industry rather than the other way around. Indeed, if European industry fails to build up its capability to produce its own information-processing products, it will not be in a position to expand beyond its borders. It will be trapped into commercializing products in Europe which would not be saleable on other markets. European firms would then become prisoners in their own fortress.

Notes

1. This paper is based on research undertaken by the LAREA/CEREM, a joint unit of CNRS and Paris X University at Nanterre under a grant from the Commissariat du Plan.
2. See L.K. Mytelka (ed.) (1991) *Strategic Partnerships and the World Economy*, Rutherford, Fairleigh Dickinson University Press.
3. The globalization of the economy has led to a world-wide oligopolization of industries resulting in a shift from internal to external growth.
4. See for instance R. Reich and E. Mankin (1986) 'Joint Ventures with Japan Give away our Future', *Harvard Business Review*, March–April, 78–86.
5. C. Oman (1984) *New Forms of Investment in Developing Country Industries*, Paris, OECD, Development Centre.
6. O.E. Williamson (1985) *The Economic Institutions of Capitalism*, New York, The Free Press.
7. On the importance and the persistence of size as a determinant of firm strategy see A. Chandler (1990) *Scale and Scope: The Dynamics of Industrial Capitalism*, Cambridge and London, Harvard University Press, Belknap Press.

8. See M. Delapierre and C.A. Michelet (1989) 'Vers un changement des structures des multinationales: le principe d'internalisation en question', *Revue d'Economie industrielle*, No 47, 27–43.

9. LAREA/CEREM (1992) *Les stratégies d'accord des groupes européens*, report on behalf of the Commissariat General du Plan, Nanterre (mimeo). Five industries were covered: automotive, biotechnology, defence, information-processing and materials.

10. See for instance: APRA data base, G.C. Cainarca, M. Colombo and S. Mariotte (1989) 'Cooperative agreements in the information and communication industrial systems', (mimeo), Milan, Politechnico di Milano, Dipartimemo di Electronica; Cali data base, J. Haguedorn and J. Schakenraad (1991) 'The Role of Interfirm Cooperation Agreements in the Globalization of Economy and Technology', CHP.FAST/MONITOR, vol. 8; INSEAD data base, G.D. Morris (1992) 'Trends in world-wide inter-firms agreements', presentation to an OECD workshop on *Globalization of the Computer Industry*; MODULI data base, R. Camagni (1988), *Cooperative Agreements and New Forms of External Development of Companies*, Milano, Centro Studi IBM, Italia.

11. This is often in order to centralize decision-making in multinational firms. In most cases the head office nationality is retained for the subsidiaries of multinational corporations involved in agreements, with some rare exceptions in diversified corporations where the subsidiary is considered to be strategically autonomous.

12. The final distribution of the overall gains between the players depends, however, on the subsequent competition following the standardization alliance.

13. Moreover, a certain number of comprehensive alliances involved European takeovers of American firms.

14. The data covered in this study is nevertheless relatively recent and does not capture a potentially large number of pre-1980 alliances, particularly with American firms.

15. These three firms were involved in only thirty-six of the surveyed alliances in the LAREA/CEREM data base of which twenty-one were with one or another of the final nine surviving firms. In any case, these thirty-six alliances are incorporated into the analysis of the major European firms.

16. The major non-European information-processing firms such as IBM, AT&T or NEC are not included in this listing since their global alliance strategies are beyond the scope of this study.

17. The General Electric Company (GEC) was involved in too small a number of alliances to constitute a statistically significant distribution.

18. On the issue of defining true partnership, see another publication from the research programme on European corporate alliance strategies financed by the CGP: M. Delapierre, 'Les accords inter-entreprises, partage ou partenariat? Les stratégies des groupes européens du traitement de l'information', *Revue d'Economie industrielle*, no 55, First Trimester, 1991.

19. For an overview of European industrial positioning in computers in the global economy see M. Delapierre and J.B. Zimmermann, *La globalisation de l'industrie des ordinateurs*, op. cit.

20. Standards organizations have an important role to play in this respect.

7 Technical alliances of Japanese firms: an 'industrial restructuring' account of the latest phase of capitalist development

Terutomo Ozawa

7.1. Introduction

These days one often hears about strategic alliances between Japanese and Western firms. This latest development in international business reflects a new era of cross-border cooperation among the major high-tech firms, particularly from the tripolar centers, namely the United States, Japan and Europe. Most noticeable, Japanese firms have suddenly become very active in this new global game of alliances, especially in high-tech industries.

The purpose of this chapter is to explore the following questions: (1) What are the driving forces for – and the functional determinants of – the sudden emergence of cross-border strategic alliances worldwide but especially on the part of Japanese corporations as the significant partners? (2) What forms of strategic alliance are used by Japanese corporations, and why are the forms so diverse and differentiated?

7.2. Major features and varieties of alliances

The most recent – and most attention-getting – example of strategic alliances in which a Japanese firm is involved is an unprecedented three way mega-alliance among the electronics giants from the United States, Japan and Germany: IBM, Toshiba and Siemens.

The three companies have teamed up on designing 256-megabit dynamic random access memory chips, or DRAMs, for computers of the twenty-first century in a bid to share the exploding costs of this fundamental semiconductor technology. Earlier, IBM and Toshiba also made a tie-up agreement to develop and manufacture flash chips, while Advanced Micro Devices (AMD) concluded a wide-ranging alliance with Japan's Fujitsu Ltd to cooperate on a new kind of memory chip and exchange some shares of each other's stock. In the meantime, as reported in the *Wall Street Journal*,

* The author is grateful to Dr Jorge Niosi for his constructive comments on an earlier version of this chapter.

'AMD's archrival Intel Corp. announced a similar agreement with Sharp Corp. in February. Notably, both IBM and AMD apparently sought out Japanese partners in flash memories without approaching each other . . . The new emerging philosophy is that U.S. and Japanese companies have complementary strengths and weaknesses in semiconductors, with the Americans strong on design and innovation and the Japanese contributing their superiority in manufacturing techniques.'[1] 'Siemens isn't considered as technologically accomplished as IBM or Toshiba, but would offer deep pockets and access to the valuable European market.'[2]

Indeed, strategic alliances are rampant in the semiconductor industry. Figure 7.1 summarizes the growing networks of alliances in this industry among the major firms from the tripolar economic powers. Just looking at these arrangements in this particular industry alone, we can still point out a number of important features of this latest form of international business:

(1) The modern growth industry as best represented by semiconductors is characterized by a high degree of oligopoly and fierce rivalry among compatriot firms as well as between firms of different nationalities. It may be hypothesized that domestic rivalry tends to be much more intense than international rivalry because of a keen historical domestic rivalry and antitrust regulations at home; hence, alliances (cooperative agreements) may occur more frequently and more extensively across national borders than inside the border. In other words, IBM is more interested in teaming with Toshiba rather than with AMD, while Sharp is more eager to secure alliance with Intel than with Toshiba or Fujitsu. Yet Japanese industry is rather an exception, since there exist *keiretsu* as well as legalized cartelization, namely close-knit domestic alliances as a feature of Japan's industrial organization. This aspect will be discussed below.

(2) Japanese partners' strengths are *manufacturing-focused*, while American partners', especially IBM's, are largely *design-and-innovation-focused*.[3] Besides, Japan's electronics industry is vertically integrated to a much greater extent than its American counterpart, which in sharp contrast is highly fragmented and specialized, with a large number of small independent merchant-chip producers and only a handful of large systems producers.[4] These differences in structural characteristics constitute the basis for alliances.

(3) These alliances are made between those vigorously competing business firms whose technological/marketing/financial capacities are more or less at a similar or comparable level of sophistication and development. The parties need to possess some strong firm-specific advantages or intangible assets if they are mutually to gain from this type of intercorporate partnership.

(4) Alliance may mean a form of 'collusion' and appears to eliminate competition. But because of the *asymmetrical* nature of tie-ups between domestic alliances and cross-border alliances, these alliances are on the whole perhaps competition-enhancing rather than competition-suppressing in the long run. This may be true, particularly if and when they are aimed at creating new generic (core) technologies that can generate what Schumpeter called 'the perennial gale of creative destruction', a dynamic force that keeps the growth of the semiconductor industry in a state of high flux and rivalry.

(5) The cost of developing a new product technology in science-based industries has grown prohibitively high – so high that any one particular corporation can no longer afford to undertake any future research all by itself. It makes sense to cooperate in generating a core or generic technology and share the cost of

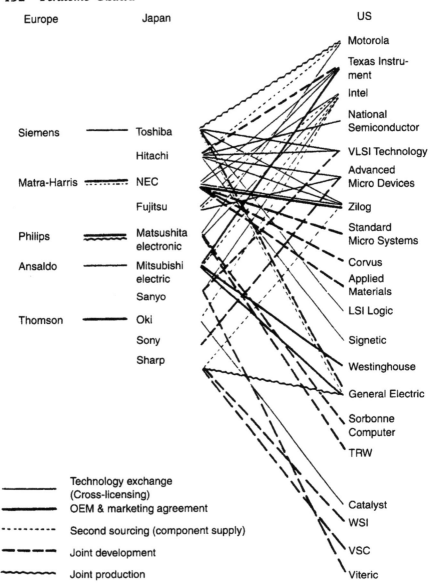

Figure 7.1 Cross-border alliances between Japanese and Western manufacturers of semiconductors (at the start of 1990)

Source: JETRO (1990)

research and development. But competition prevails in commercializing it in differentiated ways.

(6) Alliances take numerous forms such as cross-licensing agreements, OEM (original equipment manufacturing) and sales agreements, component-sourcing agreements, joint R&D and joint production. They are mostly non-equity contractual forms of business tie-ups, but a swap of small equity ownership is often combined in order to facilitate an exchange of information and to reduce the transaction cost (principal-agent, adverse selection and moral hazard) problems.

(7) Although the above examples (Figure 7.1) are taken only from the semi-conductor industry, the incidence of strategic alliances can be observed in other high-tech industries such as aircraft and pharmaceuticals as well as those already mature industries that are striving to upgrade technologically (such as automobiles, chemicals and steel).

7.3. The latest phase of capitalist development

Given the fact that any alliance requires a give-and-take relationship, both parties need to be at the relatively equal level of technological and marketing sophistication so that each can offer some superior corporate asset (firm-specific asset) in exchange to complement their respective strengths.

This means that partners are all fairly sophisticated business entities. At the macroeconomic level, the industrial sophistication level of national corporations is essentially a function of their economic development: the more advanced a nation is, the more sophisticated its business corporations in technological progress, production, and marketing – and vice versa. In other words, the nations whose firms are engaged in alliances are mostly at the forefront of modern capitalism. And *the more advanced a nation is, the more likely its firms are involved in strategic alliances across national borders.* In this sense, strategic alliances, especially those involving technological exchanges and mixing, are the high-income ('luxury') mode of international business. This sheds light on the fact that the firms from the tripolar powers are the most active participants in this latest form of international business.

In addition, it should be noted that the global trend toward this new form is essentially the latest product of evolutionary capitalism. Capitalistic production, which began with textiles and light machinery as the leading industries in the Industrial Revolution, has ever since spawned a series of representative growth industries in its subsequent stages of evolution; to iron and steel, heavy machinery and basic chemicals, to automobiles and petro-chemicals, to aircraft, to TV sets and VCRs, to computers and software. To put it simply, capitalist production was originally a *labor-dependent* system (textiles), which became a *resource-dependent* system (iron and steel, chemicals and heavy machinery), which then turned into an *assembly-dependent* system (automobiles) and most recently, an *information-dependent* system (computers and software). At present, we are in this new 'techno-logical paradigm' of capitalist development in which R&D-based knowledge and information have become key inputs for industrial activity.[5]

The presently advanced nations have continuously evolved by introducing these new industries one by one and shifting from technologically less-

sophisticated, low-productivity products (such as textiles) to more sophisticated, higher-productivity industrial activities (most recently, computers).
This gradual historical shift in industrial composition has also accompanied
a shift away from highly *competitive* markets (close to the textbook version of
perfect competition) to more concentrated ones (as envisaged by the
theoretical model of *imperfect competition*) and most recently to highly
oligopolistic ones. Information (technology)-dependent capitalism, characterized by oligopolistic rivalry at home, is creating a fertile ground for cross-
border tie-ups in knowledge-developing (and exploiting) ventures.

It is thus in the latest phases of capitalist evolution that alliances have
emerged as an effective new form of international business. For example, the
arm's-length exchanges of goods (*trade*) were a sufficient form of business for
those stages in which textiles, steel, and basic chemicals were the dominant
industries. The traditional form of *foreign direct investment* was appropriate for
resource-extractive overseas ventures during the heyday of heavy and
chemical industrialization. Now that human capital and modern science-
based technologies are the key inputs for innovation-driven industries,
corporations are engaged in this stage-specific mode of transactions, *strategic
alliances*, across national borders.

In short, strategic alliances are the latest mode of cross-border business
transactions among the modern corporations that operate in highly
oligopolistic and high-tech-oriented industries which are the latest phase of
capitalist development.

7.4. Emerged compatibility (basis) for strategic alliances

Although Japanese corporations are now active partners for alliances with
Western corporations, as seen in the IBM–Toshiba–Siemens research
agreement for 'future' microchips, Japanese participation in such an
arrangement was unthinkable, say, two decades ago. Japanese industry then
hardly had any significant common basis – or structural compatibility – for
mutual collaboration across national boundaries at the firm level.

It is only in the recent past that Japanese industry has earned the
qualifications as potential partners for strategic alliances, particularly of the
technology-sharing type, as a result of its rapid industrial upscaling both at
the economy and the firm level. Rapid structural upgrading has also
accompanies the swift rises in Japan's per capita income and technological
capacity, making Japanese industry very similar in composition to the
advanced Western economies, providing a strong common basis for direct
mutual business cooperation at the firm level.

As presented elsewhere in the 'industrial restructuring' paradigm of
international production (Ozawa, 1991a, 1991b, 1992a), the Japanese
economy has expeditiously gone through three distinctive phases of
structural upgrading, while accompanied by equally distinguishable stages of
multinational operations, and is presently on the threshold of another new
phase, as illustrated in Figure 7.2

This analytical framework captures the changing phenomenon – and
nature – of overseas investment as a function of the evolutionary stages of

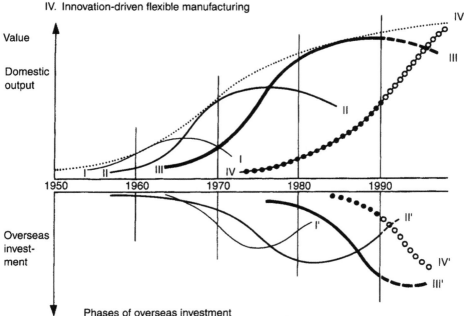

Stages of industrial upgrading
 I. Labor-driven industrialization
 II. Heavy and chemical industrialization
 III. Assembly-based manufacturing
 IV. Innovation-driven flexible manufacturing

Phases of overseas investment
 I. Low-wage labor-seeking investment
 II. Resource-seeking and house-cleaning investment
 III. Assembly-transplanting investment
 IV. Strategically localizing (alliance-seeking) investment

Figure 7.2 Japan's structural upgrading and overseas investment

Source: based on Ozawa (1991a)

industrial structure at home, each stage giving birth to a distinct stage-specific pattern of business involvement across borders.

The past three phases of industrialization and FDI are: (a) labor-intensive industrialization and the 'elementary' stage of overseas investment (1950 to the mid-1960s); (b) heavy and chemical industrialization and the 'resource-seeking' – and later, the 'house-cleaning' – stage of multinationalism (the late 1950s to the mid-1970s); and (c) assembly-based industrialization and the 'assembly-transplanting' stage of multinationalism (the late 1960s to the present). Japan is currently at the end of the third phase and on the threshold of entering (d) a new era of flexible manufacturing and the 'strategic localization/alliance' stage of global operations. Indeed, Japan has come a long way from the days of textiles and iron and steel, to automobiles, to VCRs and camcorders, to computers – each, in fact, having represented

Japan's major export items for each stage of catching-up capitalist development in a highly time-compressed fashion (see Figure 7.3).

In this latest phase, revolutionary changes are taking place in both Japan's manufacturing system (supply side) and its consumption behavior (demand side). On the supply side, Japanese industry is metamorphosing into an ever-more-efficient system characterized by computer-guided production process technologies (computer-integrated manufacturing or CIM) – what is popularly known as 'flexible manufacturing', 'lean production', or 'smart factories'. By 1990, 'one third of Japanese manufacturers have completed their introduction of CIM, with the remaining two thirds in the process of putting in such systems or studying the feasibility of doing so'.[6] Japan is leaving behind the era of limited-variety, large-lot mass manufacturing and plunging into the new era of multi-variety small-lot flexible manufacturing (Ozawa, 1991b).[7] And this focused effort on manufacturing efficiency explains why Japanese manufacturers are often sought as partners who can contribute to the quick and cost-effective commercialization and production of any new product that may come out of a joint research and product development program.

On the demand side, Japan's domestic market has been expanding very rapidly, especially for high-income products, with the fast-rising disposable income of Japanese consumers and the every-greater diversification and sophistication of their tastes. Indeed, Japan has suddenly developed into one of the most affluent, upscale markets in the world. And despite the recent decline in Japan's stock market and a sharp reduction in corporate investment, private consumption has been the major prop for the Japanese economy.[8] Japanese entrepreneurs are now innovating inward – first for domestic consumers, and when a new product has been successfully test-marketed at home, it is then exported overseas. Japan is thus becoming a major initiator of the product life cycle of many new products (especially in consumer electronics), and more and more innovations are trickling down from Japan into overseas markets.

All these latest developments mean that (1) Japanese industry has become highly sophisticated with a large accumulated stock of exportable technologies, as well as with a world-class research capacity to create new ones, and that (2) the consumers and corporate customers in Japanese markets have equally attained a sufficiently high level of sophistication whose demands and needs can be articulated and translated into high value-added, high-technology products and high-value services. In short, the Japanese economy is now on an equal – and even superior in some areas – footing with the United States and Europe to interact with in terms of both sophisticated technology and demand.

According to a recent study made by *Business Week* (August 3, 1992) on the distribution of US patents granted to the world's top companies, a list of twenty-five companies ranked in terms of number of US patents secured in 1991 included eleven Japanese companies, eleven American companies, two German companies and one Dutch company (Table 7.1). The top four positions are captured by Japanese companies.

Most interestingly, a list of the world's top fifteen companies with 'high-impact patents' (most frequently cited as building blocks in new patents)

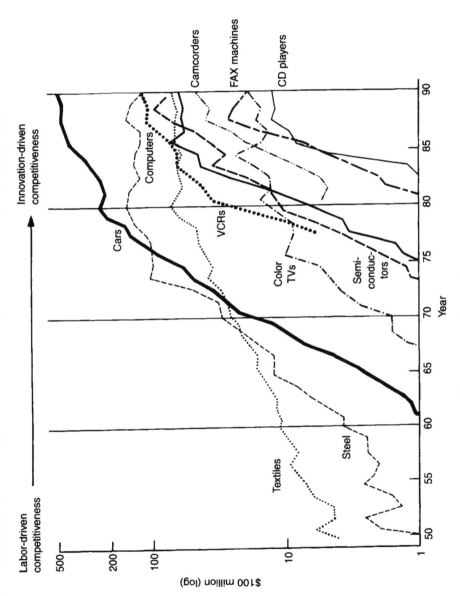

Figure 7.3 Trends of Japan's major exports of manufactures

Source: Ozawa (1992b)

Table 7.1   Top twenty-five corporations in number of US patents granted (1991)

	No. of US patents	Current impact index	Technological strength	Technology cycle time
Toshiba (Japan)	1,156	1.45	1,677	5.4
Hitachi (Japan)	1,139	1.43	1,633	5.7
Canon (Japan)	828	1.45	1,201	6.0
Mitsubishi Elec. (Japan)	959	1.24	1,190	5.1
Eastman Kodak (USA)	887	1.34	1,186	7.8
IBM (USA)	680	1.71	1,161	5.9
General Motors (USA)	863	1.32	1,139	7.9
General Electric (USA)	923	1.16	1,069	8.8
Fuji Photo Film (Japan)	742	1.42	1,056	5.8
Motorola (USA)	631	1.54	969	5.5
AT&T (USA)	487	1.84	895	5.3
Philips (Netherlands)	768	1.02	781	6.0
Nissan Motor (Japan)	385	1.91	736	4.7
Texas Instruments (USA)	380	1.87	709	6.2
NEC (Japan)	483	1.46	706	5.0
Matsushita Elec. (Japan)	561	1.24	694	5.6
Du Pont (USA)	631	1.06	669	9.7
Xerox (USA)	353	1.75	619	6.8
Fujitsu (Japan)	382	1.56	596	5.3
Siemens (Germany)	610	0.97	589	6.6
3M (USA)	374	1.39	519	10.9
Hoechst (Germany)	575	0.88	507	8.6
Minolta Camera (Japan)	315	1.61	506	5.1
AMP (USA)	275	1.84	505	7.1
Sharp (Japan)	388	1.27	493	5.4

Note: The number of patents granted by the US government is a traditional test of high-tech strength. But CHI Research Inc. has come up with more sophisticated measures, based on earlier patents cited as building blocks in new patents. The current impact index measures how often a company's patents are cited relative to those of all other companies. The 1.45 for Toshiba, for example, means its patents are cited 45 per cent more than average. CHI multiplies the index by number of patents to get technological strength, the basis for this ranking. Technology cycle time is the median age in years of patents cited in a company's new patents. The shorter the cycle time, the faster the company is developing new technology.

Source: 'Global Innovation: Who's in the Lead', *Business Week*, August 3, 1992, p. 68.

included ten American companies, four of which took the first four rankings, but only five Japanese companies (Table 7.2A). On the other hand, a list of the world's top fifteen companies who were 'closest to the cutting edge' (ie, the shortest technology cycle time, which is the median age in years of patents cited in a company's new patents) included practically only Japanese companies – with the sole exception of one American company, Intel, which ranked ninth (Table 7.2B). Thus, the emergence of Japan as a technological superpower is undeniably evident.

It should be mentioned, however, that in some specific industrial sectors such as aerospace, chemicals and computers, American corporations, as well as European corporations, still possess decisively dominant technological

Table 7.2 High-impact versus cutting-edge patents (1991)

A High-impact patents		B Cutting-edge patents	
	Current impact index		Technology cycle time
Cordis (USA)	2.25	Fuji Heavy Indust. (Japan)	4.1
Intel (USA)	2.16	Mazda Motor(Japan)	4.5
Proctor & Gamble (USA)	2.08	Pioneer Electronic (Japan)	4.5
Alza (USA)	1.96	Mitsubishi Motor (Japan)	4.6
Nissan Motor (Japan)	1.91	Ricoh (Japan)	4.6
Texas Instruments (USA)	1.87	Nissan Motor (Japan)	4.7
AT&T (USA)	1.84	Olympus Optical (Japan)	4.8
Nippon Telephone (Japan)	1.84	Nikon (Japan)	4.8
AMP (USA)	1.84	Intel (USA)	4.9
Fuji Heavy Indust. (Japan)	1.83	Aisin Seiki (Japan)	5.0
Mazda Motor (Japan)	1.81	NEC (Japan)	5.0
Mitsubishi Motor (Japan)	1.78	Sony (Japan)	5.0
Xerox (USA)	1.75	Mitsubishi Electric (Japan)	5.1
Colgate-Palmolive (USA)	1.72	Minolta Camera (Japan)	5.1
IBM (USA)	1.71	Toyota Motor (Japan)	5.2

Source: 'Global Innovation: Who's in the Lead', *Business Week*, August 3, 1992, p. 69. Original data are from CHI Research, Inc.

advantages over their Japanese competitors. On the other hand, Japan has cutting-edge technologies in automobiles, electric machinery and electronics – and manufacturing technology in general. Thus a pattern of *specialized* technological competitiveness has emerged, providing a basis for exchange and interaction in terms of comparative advantage. After all, today's technology is becoming more *fusion-derived* in development, that is, it draws on – and synthesizes – a myriad of industrial knowledge and skills created and accumulated in *different* industrial sectors.

Furthermore, the newly emerged tripolar world means, as Lester Thurow (1992) points out, that the pattern of trade among the tripolar powers is increasingly characterized by 'head-to-head' global competition as each strives to develop and retain 'critical' high-tech industries such as microelectronics, biotechnology, advanced materials, telecommunications, civilian aircraft, and computers and software. This 'head-to-head' competition is more directly confrontational than the 'niche' competition that prevailed in the postwar era when, say, Japan was selling labor-intensive manufactures or inexpensive small cars, while 'the United States exported agricultural products they could not grow, raw materials they did not have, and high-tech products, such as civilian jet airlines, that they could not build'.[9] Those were the days when America ruled the world as a hegemon.

Yet this conformity or commonality in the industrial structures of the tripolar world, which generates 'head-to-head' rivalry at the national level, is also the new basis for cross-border strategic alliances among the major corporations, since they can merge and coalesce their separately evolved technological trajectories in a mutually complementary and synergistic direction.

In short, Japan has successfully climbed up the ladder of capitalist development all the way from textiles to computers and is on an equal footing with the advanced West in technologies and demand conditions. It now possesses a common capacity to engage in intercorporate alliances as an equal partner. This is a macro-structural-level explanation of Japan's sudden and rising participation in strategic alliances.

7.5. Japan's high propensity to engage in alliances at the corporate level

In addition to the macro-structural forces that have ushered Japanese industry to the age of alliances, there are also meso-structural attributes that foster the willingness of Japanese firms to seek cooperative relationships across borders. One such attribute is the tradition of *keiretsu* formation in Japan, and another is the legalized (government-sponsored) practice of establishing cartels or associations for the purpose of capacity rationalization (eg, an orderly reduction in productive capacity in a recession-hit or declining industry) and promoting research and development in specific fields.

7.5.1. Keiretsu: a collective form of domestic alliances

There are two basic types of *keiretsu*: financial and manufacturing. The financial *keiretsu* is an inter-industry group of key firms clustered around a major bank. Six such bank-clustered *keiretsu* exist; Mitsui, Mitsubishi, Sumitomo, Dai Ichi Kangyo, Fuyo and Sanwa. On the other hand, the manufacturing *keiretsu* is an intra-industry group of firms vertically linked through procurer–supplier (farming-out) relationships under the leadership of one major final assembler. This second type of grouping characterizes such parts/components-dependent, assembly-based industries such as automobiles, electronics goods and industrial machinery. Both types of *keiretsu* are integrated on the basis of intercorporate directorship, mutual ownership of stocks (usually between 5 to 10 per cent), and long-term business relationships among the member firms.

Although member firms are independent and often even have business transactions with non-member firms outside their group, they maintain close affiliative and cooperative links within the group in order strategically to enhance their own intra-group business opportunities *vis-à-vis* other groups. Hence, while a strong spirit of cooperation pervades within each *keiretsu*, there exists fierce rivalry among them.[10] The upshot is an intricate balance between cooperation and competition, each generating benefits to Japanese industry. In this unique form of industrial organization the constituent firms are engaged in a collective form of domestic alliances.

Given such widespread practices of inter-firm affiliation and collaboration at home and the competitive advantages such domestic alliances can create, the Japanese firms are well prepared and motivated to lay out similar external links across borders. In other words, it is no surprise if they exhibit a high propensity to link up with foreign firms in business alliances.

7.5.2. Legalized cartelization

Cartels have long been sanctioned and even encouraged under the close supervision of the Japanese government for a variety of purposes. In the early postwar period, for example, Japanese exporters were allowed – and in fact, required in some cases – to form trade cartels with respect to price, quality, volume and other key aspects of trade if such need was explicitly recognized by the Ministry of International Trade and Industry (MITI) for the sake of preventing what it considered the undesirable effects of disorderly exports on domestic, as well as foreign, markets.

So-called recession and rationalization cartels are intended to reduce productive capacities in an orderly manner as they were once used in such declining industries as coal, aluminium, shipbuilding and textiles – and also to stabilize output and prices on a temporary basis when industry experienced excess supplies. Rationalization cartels also aim at promotion and diffusion of new technologies among the member firms. In the mid-1960s, the heyday of legalized cartelization, when Japanese industry and government busily prepared for liberalization of trade and investment, the number of cartels then in existence exceeded one thousand each year (for example, 1,079 in 1966; 1,040 in 1967; and 1,003 in 1968).[11]

Another form of government-supported cartelization occurs in research and development on a new strategically significant technology. A number of key large firms organize a research association to conduct joint R&D on a specific generic technology. This type of collective research is permitted and promoted by the Mining and Manufacturing Technology Research Association law of 1961. Perhaps the most famous example is the VLSI (very large scale integration) Technology Research Association set up by five Japanese firms (Fujitsu, Hitachi, Mitsubishi Electric, Nippon Electric and Toshiba) over the four-year period of 1976–9 in order to develop the manufacturing process technology for VLSIs (a single chip that could contain one megabit at that time). Many other such research associations have been organized periodically, involving optoelectronics, fourth and fifth generation computers, next-generation industries' technology, fine ceramics, flexible manufacturing and work robots.[12]

These joint research efforts have no doubt contributed to the rapid rise in Japanese technological level not only because of the creation of specific new technologies but also because they further spurred industry to focus on technological process. As Okimoto (1989) emphasizes,

... quite apart from the question of breakthroughs, national research projects appear to serve a variety of instrumental functions. Indeed, the value of national projects may reside as much in their secondary effects – corporate commitments, technological diffusion, and stepped-up market competition – as in their primary goals – advances in state-of-the-art technology. Assessments of their long-term effectiveness must take both primary and secondary effects into account. [p. 72]

Another instrumental function is the realization on the part of the Japanese firms that external cooperation in research with outside entities (including competitors and government institutions) on a brand-new technology which, once developed, they can share in their differentiated applications is a viable supplement to internal research of their own. This facet is described by Goto and Wakasugi (1988):

> ... the system served as a focal organization to enable the individual firms *to use resources of other organizations*. Other organizations, here, imply government, national and public research institutes, other firms in the same industry, and suppliers of parts and equipment, while resources refer to research funds and research personnel ... Had these firms undertaken the same research on their own, they might not have been able to avail themselves of government subsidies. As for research personnel, in view of low labor mobility in Japan, including that of research personnel, the interaction among research personnel from national and public research institutes, other manufacturers within the industry, suppliers, and so on that took place under this system could have been important in its own way. [emphases added] [p. 199]

In other words, research associations provide a forum for external networking, one of the most important mechanisms of innovations identified by empirical studies (Freeman, 1992): 'Linkage with external sources of scientific and technical information and advice: Successful innovators, although typically having their own in-house R&D, also made considerable use of other sources of technology. Failures were characterized by the lack of communication with external technology networks, whether national or international.' (Freeman, 1992, p. 95)

As is with the *keiretsu*, the prevalent use of these cartels and associations has no doubt sensitized the Japanese firms to the strategic significance of forming cooperative links with other firms. In this respect, one may even argue that 'the characteristics of Japanese industrial organization have facilitated Japanese participation in strategic alliances'.[13] This is not only at home but across the national borders as well.

7.6. Stages of development and strategic alliances

Referring back to the 'structural upgrading' pattern of Japanese industry, we can observe that the emergence of strategic alliances is associated with the latest (third and fourth) stages of industrialization and international business, represented by the stage of 'assembly-based' manufacturing with the 'assembly-transplanting' type of overseas operations and that of 'innovation-driven' flexible manufacturing with the 'strategic localization' phase of global business. For example, when Japan was in the stage of heavy and chemical industrialization (the late 1950s to the mid-1970s), *inter-industry* trade was clearly the most desirable form of international business; Japan simply imported raw materials, processed them at home and shipped back finished goods to the world market. Japan was basically a processing workshop. Its overseas investments were therefore confined to the conventional (non-strategic) form of investment in the overseas extractive sectors (*resource-seeking* investments in the exploration and mining of mineral resources and the extraction of oil and natural gas) on the upstream end of the workshop activities and to the overseas marketing facilities (*trade-supportive* investments by trading companies and manufacturers in sales and procurement networks) on the downstream end.

It was essentially only after Japan's industrial upgrading had reached the stage of 'assembly-based' manufacturing that Japanese firms began to engage in the unconventional, less-equity-oriented, and strategically arranged forms of direct overseas business such as joint production, original equipment manufacturing (OEM), 'design-in' agreements, joint product development and other strategic forms of cross-border business arrangements.

Assembly-based industries, as best exemplified by automobiles and consumer electronic goods such as TV sets and VCRs, may be called 'differentiated Smithian industries' (Ozawa, 1991a) because products are highly differentiated in terms of design features, quality, options and prices, and these industries are highly dependent on *economies of scale*; yet, at the same time, the potential of *scope economies* is large, especially on the marketing end of the corporate activities where a full line-up of product variety is often required to satisfy the diversified tastes of consumers. As emphasized by Adam Smith, an extension of the market through exports, particularly when the domestic market is small, is a critical factor in gaining from both scale and scope economies. As might be well expected, Japanese car makers whose domestic market was initially small, for example, pushed through exports the limits of scale and scope economies to new heights – soon overtaking America's auto industry as the world's large car maker. Yet such an export-focused expansion soon caused trade frictions in the US and European markets at which exports were targeted.

As a way of retaining their export markets, Japanese car makers had no choice but to set up local production in their major export markets in North America and Europe. Other assembly-based industries such as semi-conductors and consumer electronics likewise experienced the same fate. Given the fact that these assembly-based industries in Japan are built on an extensive multi-layered system of subcontracting in the production of parts, components and accessories at home, their overseas production initially took the form of final assembly operations or 'screwdriver' plants. Sub-assemblies, parts and components continued to be exported from Japan.

The lack of vertical integration in overseas subsidiaries inevitably leads to the demand from the host country for procurements of locally produced parts and components – and soon a threat or an actual imposition of local-content requirements. Understandably, local reactions to these screwdriver plants are unfavorable so long as they are owned and operated by foreign manufacturers, especially by those who have injured local competitors through exports. Yet, interestingly enough, these plants are less controversial when they are owned and run by local interests. Hence, various forms of a trade-conflict-avoiding – strategically localizing – strategic alliance have come into existence.

Consignment production or a *joint production* agreement is such an arrangement, under which a local firm assembles imported subassemblies ('knockdown' kits) of a foreign competitor's model – and most often markets it as its own product line under its own brand. This form of strategic alliance is essentially a scheme to share in scale-based scope economies between foreign multinationals and local producers; that is, the former retain scale economies in components production, while the latter gain from scale and scope economies (joint production and joint marketing) by utilizing the existing local assembly lines and marketing facilities. Joint production or production sharing is also a conflict-avoiding scheme designed to renovate and reactivate idle local production facilities (thereby making scale economies exploitable) that exist in the host economy and simultaneously to exploit scope economies in marketing (by completing a full line-up of product variety).[14]

Honda Motor Co., for example, had a consignment production contract with the Rover Group in the UK under which the latter assembled Honda's Ballade cars and marketed them as Rover 200s. Suzuki Motor and Daihatsu Motor also have had similar production consignments with the local automakers in Italy. More recently, Honda and the Rover Group have set up a new plant in Swindon, UK along with a stock swap of 20 per cent interest, to deepen their ties in R&D and production-sharing. The similar arrangement is seen in the GM–Toyota venture in California (New United Motor Manufacturing Inc. or NUMMI), the Chrysler–Mitsubishi venture in Illinois (Diamond-Star Motors or DSM), and the Ford–Mazda venture in Michigan (Auto Alliance International or AAI). The latest development is the agreement among Mitsubishi Motor, Volvo and the Dutch government to transform Volvo's Dutch venture (Volvo Car BV is currently 70 per cent owned by the Dutch government) into a three-way joint venture with the participation of Mitsubishi Motor. They are reportedly aimed at a joint production of 'vehicles with different bodies but similar insides'. The Japanese partners for all these joint production and marketing ventures have so far been on the production end of the equation, a reflection of their strong competitiveness in manufacturing.

Another recent development in strategic localization is the procurement or sourcing agreements for auto parts between Japanese automakers and American parts suppliers. A recent agreement with Toyota's purchase contract for charcoal canisters with Acustar Co., Chrysler's affiliate. Toyota planned to purchase 400,000 units for the Camry model assembled at Toyota Motor Manufacturing, U.S.A. Inc., in Kentucky. This is part of the Japanese auto industry's efforts to implement the US–Japan auto-parts agreement (made on the occasion of President Bush's visit to Tokyo in the spring of 1992) to raise the purchases of American-made parts by Japanese factories in the US from $7 billion in 1990 to $15 billion in 1994 and to increase parts-imports by the automakers in Japan from $2 billion to $4 billion at the same time.

As is already well known, Japanese automakers' competitiveness derives from their unique relationships with their parts suppliers, relationships that are based on the joint development and 'just-in-time' delivery of model-specific parts, components and accessories from the very beginning of product development. This Japanese procurement contract is known as the 'design-in' agreement, one of the major unique features of collaborative business practices conducted within a *keiretsu* group. At the end of 1991, Toyota had these joint development 'design-in' projects with as many as 119 US suppliers and was negotiating with another 187 auto parts makers.

Nissan had twenty-two design-in partners; Mitsubishi thirty-two partners; Honda sixty-five; and Mazda sixty-three.[15]

In addition, another tack to avoid trade friction is being employed by many Japanese manufacturers of photocopiers, video cassette recorders (VCRs), color TV sets, fax machines, computers, printers, camcorders, machine tools and other successful exports. They are resorting to what is popularly called *original equipment manufacturing (OEM)* contracts with leading local manufacturers or distributors who are incapable of competitively producing comparable products but are interested in marketing under their own brand names the products made in Japan. The models produced under OEM are differentiated from the producers' own export models. Under this arrangement, economies of scale and scope are split up between the partners, scale economies (via joint production) being retained by Japanese manufacturers, while scope economies (via joint distribution) are exploited by Western firms.[16]

OEM may be regarded as 'disguised' exports but it can also be considered as an intermediate step between exporting and foreign direct investment, just as licensing is. From the point of view of OEM exporters, the OEM contract is an effective way of delegating marketing functions to foreign firms and learning foreign preferences, thereby reducing the marginal cost of a possible entry into local production in the future. OEM importers, on the other hand, may be induced at a later time to set up a joint venture to manufacture the product locally if the OEM arrangement proves successful. OEM is no doubt responsible for a large volume of intracompany trade. One estimate shows that as much as one-third of Japanese manufactured exports to the US are OEM-created (Morita, 1986).

The more rapid the pace of technological progress and innovation (hence, the shorter the product cycle) and the more locationally clustered the incidence of innovation (hence, the greater the possibility of trade conflict), the more frequent the occurrence of the OEM agreements. Scale economies are often responsible for the willingness of innovators to accept OEM contracts for the sake of securing scale-satisfying output and delegating marketing functions to local distributors who can reap scope economies in their product line-up. This willingness is perhaps much stronger for small-scale manufacturers. OEM can be construed as an international division of corporate value-adding functions between production and marketing, a sharing scheme designed to exploit both scale and scope economies.

Mass-production assembly industries are always confronted with a conflict between scale and scope economies. In fact, Japan's *keiretsu* system can serve as an institution in which scale and scope economies are exploited within the group. As seen above, across-border strategic alliances can also provide a solution (even if only partial) to this conflict. In short, the growth stage of assembly-based manufacturing with the 'assembly-transplanting' type of overseas operations (Phase III of structural upgrading) has given birth to the cross-border strategic partnerships designed to reduce trade conflict and at the same time to reap any possible scale/scope economies.

Another key area in which Japanese multinationals are fast becoming active is localized R&D activities. Overseas transplanted production, especially when local content and localization of management are demanded, requires adaptive development efforts; intermediate goods need to be re-designed and re-engineered, depending upon the supply capacities of local support industries. Product designs are often modified to meet the local market conditions. These tasks can be better performed by local personnel who are familiar with their own localities (Ozawa, 1991b).

Associated with Japan's latest stage of industrial upgrading, ie, the phase IV of flexible manufacturing with overseas 'strategic localization' operations, is the increasing incidence of technology-focused strategic alliances, as best represented by the latest IBM–Toshiba–Siemens joint research agreement, in which partners' R&D capabilities are pooled for a particular 'generic' technology development. But they are expected to compete in applying such a generic technology to differentiated downstream product development. This is the most recent stage-specific form of international business, an entirely new form of alliance which is not directly related to Japan's overseas investment activities, though such an agreement may lead to the establishment of joint ventures later on.

In the meantime, Japanese multinationals themselves are taking up localized R&D in connection with their overseas manufacturing ventures. They are setting up research centers overseas, which are intended to capitalize on unique indigenous technological resources in the host economies. Nissan's British-made Micra (a subcompact), for instance, won the 1992 car-of-the-year award in Europe. Many new car models are designed and engineered not only for local markets but for the Japanese market as well. This import-back scheme may be called a 'develop and manufacture locally and then import back' arrangement. Honda is importing back into Japan its American-designed/developed Accord station wagons. Japanese firms are increasingly eager to employ this approach to internalize access to their rapidly growing home markets.

This type of R&D takes the form of wholly owned operations or strategic alliances with local interests. A 1989 survey conducted by Japan's External Trade Organization (JETRO) indicates that 150 of the responding 485 Japanese ventures in the United States (or 30.9 per cent of the respondents) conduct some R&D-related functions locally, and that thirty-four of them (or 7 per cent) operate separate local research centers, while nineteen (or 4 per cent) are engaged in *joint R&D projects* with local firms – thus about 40 per cent of them, taken together, are carrying out research activities in one way or another.[17] Another survey by JETRO for Europe also reveals that as much as 59 per cent of the 227 responding Japanese ventures in Europe are delegating at least some segments of research activities locally.[18] Technology-creating alliances with local corporations and research institutions are thus expected to rise with the spread of Japanese manufacturing investments abroad.

7.7. Summary and conclusions

Japanese industry has gone through structural metamorphoses from the early postwar labor-driven stage to the latest innovation-focused stage of economic growth. Its modality of international business operations has also undergone corresponding changes. Strategic alliances are the most recent form of international business Japanese industry has begun to adopt, only after it reached the stage of assembly-based manufacturing and assembly-transplanting overseas investment activities. Initially, such forms as consignment production, production-sharing-cum-separate-marketing, design-in-parts-procurement and OEM appeared as means of avoiding trade conflicts and simultaneously capturing scale and scope economies.

Japanese industry is at present evolving into another new stage of industrial upgrading characterized by flexible manufacturing and a high intensity of R&D. At this stage of capitalist development, technological resources are being created and managed in terms of education, on-the-job training, corporate R&D, formation of government-facilitated research associations and joint R&D agreements (strategic alliances which are the latest phase of intercorporate partnerships) not only with compatriot firms but also with foreign firms (as seen in the rising number of this type of alliances in the electronics industry). In sum, strategic alliances are the stage-specific manifestation of the latest structural metamorphoses of capitalist development observable in the industrially advanced economies that now constitute the tripolar world economy.

Notes

1. The above quotes are from *Wall Street Journal*, July 14, 1992, p. B1.
2. *Wall Street Journal*, July 13, 1992, p. B5.
3. It should be noted, however, that it was Toshiba that 'invented the flash chip in the mid-1980s, but fell behind [Intel Corp.] when it decided to focus on the more conventional dynamic random access memory chips' (*The Wall Street Journal*, June 22, 1992, p. 8).
4. 'The characteristic fragmentation and specialization have led to steller advances by permitting smaller producers to bring innovations to market (whether in chips, tooling, or systems) and larger producers to concentrate their resources in their areas of greatest strength. The weaknesses of the fragmented structure – duplication of R&D and lack of sustained investment – were only recently exposed to the light of competition against a differently organized industry. The advantages of greater integration can best be seen in the success of Japanese firms, both technologically and in the market, in seizing the chip industry's leadership position, thereby positioning themselves for success in final systems markets.' [Borrus, 1988, p. 30]
5. This changing composition of capitalist development corresponds to the changing endowment proportion of three major factors used in a nation's overall industrial activity: resources (both natural and labor), physical capital and human capital. In other words, the advanced nation has grown by upgrading its structure as its factor and technological endowments change with the accumulation of physical and human capital (relative to resources); *the higher the per capital gross national product, the larger the per capita stock of physical and human capital relative to that of resources and the larger the per capita stock of human capital relative to that of physical capital.*
6. 'CIM – The Manufacturing/Information Wave of the Future', *Tokyo Business Today*, **58**, No. 8, August 1990, p. 48.

7. The competitive implications of this development are clear. Japanese industry will be able to compete in the world market in terms of many more product varieties, higher quality and a speedier delivery of products, rather than – or in addition to – lower prices. This latest industrial activity will enhance Japan's capacity to differentiate to a much more finely calibrated extent the physical, functional and even psychological attributes of products so as to suit the varied needs and wants of customers and to offer them in a more timely manner. The thrust of Japan's industrial technology is thus definitely to build 'smart factories'. (Ozawa, 1991b)

8. The importance of domestic demand as a key determinant of national competitive advantage cannot be overemphasized. Michael Porter (1990, p. 89) observes:

> A nation's firms gain competitive advantage if domestic buyers are, or are among, the world's most sophisticated and demanding buyers for the product or service. Such buyers provide a window into the most advanced buyer needs – the presence of sophisticated and demanding buyers is as, or more, important to sustaining advantage as to creating it. Local firms are produced to improve and to move into newer and more advanced segments over time, often upgrading competitive advantage in the process.

9. Thurow (1992), p. 29.

10. In other words, the principles of cooperation and competition are simultaneously operative in the *keiretsu* system (Yoshida, 1992). In fact, Ferguson (1990) even advocated the adoption of the *keiretsu* approach by American and European firms as a way of restoring Western competitiveness in the electronics industry. But the *keiretsu* system has its own undesirable sides (Cutts, 1992).

11. These numbers are cited in Lincoln (1984), p. 27.

12. For an analysis of research associations, see, for example, Goto and Wakasugi (1988), Imai (1988), and Okimoto (1989).

13. National Research Council (1992), p. 12.

14. Scale and scope economies as determinants of strategic alliances are discussed in Ozawa (1992c).

15. As reported in *The Japan Times* Weekly International Edition, December 2–8, 1991, p. 18.

16. This type of trade-friction-avoiding tie-up in the form of OEM may be considered as a 'crude' form of strategic alliances. For example, Korean and Taiwanese firms are still largely in this stage of alliances with Western and Japanese firms, just as Japanese firms were when the Japanese economy was in the 'assembly-based manufacturing' stage of structural upgrading. A more sophisticated form of partnership is based on technological exchanges and joint knowledge production between the firms involved. Indeed, some writers use this narrow definition of strategic alliances:

> First, [strategic alliances or 'interfirm technology cooperation agreements'] focus on those agreements among independent firms which involve knowledge-production or sharing activities, whether these are oriented towards the development of new products, new production processes or new routines within the firm or in its management of inter-firm contractual relationships . . . Second, alliances are regarded as strategic when they seek to improve the future competitive position of the firm. [Mytelka, 1991, p. 1]

17. JETRO (1990a), pp. 34–5.

18. JETRO (1990b), pp. 49–51.

References

Borrus, Michael G. (1988) *Competing for Control: America's Stake in Micro-electronics*, Cambridge, Mass., Ballinger.

Cutts, Robert L. (1992) 'Capitalism in Japan: Cartels and Keiretsu', *Harvard Business Review*, 70, 4, July–Aug., pp. 48–55.

Ferguson, Charles H. (1990) 'Computers Keiretsu and the Coming of the U.S.', *Harvard Business Review*, 68, 4, July–Aug., pp. 55–70.

Freeman, Christopher (1992), *The Economics of Hope: Essays on Technical Change, Economic Growth and the Environment*, London, Pinter Publishers.

'Global Innovation: Who's in the Lead', *Business Week*, August 3, 1992, pp. 68–73.

Goto, Akira and Wakasugi, Ryuhei (1988), 'Technology Policy', in R. Komiya, M. Okuno, and K. Suzumura (eds.), *Industrial Policy of Japan*, New York: Academic Press, pp. 183–204.

Imai, Ken'ichi (1988) 'Industrial Policy and Technological Innovation', in R. Komiya, M. Okuno and K. Suzumura (eds), *Industrial Policy of Japan*, New York, Academic Press, pp. 206–29.

JETRO (1990s), *Zaibei Nikkei Seizogyo Keiei no Jittai* (Business Conditions of Japanese-affiliated Manufacturing in the United States), Tokyo, JETRO.

JETRO (1990b), *Zaiou Seizogyo Keiei no Jittai* (Business Conditions of Japanese Manufacturing in Europe), Tokyo, JETRO.

Lincoln, Edward J. (1984), *Japan's Industrial Policies*, Washington, DC, Japan Economic Institute of America.

Morita, Akio (1986) *Made in Japan*, New York, New American Library.

Mytelka, Lynn K. (1991) *Strategic Partnerships: States, Firms, and International Competition*, Rutherford, Fairleigh Dickinson University Press.

National Research Council (1992) *U.S.–Japan Strategic Alliances in the Semiconductor Industry*, Washington, DC, National Academy Press.

Okimoto, Daniel I. (1989) *Between MITI and the Market*, Stanford, Stanford University Press.

Ozawa, Terutomo (1991a) 'Japanese Multinationals and 1992' in B. Burgenmeier and J.L. Mucchielli (eds), *Multinationals and Europe 1992*, London, Routledge, pp. 135–54.

Ozawa, Terutomo (1991b) 'Japan in a New Phase of Multinationalism and Industrial Upgrading: Functional Integration of Trade, Growth, and FDI', *Journal of World Trade*, 25, 1, February, pp. 43–60.

Ozawa, Terutomo (1992a) 'Foreign Direct Investment and Economic Development', *Transnational Corporations*, 1, 1, February, pp. 27–54.

Ozawa, Terutomo (1992b) 'Structural Upgrading and Concatenated Integration: The Vicissitudes of the Pax Americana in Tandem Industrialization of the Pacific Rim', paper presented at the Global Business Seminar, Sapporo, Japan, August 3–7 1992.

Ozawa, Terutomo (1992c) 'Cross-Investments between Japan and the EC: Income Similarity, Product Variation, and Economies of Scope', in John Cantwell (ed.), *Multinational Investment in Modern Europe: Strategic Interaction in the Integrated Community*, Cheltenham, Glos., Edward Elgar, pp. 13–45.

Porter, Michael (1990) *The Competitive Advantage of Nations*, New York, Free Press.

Thurow, Lester (1992) *Head to Head: the Coming Economic Battle Among Japan, Europe, and America*, New York, William Morrow.

Yoshida, Kosaku (1992) 'New Economic Principles in America – Competition and Cooperation: A Comparative Study of the U.S. and Japan', *Columbia Journal of World Business*, 26, 9, pp. 30–44.

Part III:
Adoption of new technologies and new productive organization

8 The Japanization of industry: a review of developments in the UK and Canada*

Jonathan Morris

8.1. Introduction

This chapter's focus differs from others in this volume in that it is explicitly about social innovations within the enterprise rather than new technology policy or technical alliances. The chapter will review current research on the extent of Japanization in Canadian and UK industry, including the author's own recent endeavours. As such it is divided into three substantive sections. The following section will define Japanization and address some of the pertinent conceptual and theoretical issues. Sections 8.3 and 8.4 will report on empirical research, with the former concentrating on case study and research material in Canada and the latter on Japanization in the UK.

8.2. Japanization: some conceptual and theoretical issues

The concept of 'Japanization' emerged in the 1980s in the UK to explain the transfer of what seemed to be discernible Japanese management techniques to Western enterprises (Oliver and Wilkinson, 1988; Turnbull, 1986). As such it was part of a wider attempt to explain changes that were occurring in the organization of production, industrial organization and the management of human resources. While there would seem to be little disagreement that major changes have occurred, the exact nature of these changes and the labels ascribed to them has been the focus of considerable debate.

Broadly, although far from exclusively, three major paradigms have emerged. First, there is the Japanization concept, which has found greatest currency in the UK and Northern America and which will be returned to later. Second, there are the concepts of lean production and post fordism, again with a North America/UK focus and with many similarities to the Japanization debate. Finally, there are a series of what might be termed 'continental European perspectives'.

The lean production focus, for example, argues that Japanese

* I wish to thank Nick Bacon of Loughborough University and Paul Blyton, Max Munday and Barry Wilkinson of Cardiff Business School for their joint contributions to the research cited in this chapter.

manufacturing systems, incorporating just-in-time and total quality management, offers workers the opportunity to work 'smarter rather than harder', that the workers become more highly skilled and have greater autonomy and control (Womak *et al.*, 1990). Meanwhile, there are a number of differences between the different continental European perspectives, but they have a number of common factors. First, there is little consensus that the changes are being driven from Japan, unlike the other two main concepts. These, mainly German-based theories, argue that new production strategies are being employed which mark a fundamental break with Taylorism and a re-emergence of the importance of labour in the production process, with labour reskilled and retrained and a new type of skilled worker being central to the core of production (Kern and Schumman, 1987). Sorge and Streek (1988) offer a similar explanation, although they place more emphasis upon the permissive role of microelectronic-based process technology which allows for a blurring of the distinction between large- and small-batch production.

To return to Japanization, the central focus for this debate has been, as stated earlier, the UK and North America. This is no coincidence, as the bulk of Japanese manufacturing investment in industrialized countries has been in North America and, in a European context, the UK. Moreover, the UK and North America have been arguably far more pressured and open to Japanese competition than markets which have been protected either by the strength of indigenous producers (such as Germany) or by trade barriers (such as Italy or France).

It is worth dwelling for a short while on what the Japanization concept actually comprises and entails (for a lengthier discussion, see Oliver and Wilkinson, 1988, 1993). For Oliver and Wilkinson, Japanization refers essentially to Japanese management practices. (Others, such as Ackroyd *et al.*, 1988, have a wider conceptualization of Japanization as deeply embedded in specified social, cultural and institutional forms.) Thus this would include the introduction of a series of independent practices such as total quality, just-in-time and harmonization (see also Wood, 1991). However, these practices are not merely introduced in an *ad hoc* way but are integrated and supportive and therefore inter-dependent. Broadly, these practices cover manufacturing methods, including total quality control and just-in-time production; personnel policies, involving employment contracts, recruitment, training, payment and reward systems, and, finally, supplier relations.

Ackroyd *et al.* (1988) make a useful distinction between three types of Japanization – full, direct and mediated. Full Japanization refers to the reproduction of Japanese economic structures, direct Japanization refers to the transfer of Japanese manufacturing systems via direct investment, while mediated Japanization is the process of transfer, via emulation, to non-Japanese firms. It is the latter two – direct and mediated – which will provide the main focus of this chapter. In a sense both of these types of Japanization are 'mediated', in that the process of transfer is inevitably channelled and altered through the particular institutional arrangements of the host country. This will be a subsidiary aim of this chapter, to explore and tease out the differences in transfer.

8.3. Japanization: the Canadian evidence

The empirical evidence for Japanization in Canada is perhaps more scanty than that for the UK. This is not to say that Japanization is not occurring, rather there does not seem to be quite the depth of empirical research. Nevertheless there is an emerging literature on the subject. Moreover, as is the case in the UK, the majority of the research conducted on the Japanization of Canadian industry has focused upon the automobile sector, although other sectors have been researched and will be discussed here. This is unsurprising for several reasons; first, this has been the sector which has been most under attack, together with consumer electronics, in Canada and North America generally, both from Japanese imports and from the so-called 'transplants'. Second, automotives is perhaps the key manufacturing sector in Canada, and in Ontario and Quebec in particular (Holmes, 1991a; b).

Finally, many of the key parts of the Japanese manufacturing systems, particularly just-in-time, were first fully implemented in the Japanese automotive industry, and more specifically at Toyota (Monden, 1983). As Holmes (1991a) argues: 'As a consequence, the automobile industry has become the focal point of the debate in North America regarding the transferability of Japanese forms of production and work organisation and the need to remake labour–management relations to produce a more co-operative industrial relations system' (p. 129).

The Japanese manufacturing presence in Canada includes three automotive transplants: Toyota employ 1,040 at their Cambridge, Ontario facility, GM–Suzuki have a joint venture (CAMI) at Ingersoll, Ontario and Honda employ 1,500 at their $450 million facility in Alliston, Ontario, which is their sole North American producer of the Civic hatchback. In addition there are an estimated twenty automotive component plants either under full or part Japanese ownership (Morris, 1991b). Automotives and auto-components thus make up the bulk of the estimated forty-five Japanese manufacturing investments in Canada (JETRO, 1991).

In contrast to the UK, and perhaps even more so to the USA, the Canadian research evidence is limited, both in terms of its overall coverage and in the industry and sectors under study. As I have already noted, for example, the work has almost exclusively concentrated on the automotive sector, although this is to a certain extent true of the research profile in the USA and Europe. Despite gaps in the research, however, and the need for both more research and a greater sectional spread, there are several excellent studies, particularly concentrated on the automotive sector.

8.3.1. Direct Japanization

There are four main areas of activity in the study of Japanese foreign direct investment (FDI) in Canada. First there is the report of the Japanese External Trade Organizations on Japanese FDI, second there is the work of Edgington (1990). These two studies are essentially descriptive overviews of Japanese FDI, rather than offering any analysis of the extent of the introduction of Japanese work and industrial practices in Canada. Nevertheless, they offer an initial insight into the scope and nature of Japanese involvement in the Canadian economy. The third and fourth studies offer a greater indication of the transfer of Japanese management practices, including the study of Morris (1989; 1991b), covering research manufacturing facilities in Canada and the single plant study of Robertson *et al.* (1991) which while being hampered by focusing upon one plant in one single industry is probably the most balanced account of a Japanese transplant made in either North America or Europe.

The JETRO (1991) study indicates that there were 340 Japanese-affiliated firms in Canada, of which 226 responded to their survey. This latter total included forty-five manufacturers which are, perhaps, of most interest in a review of this type. The survey points to an average of 109 employees per plant, with big increases in firms in the automotive and auto parts firms over the previous survey. Average manufacturing plant size was, understandably greater, at 338, again an increase over the previous survey but with a decline in the number of Japanese staff per plant. Despite this increase in employment the major problem of the firms surveyed was 'an inability to secure quality employees', although the precise nature of this is unclear. There is evidence from the survey of a 'deepening' of the activities of Japanese affiliates with 64.2 per cent reporting a local content rate of 50 per cent or more for raw materials or parts, a considerable increase over the previous survey.

In terms of geographical location, the overwhelming concentrations are found in Ontario (58.2 per cent) and British Columbia (33.5 per cent), which is understandable given the dominance of the former in Canadian GDP and its prominence in key sectors such as financial services and automotives and the latter's close historical links to Japan. While there was some activity pre-1979, the majority of Japanese affiliates located in Canada in 1980 or after, with rapid increases between 1987 and 1989. The majority of manufactures were exported, primarily to the US, and in particular from the auto and auto parts firms.

As indicated earlier, the Edgington (1989) study is essentially a review of data and previous research. This work again points to a rapid increase in Japanese activity in the Canadian economy in the 1980s and to a considerable diversification away from raw material extraction into a wider range of activities involving both production and services (see also Blain and Norcliffe, 1988). Nevertheless, with the exception of a recent surge of manufacturing investment in the 1980s, Japanese investment has been extremely trade-oriented, either through securing access to raw materials or the provision of financial services.

Edgington focuses on the four sectors which are key to Japanese FDI in Canada, particularly after 1985: finance and banking, automobile production, pulp and paper manufacturing and services and property. Again the automotive industry is perhaps of most interest here, with the three 'transplants' (Toyota, Honda and GM–Suzuki) plus the transplants, the vast majority of which are concentrated in the 'golden triangle' of Southern Ontario. The other prominent manufacturing sectors are chemicals and allied industries, steel, general machinery and electronics, but these are overshadowed in both investment and employment terms by the auto investments.

The Morris (1989) study departs significantly from the first two in that it attempts to answer some questions surrounding the issues of the transferability of Japanese management systems (personnel issues, buyer–supplier relations and production and work organization) to a Canadian setting (see also Morris, 1991a, 1991b). The study reports, albeit in a fairly extensive rather than intensive fashion, on sixteen Japanese (manufacturing) transplants. Again the study was biased towards the auto and auto parts industry (ten of sixteen firms), which is unsurprising given their overall dominance of the transplants, but also included firms in the furniture, sports equipment, metal manufacturing, mechanical engineering and consumer electronics sectors.

Recruitment and training was the first issue addressed which in turn was part of a wider issue of total quality control in that it reflects a willingness to commit finance and time to the human resource (see the findings of the JETRO study quoted earlier). The three large automobile producers were perhaps the best illustrators of the Japanese commitment to recruitment. 'Attitude' was, for example, the main recruitment criteria at the Honda plant, but nevertheless 90 per cent of the workers at the Alliston plant had a Grade 12 education and 40 per cent a community college diploma or university degree. Potential workers faced three interview schedules. At CAMI (GM–Suzuki) twenty-eight hours were set aside for aptitude tests, dexterity, problem-solving and human relations skills. The company also sent 200 of its workers for training in Japan. Toyota follows a similar policy.

In the field of production relations, the Morris survey pointed to attempts to replicate the Japanese model in the Japanese plants; the CAMI plant, for example, is a model of Suzuki's highly successful Kasei plant, including even the early indications of the implementation of quality circles, with eight plants introducing them, although not without early teething troubles.

Many of the plants also displayed the more obvious manifestations of Japanese practice. At Honda, for example, all workers were termed associates and wore the same uniforms. There was also evidence of much greater flexibility at the shop floor level. Honda workers, for example, were employed to carry out a range of functions without rigid pay classifications. Japanese plants have also introduced the notion of team working; at Toyota, for example, functions were carried out by teams of between four and eight multi-tasked workers in which the team leader played a crucial and pivotal role.

The third main strand of the implementation of Japanese practices was in the area of buyer–supplier relations. This was aided by the attraction of a significant number of Japanese-owned suppliers to Canada, in addition to the larger number of Japanese suppliers in the US. In the three auto transplants, for example, there were moves towards closer collaboration and long-term trust relations. Just-in-time supply systems were being implemented by half of the plants, all but one of which (a CTV producer) were in the automotive sector. In the main the just-in-time system was of a daily delivery rather than a multiple deliveries per day type. The system in operation at the CAMI plant was illustrative of these initial moves. Just-in-time deliveries started on selective components, and the majority of suppliers were within a four-hour drive time. Certain of the CAMI suppliers were, however, considerably closer and were supplying multiple deliveries daily.

Certain of the firms' policies indicated the introduction of other Japanese buyer–supplier systems. At CAMI, for example, as with other of the auto transplants, there was an attempt to introduce long-term relationships with a small number of key suppliers grouped into a first tier.

In direct contrast to the Morris study, the research of Robertson, *et al.* (1991) is an intensive, and in some ways unique, piece of work on one plant, CAMI. The project was union-initiated (CAW) with management support and had two aims: first, to review the implementation of Japanese management systems at the plant; and second, to chart workers' responses to such systems.

CAMI is a GM–Suzuki joint venture located at Ingersoll, Ontario, and is Canada's only unionized Japanese auto transplant (and only one of four in North America). The study was longitudinal, with four intensive research visits over two years. The 1991 work reports on the first and second visits, at the start of production and eight months later. Its focus is explicitly on the organization of work and shopfloor production relations.

The CAMI production system is based around 'four pillars': standardized work, *Kaizen* (or continuous improvement), flexibility and team working. Extremely rigid work standards are continuously changed through *Kaizen*. This is facilitated through extreme flexibility of workers within the context of a team which:

provides a vehicle for job rotation, training and productivity improvement activities. Second, it provides a supervisory system in which peer pressure is combined with more traditional supervision. Third, the team (by its very existence and dynamic) will serve both a social function and as a vehicle for communicating management values. Finally, the team serves a production function with the expectation that people are not performing an exclusive job. [p. 10]

While these are recognizably Japanese forms of production organization, the plant represents an amalgam of Japanese and Canadian practice, not least in the role of the union. The role of the union is very different from what might be expected in a Japanese plant, but equally the contract signed was very different from those the CAW has negotiated at other GM plants, with an acceptance of teamwork, reduced job classifications and flexibility (see Holmes' research reported below).

This is a brief summary of the transfer of Japanese methods and is not unique in the literature. What is innovative is the response of the workers to such implementation. The research concentrates on two crucial areas, *Kaizen* and teamwork. *Kaizen* is crucial to the management philosophy, the 'kaizening' of jobs is the responsibility of all employees and is portrayed as empowerment. Various methods are employed such as quality circles and suggestion schemes. The research indicates that between the first and second rounds of interview there was growing disillusionment with the *Kaizen* system, manifested in a reduction in suggestion programme participation, a decline in quality circle teams, roving non-production *Kaizen* teams and resentment among workers. However, as Robertson *et al.* acknowledged, 'some work teams have been able to use kaizen to make work easier and less stressful' (p. 23).

Workers were broadly supportive of team working in both rounds of interviews. However, the reasons for this differed between rounds, with a growing feeling of peer pressure and work intensification in the second round. The reasons for its popularity indeed were slightly negative (from a managerial perspective) in that it engendered solidaristic worker attitudes.

What is evident from this research is that Japanese management practices have been transferred in a modified form in terms of work organization (if not personnel issues). The implications for workers are perhaps mixed, with both positive and negative elements.

8.3.2. The Japanization of Canadian industry: the emulators

The case studies of emulators of Japanization of Canadian industries fall into two groups. First, there is the closely related work of Holmes and Kumar on the Canadian automobile industry and second, the work of Blyton *et al.* on the Canadian steel industry.

Holmes (1991a) has pointed to a Canadian auto industry in the 1990s which is far more differentiated, for example, in its payment systems. This, he argues has led to increasing flexibility and increasingly unregulated labour-market competition. Whereas pre-1970 the industry had been characterized by strict wage rules, connective bargaining and strictly defined multiple job classifications, the huge investment in the 1980s was tied to new forms of automation and reorganization of work and production, quality circles and relational contracting.

Whereas this was a pan-North American phenomenon, Holmes notes a distinctive difference between Canada and the US, with the CAW strong and increasing membership and the UAW weak and losing members. This has had notable implications for the introduction of Japanese production organization, but nevertheless the new union–company agreements have allowed management to deploy workers in a much more flexible way.

At General Motors, for example, Holmes notes that there have been moves from traditional 'concession bargaining' to so-called world 'class contracts'. The latter include provisions for profit-sharing and lump-sum payments instead of annual increases, increased flexible work, simplified seniority systems and job redesign and blurring and reduced job classifications. This has been introduced at all new GM plants and in parts of existing plants. While the CAW has been in a much stronger position to resist changes than the UAW, Holmes notes that resistance is crumbling, especially in the realm of teamworking.

At the massive GM 'Autoplex' facility in Oshawa, for example, the various new technologies will encourage continuous employee involvement in production problems with work groups of between eight and fifteen operators ('teams' in some cases). The Autoplex will have a JIT inventory system which will be extended to parts suppliers who will have to meet the requisite quality standards and will be encouraged to collaborate in design at an early stage. Some 40 per cent of parts will be produced within a forty-minute drive time (Kumar, 1988).

Japanization has also been introduced in other sectors of Canadian industry. The study of Canadian steel by Blyton *et al.* (1989) was part of a wider research project on flexibility in a variety of industrial and service sectors. The focus, therefore, was not on Japanization *per se*, although many of the questions and the results offer some useful insights. It concentrated on the two largest, fully integrated producers and two minor provincially owned companies (see a summary in Morris, 1991b).

In particular, the Blyton *et al.* study pointed to increasing quality demands and adoption to just-in-time production schedules. As a semi-finished goods producer, the steel industry is not driving these demands as such but is being driven by the end-users, and the automobile industry in particular. The steel industry in turn has had to smooth production planning and respond much more quickly to changes in client demands.

Blyton *et al.* also found new relations being forged between producers and clients: product design, for example, was often more collaborative or even client-led and customers were insisting on site checks for quality standards. The Japanese auto producers, for example, have been relatively slow to turn to Canadian steel producers and have indicated that quality standards must first be met before Canadian steel replaces more expensive Japanese imports.

Changes in workforce composition accompanied such developments: the steel companies were, for example, concentrating upon a core workforce with moves to upgrade and/or retrain existing workers and, where possible, to recruit workers with higher educational standards. Moreover, in-process controls were being introduced, with measurement and monitoring of production throughout the process, including systematic and formal attention given to the quality of each employee's work. As part of this programme, for example, Dofasco sent hundreds of its employees to study best practice in Japan and since 1984 has implemented statistical process control (SPC) training and quality awareness seminars. Stelco employees have also had detailed quality responsibility, including SPC training, as part of a programme of a smaller but more highly skilled workforce.

8.4. Japanization in the UK

8.4.1. Japanese FDI in the UK

The UK has been the major focus for direct Japanese investment in the EC. Japanese direct manufacturing investments rose from a small total of twenty in 1980 to fifty in 1987 and by 1991 there were approximately 160 such investments (Oliver and Wilkinson, 1993). The key sectors remain electronics, automotives and components and, to a lesser extent, chemicals and plastics. Employment at these facilities was 50,000 in 1990, but this figure is likely to have undergone a rapid increase with the expansions of existing plants and with new plant openings, notably those of Toyota and Honda.

It would not be exaggerating to say that this Japanese investment has revolutionized work organization and industrial relations, both in its direct impact and in its 'demonstration' and 'best practice' effect. Two pieces of research will be presented here to indicate the extent of the transfer of Japanese practice. The first is an extensive study of Japanese investment in the largest recipient region, Wales, and the second is a case study of one of the most prominent Japanese investments in the UK, the Nissan car plant in Sunderland.

One of the most recent and comprehensive studies of the implementation of Japanese forms of work organization is found in the study of Morris, Munday and Wilkinson (1992; 1993) on Japanese transplants in Wales, one of the key European regions for Japanese investment. The study was comprised of intensive interviews at twenty-three plants with over eighty managers. Although plants were drawn from a variety of industrial sectors, the vast majority were found in electronics or related supply industries (parts, plastic mouldings etc.). In all of the companies visited, managers were well versed in Japanese production methods and there have been significant attempts to transplant just-in-time production and total quality control on to Welsh soil. The most popular forms of transfer were just-in-time production (fifteen of twenty-two), and team-based organization (eighteen), although other aspects such as quality circles, statistical process control techniques and individual fault training were also in evidence.

Personnel management practices were typically supportive of a form of work characterized by team responsibility, flexibility, and discipline and quality consciousness. Attitude to flexible working and quality was, for example, the main criterion for selection for shopfloor workers. Workers were in the main put through intensive induction programmes and in general there was a strong training emphasis. Appraisal systems were common, and, more importantly, were supportive of the working practices described above, attention being focused upon employee attributes such as flexibility, teamwork, responsibility and attitude. Communications were taken seriously in all of the companies studied, through small group activities, daily team briefings or company newsletters. Such open communications were already facilitated by single-status terms, conditions and facilities, which were widely in evidence.

The personnel practices described helped to generate the disciplined and flexible workforce necessary for efficient, high-quality production. Appropriate industrial relations systems on the other hand were supportive of the working practices required of employees and provide the high degree of industrial relations stability which is crucial in the absence of stocks. Trade unions were recognized in twenty-one of the twenty-three companies which is broadly typical of Japanese investors in the UK but not true of such investment either in Canada or the US. However, the nature of trade union recognition differs markedly from traditional British patterns. All but three of the agreements were single-union recognition deals (typical UK plants have multi-union deals), while two were take-overs with existing recognition arrangements being maintained. The most evident features of collective agreements were binding arbitration and flexibility clauses, the latter in particular being innovative in a UK context.

The broad trends outlined in the Japanese plants in Wales were found elsewhere in the UK, and specifically at the Nissan car plant. This plant in Sunderland started production in 1986 and received unparalleled UK media attention as the first Japanese car plant in the EC and one which was set to break the mould of traditional UK work organization and industrial relations practices. It also represented, both in investment and employment terms, the largest Japanese UK investment (Garrahan and Stewart, 1992; Oliver and Wilkinson, 1992; Wickens, 1987). From the outset, Nissan aimed to adopt a philosophy alien from traditional British production organization, including new production and work organization concepts, personnel and industrial relations practices and supplier relations.

The working practices at Nissan were to include, according to Wickens (personnel manager at Nissan) a tripod – including teamwork, quality and flexibility. Teamwork was to revolve around team leaders, with total responsibility for their work areas. Flexibility was to be facilitated through a minimum (two) of job classifications and no specifications *per se*. Teams were also expected to initiate production improvements through *Kaizen*. Quality, meanwhile, was the responsibility of both teams and individuals, with considerable peer pressure (Garrahan and Stewart, 1992). Garrahan and Stewart's (1992) study of worker attitudes at Nissan found contradictory feelings of solidarity (much the same as at CAMI) but also reports of intense work pressure.

The ability to achieve such a transfer was aided considerably by a rigorous selection and training procedure. However, this was also reinforced by a facilitative industrial relations structure. The Nissan plant is unionized, but Garrahan and Stewart (1992) argue that the nature of the single-union agreement (with the AEU) makes the union position extremely weak. It is not a 'no strike' agreement *per se*, but termed a 'minimum disruption' agreement, which is tantamount amount to the same thing. The union has no direct bargaining mechanism at Nissan; this is carried out through the company council, which represents all employees, non-union and union, manual and non-manual. Garrahan and Stewart (1992) comment that this is not independent unionism but tacit recognition allied to marginalization.

The final area of 'Japanization' at Nissan is in the area of buyer–supplier relations (Morris and Imrie, 1992). Nissan have opted for a quasi-Japanese model of close links with a small number of key selected suppliers, including a number of Japanese component transplants. Relations with suppliers are long term, close and collaborative, but the selection system is rigorous and exhaustive, including financial, quality and industrial relations audits, as are the control systems in place consequent upon selection.

8.4.2. *The UK emulators*

Manufacturing firms across the spectrum of British industry are attempting to emulate Japanization (Oliver and Wilkinson, 1988; 1993). As in the Canadian case, the best documented evidence of this is found in automotive industry because of its size, importance and openness to Japanese competition. This industry will therefore provide the second of the case studies. The first case study will be the UK steel industry, in which vigorous attempts have been made to Japanize.

The UK steel industry has been through fundamental changes in the past decade, including a scaling down of capacity, substantially reduced manning, major technological changes, a move to far higher quality standards and an ownership change (nationalized to privatized). As a result of these developments, and accompanying them, there have been major changes in work organization (Morris *et al.* 1992).

The steel industry in the UK, and indeed across Europe, has had rigid forms of work organization characterized by gang working with a strict hierarchy based on seniority promotion and distinctive demarcation. Essentially when a new production worker joined the industry, he joined a gang of typically six workers in one functional area as the most junior member. The only promotional route for this new worker was when somebody left the gang and he then stepped up one place. At the top end of the gang a worker might be forty or fifty years old before achieving the top position, such as chief rollerman. There was a little fluidity in the system: during an absence for example, a worker might step up one place on a temporary basis. This strict hierarchical system has a tradition extending back into the last century and has had a powerful inertia of its own, especially for those at the top end of the gang with many years' service. In addition to this structure for production workers, the industry was also characterized by a plethora of craft workers whose skills and jobs were heavily demarcated; in the BS Llanwern plant, for example, there were over seventy grades in the 1970s.

Against this backcloth, British Steel management have been attempting to introduce radical changes to work organization. Management have been working against the long-standing work organization methods but in a position of considerable strength given massive financial difficulties, job losses, plant closures, a distinctive shift in bargaining strength and union weakness and disarray.

The three main changes in work organization, all distinctively Japanese, have been a general reduction in demarcation, a move to multiskilling of craftsmen and the introduction of teamworking. In the first of these changes, management has been the most successful, tying flexibility agreements to bonus payments, and including a distinct blurring of the craft–production divide with production workers carrying out routine maintenance tasks.

Multiskilling has proved a more difficult arena. Essentially BS management have reduced skilled workers to two categories, an electronics/electrical craftsman and a mechanical craftsman. This was a lengthy and expensive process in terms of costs of training and retraining and met with the considerable resistance from craft unions over pay, selection of candidates and the number of candidates to be retrained. However, multiskilling is now being implemented across most of the BS sites.

Teamworking has proved the most problematic facet of the new working organization. Given the massive attack on union strength and shopfloor worker and despite union weakness, workers have so far successfully resisted its introduction. Indeed, teamworking has only been introduced in experimental parts of plants where major new technology has been introduced, as a quid pro quo for that investment being made. In the longer term it would seem that teamwork will be introduced, especially in a context of extremely depressed steel markets and the resultant competitive pressures. However, this will be a lengthy process with considerable continued union and shopfloor opposition.

While Japanization has been evident in the steel industry, perhaps the most obvious examples have been found in the automotive industry. As was the case in Canada, existing auto producers in the UK have been faced with extreme competition from Japanese imports and transplants and have attempted to circumvent such competition by emulating Japanese practices. Essentially, the 'indigenous' UK car industry should read the existing, that is non-Japanese industry, with three main producers, the US firms GM and Ford and the UK firm Rover.

All three firms made major attempts in the 1980s to alter work organization and industrial relations to a more Japanese model, although firm strategies and union responses have differed in the three. This process started at the Rover Group in the 1980s and was hastened considerably with the group's links with Honda Motor (there is now a co-ownership deal). By 1980 for example, job classifications had been considerably reduced, in the early 1980s teamworking was being implemented and by 1985 quality control responsibility was devolving to the operator level (Oliver and Wilkinson, 1993). However, not all Japanese practices were well received and successful: quality circles, for example, met with very limited success.

In early 1992, however, after a nine-month negotiation process with unions, Rover implemented a package of Japanese-style measures, including the removal of remaining job demarcations; a major flexibility clause; a cut in bargaining units to one; the introduction of *Kaizen*; common terms and conditions for all employees; 'jobs for life' and a binding arbitration clause.

Ford in the UK have also attempted to introduce a Japanese-style package, dating back to their 'After Japan' productivity campaign in the late 1970s when, among other items, quality circles were introduced. As Oliver and Wilkinson (1993) note, despite early productivity improvements, within two years the programme was resisted by the unions, which withdrew their support due to a lack of consultation. Nevertheless, throughout the 1980s Ford attempted to introduce Japanese practices, including just-in-time, total quality and flexible working. A 1985 agreement, for example, cut job classifications from 550 to fifty-two (Oliver and Wilkinson, 1993).

In 1988, however, Ford attempted to introduce further reforms, including teamworking. When tied with a pay deal, however, this culminated in a major strike, which resulted in considerable concessions from the company. A major contribution to this situation was the fact that the implementation of a European-wide Ford just-in-time system had resulted in a strike in one country, paralysing production throughout Europe through a lack of components.

Despite this setback, Ford has made further attempts to introduce new working practices and the victory may seem a pyrrhic one for the unions as Ford investment activity has been shifted away from the UK, notably to Spain and Germany. In a similar fashion, General Motors has used 'divide and rule' tactics between European plants, plus the carrot of major investments, to introduce new working practices, both in its UK and continental European operations (Martinez Lucio and Weston, 1992).

8.5. Conclusion

As this chapter has outlined, there is growing evidence of the transfer of Japanese manufacturing methods and working practices to both Canada and the UK. This transfer process is being achieved both through the so-called 'transplants' and through existing producers emulating elements of the Japanese system.

Such a transfer is having far-reaching consequences for industries and workers in both countries. However, we should not overestimate the scale or nature of transfer for a number of reasons. First, the transfer would seem to be most prominent in certain key sectors, notably automotives, electronics and engineering. Second, this is clearly an extremely modified form of transfer. Ogasawara (1992), for example, has recently outlined the extremely complex payment and appraisal system operating in Japanese companies, but there is little evidence of this being transferred. Finally, there is a clear mediation process occurring, with different elements of Japanese practice being transferred to different countries, albeit as part of a wider package. This transfer is thus being mediated through institutions including the legal framework, social and economic forces and industrial relations' structures and is clearly most evident in greenfield Japanese transplants.

References

Ackroyd, S., Burrell, G., Hughes, M. and Whitaker, A. (1988) 'The Japanization of British Industry', *Industrial Relations Journal*, 19, 2, 11–23.

Blain, R. and Norcliffe, G. (1988) 'Japanese investment in Canada and Canadian exports to Japan 1965–1984', *Canadian Geographer*, 32, 141–50.

Blyton, P., Ursell, G., Gorham, A. and Hill, S. (1989) *Human Resource Management in Canadian and UK Work Organisations, Strategies for Workplace Flexibility*, Interim Report to Canadian High Commission, London, 2 vols.

Edgington, D. (1990) 'Recent trends in Japanese Investment in Canada', paper presented to the Canadian Association of Geographer's Annual Meeting, Edmonton, June.

Garrahan, P. and Stewart, P. (1992) *The Nissan Enigma: Flexibility at Work in a Local Economy*, London, Mansell Publishing.

Holmes, J. (1991a) 'From uniformity to diversity: changing patterns of wages and work practices in the North American automobile industry' in P. Blyton and J. Morris (eds), *A Flexible Future?*, New York and Berlin, De Gruyter.

Holmes, J. (1991b) 'The globalisation of production and the future of Canada's mature industries: The case of the automotive industry' in D. Drache and M. Gertler (eds), *The New Era of Global Competition*, Montreal and Kingston, McGill–Queens University Press.

JETRO (1991) *Third Survey of Japanese-Affiliated Firms in Canada*, Toronto, JETRO.

Kern, H. and Schumman, M. (1987) 'Limits of the division of labour: new production and employment concepts in West German industry', *Economic & Industrial Democracy*, 8, 151–70.

Kumar, P. (1988) 'Changing labour relations in the auto industry: a case study of General Motors of Canada', unpublished paper, School of Industrial Relations, Queens University, Kingston, Ontario.

Martinez Lucio, M. and Weston, S. (1992) 'The attempted restructuring of worker representation under different industrial relations systems: a post modern convergence?' in *Proceedings of the Employment Research Unit Conference*, Cardiff Business School, September.

Monden, Y. (1983) *Toyota Production System*, Atlanta, Industrial Engineering & Management Press.

Morris, J. (1989) *The Changing Industrial Structure of Canada in the 1990's: The Role of Japanese Foreign Direct Investment*, Final Report to the Canadian High Commission, London.

Morris, J. (1991a) 'A Japanisation of Canadian Industry?' in D. Drache and M. Gertler (eds), *The New Era of Global Competition*, Montreal and Kingston, McGill-Queens University Press.

Morris, J. (1991b), 'Japanese manufacturing investment in Canada' in J. Morris (ed.), *Japan and the Global Economy*, London, Routledge.

Morris, J., Blyton, P., Bacon, N. and Franz, H.W. (1992) 'Beyond survival: the implementation of new forms of work organization in the UK and German steel industry', *The International Journal of Human Resource Management*, 3, 307–29.

Morris, J. and Imrie, R. (1992) *Transforming Buyer–Supplier Relations: Japanese Style Industrial Practices in a Western Context*, London, Macmillan.

Morris, J., Munday, M. and Wilkinson, B. (1992) *Japanese Investment in Wales: Economic & Social Consequences*, Cardiff Business School, UWCC, Cardiff.

Morris, J., Munday, M and Wilkinson, B. (1993) *Japanese Investment in the EEC: Evidence from a Key Region*, London, Athlone.

Ogasawara, K. (1992) 'Japanese personnel appraisal: individualized race for power and imposed involvement', paper presented to conference on *Japanese Management Styles: An International Comparative Perspective*, Cardiff, September.

Oliver, N. and Wilkinson, B. (1988) *The Japanisation of British Industry*, Oxford, Basil Blackwell.

Oliver, N. and Wilkinson, B. (1993) *The Japanisation of British Industry*, Oxford: Basil Blackwell (second edition).

Robertson, D., Rinehart, J. and Huxley, C. (1991) *Team Concept: A Case Study of Japanese Production Management in a Unionized Canadian Auto Plant*, Willowdale, Ontario, CAW.

Sorge, A. and Streek, W. (1988), 'Industrial relations and technical change: the case of an extended perspective' in R. Hyman and W. Streek (eds), *New Technology and Industrial Relations*, Oxford, Basil Blackwell.

Turnbull, P. (1986) 'The Japanisation of production and industrial relations at Lucas Electrical', *Industrial Relations Journal*, 17, 193–206.

Wickens, P. (1987) *The Road to Nissan*, London, Macmillan.

Womak, J., Jones, D. and Roos, D. (1990), *The Machine That Changed the World*, New York, Rawson McMillan.

Wood, S. (1991) 'Japanization and/or Toyotaism?', *Work, Employment & Society*, 5, 567–600.

9 What about concurrent engineering?

Thomas Durand

9.1. Introduction

The management of innovative projects is certainly not absent from the literature on the management of innovation but in our view is not sufficiently treated. This chapter deals with what is called concurrent or simultaneous engineering, ie new organizational processes for developing new products. Concurrent engineering relies on strong and permanent interactions between the functions during the whole design and development process. It aims at breaking the tight partitioning which tends to prevail among the various actors of the organization and which usually leads to successive relays from one function to another as the project unfolds. Simultaneous engineering, instead of calling for such a sequence in time, is based on a parallel and articulated development mode.

Carter (1992) reports that the term 'concurrent engineering' was first used in 1986 in a report from the IDA, the Institute for Defense Analysis. The R-338 IDA report explained the systematic method of designing at the same time both a new product and its downstream production and support processes. This followed a 1982–7 effort from DARPA (Defense Advanced Research Projects Agency) to improve concurrency in the design process.

Along these lines, research in management on concurrent engineering for development projects has been initiated rather recently. Most of the resulting contributions turn out to be descriptive and rather convergent: the firms which have adopted such processes seem to build a competitive advantage as they are able to develop new products and the corresponding new production processes under particularly good conditions in terms of lead time and cost.

Yet, it should be noted that the literature on this subject does not seem to allow for much debate, questioning of new hypotheses, raising of new issues, or discussion of counter-examples. Some nuances may be expressed here and there, eg to underline the contradiction between concurrent engineering and total quality; still most of the literature seems to insist on the positive aspects of concurrent engineering.

We feel puzzled and suspicious about such unanimity. In the present chapter, our purpose is to bring an empirical contribution to the questioning of this apparent alignment of the literature on concurrent engineering and in turn to cover four subjects: crisis as a learning mode, the role of the champion in the innovation process, the level of formalization needed for concurrent engineering and the evolution in the structuring of inter-functional project groups.

We will first discuss the concept of concurrent engineering, relating it to organizational forms, including product development groups or project teams. We will then present the case of a large consumer goods company whose decentralized structure allowed for the implementation of several experiments in simultaneous development. This case will then make it possible to comment on the four subjects mentioned above (crisis, the champion, formalization, project groups) before a brief conclusion.

9.2. Project management and concurrent engineering

Project management for the development of new products is normally faced with a major difficulty: how to integrate the complementary, although different, views of the various entities involved in a project. Figure 9.1 recalls the traditional chain between the different entities such as suppliers and the purchase function upstream and the marketing and the sales force downstream linking the organization to the customers. 'Normal' operations require that some day-to-day integration be made among these functions: this is the task of general management.

However, managing change, eg managing the development of a new product, requires a different integrative role: each function has to bring some input into the product development at appropriate times. A specific organizational mode has thus to be adopted. A product manager, a project leader or a 'product development team' are typical ways to organize such integration and coordination tasks. Let us be more precise about the various organizational forms which firms adopt to manage product developments.

9.2.1. Structural organizational forms

Figure 9.2 calls upon Kline and Rosenberg (1986) to present the links between research and the chain of innovation: the research function is primarily considered a source of competence which feeds the innovative process as and when needed. Obviously, if the available competencies are not sufficient to solve the problems encountered at any stage of a development project, then a need for research work may be identified. The results of this R&D work (arrows 3) may not always provide a solution to the problem (arrows 4 are thus shown as dotted lines).

Also, Kline and Rosenberg emphasize that design, rather than research, is at the very heart of the innovative process. They stress the crucial importance of the multiple and complex feedback loops between each and every different stage of the process and hence between each and every different actor involved in the project. The efficiency of these feedback loops, articulations and interfaces is precisely the main issue of project management for new products. How can one put in place an organizational scheme well suited to coordinate and integrate the complementary and diverging views of all the different actors involved in the project?

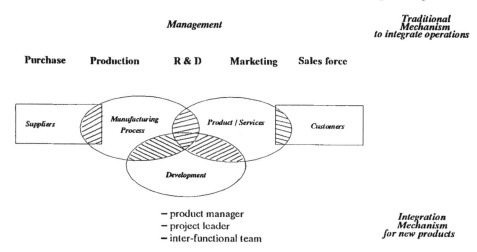

Figure 9.1 Functions and integration

Dean and Susman (1989) have identified four ways to help design new products likely to be efficiently industralized. The first consists of giving the production unit the right to veto new products which they regard as 'poorly designed', ie difficult and costly to industrialize and manufacture. The second consists of appointing an 'integrator', acting as a mediator between the different functions. The third leads to the setting up of project groups including representatives from the different functions involved. The fourth consists of creating a new department or business unit in charge of the new product and its manufacturing process.

Beyond the basic question of whether new products may be easily industrialized or not, we feel it necessary to enlarge the issue to question as well the marketability of the product, its maintainability, the difficulty in gaining access to supplies, etc: ie the problems that the newly designed product may cause to the various actors in the firm; not just to manufacturing *per se*.

With this broader perspective in mind, we can now go back to Dean and Susman's four coordination mechanisms. Giving a right of veto to each function very quickly proves inefficient. Appointing a mediator – integrator – is a frequent practice (project leader/product manager). But this approach is often biased due to the functional position of the integrator. The fourth method, which integrates the various functions in a single department, is not easy to implement as it may well imply reorganizing the company in micro-profit centres each time a new project emerges. Companies tend increasingly to rely on Dean and Susman's third approach, based on inter-functional project groups. We will come back to this topic later. These four ways of coordinating among functions to develop new products and manufacturing processes, as derived from Dean and Susman, correspond to structural organizational forms. Each may actually use more or less simultaneity or synchronization or concurrency in the design process.

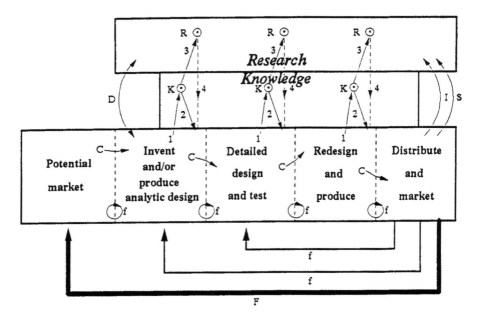

Chain-linked model showing flow paths of information and cooperation

Symbols on arrows:

    C = Central chain of innovation.

    f = Feedback loops.

    F = Particularly important feedback.

K–R = Links through knowledge to research and return paths.
        If problem solved at node K, link 3 to R not activated.
        Return from research (link 4) is problematic – therefore dashed line.

    D = Direct link to and from research from problems in invention and design.

    I = Support of scientific research by instruments, machines, tools, and procedures of technology.

    S = Support of research in sciences underlying product area to gain information directly and by monitoring outside work.
        The information obtained may apply anywhere along the chain.

Figure 9.2   Chain link model

Source: Kline, S.J. and Rosenberg, N. (1986)

9.2.2. Organizational processes for faster coordination: concurrency

The basic principle of concurrency is to reject the usual sequence that starts with a marketing idea, then leads to the design of the product before its industrialization and its introduction in the market-place.Figure 9.3 presents this so-called 'pipe-line' model which offers a perfect overall coherence but involves the downstream functions at too late a stage. In this scheme, if

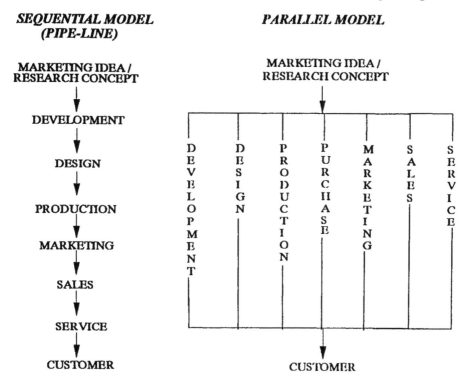

Figure 9.3 Models of innovation development

major difficulties arise in the course of the industrialization or commercialization phases, the project is more or less sent back to the starting line. It may thus take for ever before the product finally reaches the market.

Concurrent engineering means asking each player from the organization to become part of the project right from the beginning according to a parallel model, also depicted in Figure 9.3. Here, each actor can at any time express his/her concerns, suggestions or constraints, and thus influence the development of the project in real time. As an illustration of this, a buyer may insist on asking the R&D people as well as marketing to substitute some packaging material for a more standard one because he/she knows the supplies will be much more cost competitive.

Additional costs will obviously appear in organizations using concurrent engineering: representatives of each function will have to be involved in the project much before and long after their own perspective, expertise and opinion are absolutely required. Besides, some developments (eg in the field of industrialization) may well have to be revisited several times because of modifications to the product imposed by the marketing or R&D teams. This means that there is a strong contradiction between concurrent engineering and total quality. Indeed total quality principles would require

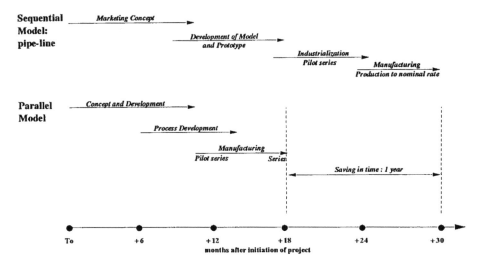

Figure 9.4   Project lead times

the organization to avoid any revisiting, any redesigning. 'Do it right the very first time' does not fit very well with the intrinsic iterative nature of design and development.

Morris and Hough (1987) typically recommend the avoidance of concurrency, which they assimilate to 'the practice of initiating some production activities prior to the completion of full scale development', later recognizing concurrency as 'the simultaneous and interrelated development of design and production to a tight schedule'. They claim this leads to project overruns.

It is striking to note that concurrent engineering is becoming increasingly popular at a time when the Japanese concept of total quality is also becoming widely accepted and implemented. Note here that, in some sense, concurrent engineering is to total quality in development projects what a market economy is to a planned economy. Concurrent engineering allows for trial and error corrected in real time, generates some wastes – non quality – but converges faster toward a sound industrializable and marketable product: this is in a way similar to what the market economy can offer to a planned economy. Despite their inherent partial inefficiencies, market mechanisms have proven to operate overall as a much better economic filter than central planning.

When using parallel development, the above-mentioned additional costs and modifications, due to inevitable iterations in the design process, together with the apparently useless participation of each main function during the whole project, actually yield an important shortening of the time usually needed for the launching of a product (see Figure 9.4). This strongly iterative parallel process, apparently straying away from total quality principles, is claimed actually to speed up the availability of the product on the market and reduce the development costs.

Enlarging the perspective, one may recall the fluid and intermediate phases identified by Abernathy and Utterback (1978) in their model of technical change describing the dynamic, iterative search for dominant designs for both the product and its manufacturing process. One may argue that these two first phases of an Abernathy and Utterback cycle are part of the process. This would imply that the design period should actually be expanded significantly to include the moment when dominant designs emerge. In that respect, production and market launch obviously take place much before a dominant design is reached.

Although this enlarged perspective goes much beyond the scope of the present chapter, interestingly enough it raises the issue of the reference to be used for lead time and costs when assessing concurrent engineering against standard practices. This might actually shed some light on the comment by Morris and Hough (1987) about project overruns due to inadequate concurrency. In their view, what is 'premature production'? Is it when production occurs 'prior to the completion of full scale development'? What then is real 'full scale development'?

A connected theme has to do with the difference between lead times and development costs. Although correlated, both may not necessarily be reduced through concurrent engineering processes. It seems that the literature emphasizes more lead time reductions than cost savings even if cost savings are often cited. Still, as will be shown, implementing concurrent engineering may prove difficult. The simultaneous development implies that each function fully agrees with this approach: Dean and Susman (1989) correctly emphasize that it means, for instance, replacing validation and control routines by cooperation and information exchanges in the organizational processes. This also implies developing new communication and relation skills, and, as a consequence, setting up a reward system for these skills that values such behaviours and competence. Organizational inertia is known to appear with such process changes as some form of unlearning is required to make it possible for the organization to relearn. We will come back later to this point, to underline how a crisis may help accelerate the unlearning process, reopening up learning capabilities.

Several articles have described how simultaneous development has been applied by different firms. The approach became popular in Japan, where it was first applied to two major industrial fields, the car industry and consumer electronics. In these fields, Japanese companies developed in the eighties a significant competitive edge by sharpening their ability to develop, industrialize and commercialize new products with lead times much shorter than those of Western competitors. Strategic time to market, and its inevitable acronym STTM, became well-known managerial slogans. Clark and Fujimoto (1991) describe in detail the case of the car industry. Other examples are discussed by Jelinek and Shoonhoven (1990), Hayes, *et al.* (1988), Midler (1991), Navarre (1989) and Teece (1989). It should be noted that most of these contributions one way or another present concurrency in the context of interfunctional product development groups – or vice versa. We are going to show why this should not be regarded as a surprise.

Structural forms ／ Organizational processes	Veto rights	Mediator/ integrator	Interfunctional project team	New Department - Restructuring
Pipeline	Standard iterative pipeline	Sequential mediation	Uncoordinated pipeline teams	Micro pipeline
Intermediate	Contention mode	Shuttle mediation	Sequential coordinated teams	Shortened coordination in Micro units
Parallel	Neutralized organization	Real time mediation/ parallel integration	Concurrent engineering in interfunctional teams	Structural concurrent engineering

(Concurrency — vertical axis)

Figure 9.5 Concurrency and organization: process and structure

9.2.3. *Concurrent engineering and forms of organization*

Concurrency, as an organizational process to shorten and facilitate coordination among the functions involved in a development project, may operate in various structural settings. More specifically Figure 9.5 matches the four structural forms discussed earlier to the degree of concurrency involved. Indeed concurrency falls along a continuum, from a pipe-line type of sequence to fully parallel developments. Figure 9.5 thus combines the structure and process dimensions: it maps out the various organizational solutions which may be adopted to coordinate and integrate the complementary and diverging views of all actors involved in a development project.

It starts in the north-west corner with *standard iterative pipe-lining,* ie sequential design and development with some form of a right of veto for the function 'receiving' the project at a given stage. This is typically what better coordination mechanisms are trying to prevent. If concurrency increases, still with veto rights, the organization tries to run its development projects through a *contention mode,* ie continuously identifying and solving small conflicts in the projects thus avoiding full blockage. This may actually lead to a *neutralized organization,* unable to keep its projects moving as successive vetoes halt any design progress.

When a mediator or an integrator is in charge of a project, it may keep a *sequential mediation* approach, simply helping the relaying of the project from one function to the next, or he/she may accelerate the iteration, operating in a *shuttle mediation* mode, or even in a *real-time mediation* yielding some form of *parallel integration.*

Similarly an 'Interfunctional Project Team' may remain essentially *uncoordinated,* operating as a *pipe-line team,* or may indeed be coordinated but still operating the various phases of the development project in sequence – what we call a *sequential coordinated team.* When the project team uses a concurrency approach then we clearly face *concurrent engineering in interfunctional teams.* This is probably what most people have in mind when they refer to concurrent engineering.

The last column of the table shown in Figure 9.5 deals with the creation of a specific new department for the project, ie a business unit of its own. If this micro department simply operates according to the standard sequential development process, we call it a *micro pipe-line* mode. If rendered more iterative, the process is rather fast since the organized unit is smaller, meaning *shortened coordination in micro units.* When full concurrency is used in such newly created small departments, we shall call it *structural concurrent engineering,* ie not only is concurrency looked for in the organizational process but also in the organizational structure: the structure is permanently modified – while it was only temporarily adapted with interfunctional project teams. The whole table shown in Figure 9.5 thus illustrates how much concurrency may be involved in various organizational settings. The shaded part of the table indicates the situations where some form of concurrent engineering is actually encountered.

It should be recognized at this stage that the four organizational forms used to build the mapping tend to be somewhat related to concurrency: the structure obviously affects the process. Indeed mediators, and even more so interfunctional project teams or new business units, tend structurally to link up the functions and thus make it easier for concurrency processes to take place. As mentioned earlier, most of the cases discussed in the literature about concurrency deal with interfunctional project teams. We can see now how these are two different concepts (one functional, the other structural) but clearly related, at the very heart of the shaded zone shown on our map of Figure 9.5.

Along the same lines, we would like now to report on the case of a large European consumer goods firm operating in a field less famous for its rate of innovation than the car or electronics industries.

9.3. The painful learning of concurrent engineering at EURO Inc.

The EURO Inc. Company stands among the leading firms in Europe in its consumer goods industry. Its structure is largely decentralized and each business is organized as a profit centre. The managers of one of the main divisions were rather concerned in 1986 about the launching of a particularly innovative product which had been put on the market three months earlier by a small competitor. This product, PX, was likely to cannibalize an important part of EURO Inc.'s leading products in this business. Besides, the development of PX, which had a 'young, sports and health' target, could strongly affect the image of EURO Inc. by actually positioning the firm in the out-of-date and non-sporty traditional segments of the market.

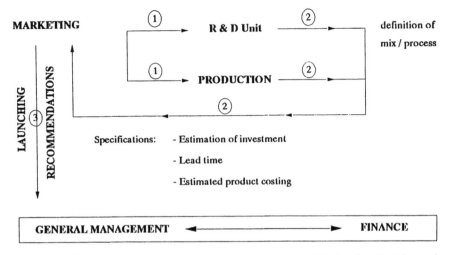

Figure 9.6 Product development procedures up to 1987 in the division of EURO Inc. to launch a new product

The corresponding division of EURO Inc. was on the alert. The marketing group issued a development proposal for a product PA, which would be an improved 'me-too copy' of PX. The proposal required the development of a similar product but with significantly different packaging. The idea was to use a new packaging concept that would differentiate PA from traditional products more clearly than a mere modification of label. This proposal implied significant industrial investments for the new lines because of the new type of packaging. The marketing group also considered that it would no longer be possible to play a significant role in the market if the product were not made available within the next eighteen months.

Figure 9.6 shows the procedures which were in use within EURO Inc. at that time to launch a new product. Of a sequential nature, they implied a lead time of about one to three months from the first request issued by the marketing group up to the first answer from production as to the industrial feasibility of the product. Should a disagreement be identified, the process would start again with a similar time scale.

The R&D and production managers reacted to the request from the marketing group. R&D had previously developed a product technology close to the needs identified by the marketing people. Production however had a more complex answer. They explained that twenty-three months would be needed to design, acquire and install a new line as required. They consequently proposed another solution that would maintain the traditional packaging but with changes in the colours of the labels on the packages. They would thus be able to re-use the existing lines with minor modifications. Their counter-proposal would necessitate an industrial investment about half of that imposed by marketing's initial request and the product would be available within sixteen months. Besides, this solution would be more flexible as it would still be possible to come back to the previous configuration of the line (eight to nine hours only for modifying the equipment and retooling) should the sales of PA prove lower than expected.

The marketing group strongly reacted to this counter-proposal and rejected it. The production's offer denied a key element of the marketing group proposal, namely a strong need for differentiation of PA from PX. Even though time was running out, the marketing group intended to reformulate its request and start another loop when the general management decided to step in with a simple straightforward slogan: 'The most important thing, now, is to gain time!'

An inter-functional project group was set up, including representatives from production, R&D, marketing, purchasing and commercial units. This group was to report directly to the general manager of the division. It was the start of a rediscovery at EURO Inc., of the increased efficiency of team work conducted by a group specifically organized for and dedicated to a clear, single task.

What followed was almost miraculous. The conflict between marketing and production was solved. The solution was fairly well accepted by all parties involved. The new product was made available in record time. The sales volume exceeded the wildest hopes. The competing product, PX, was almost driven out of the market within a few months despite renewed efforts to resist. The PA product of EURO Inc. in 1992 represented one of the largest sales of the division. Furthermore, beyond this happy ending, the project group set up for the occasion led the division in proposing a new approach for developing new products. This approach was based on formalizing the concurrent engineering concept as it was re-invented on the job during the PA product launch.

This procedure was described in a thick report. Five main steps were identified (design, development, decision, manufacturing, marketing and launching), each of them organized in parallel sub-steps addressing one of the functions involved. In total fifty or so sub-tasks were identified which are depicted in a symbolic way in Figure 9.7. The procedure thus clearly became rather heavy in its formalization. Today, those who promoted this approach are conscious of the fact that it is not so important to have the project go systematically through the fifty steps but actually to use this list as an *aide-mémoire* and make sure that no step has been overlooked.

As progress is being made along the fifty steps, leadership on the project moves from one function to another without the other functions abandoning the project. At the same time, the championing of the project remains in the hands of a specific actor, usually the product manager, who keeps coordinating and pushing the project along. This introduces a subtle distinction between the leadership on the project at any stage (some form of recognition of the function which plays a leading role at that stage) and the championing (a clear recognition that there is a need for a pushy actor who feels even more concerned than the others about the success of the project). On the map of Figure 9.5, this procedure falls into the 'Concurrent Engineering in interfunctional teams' situation.

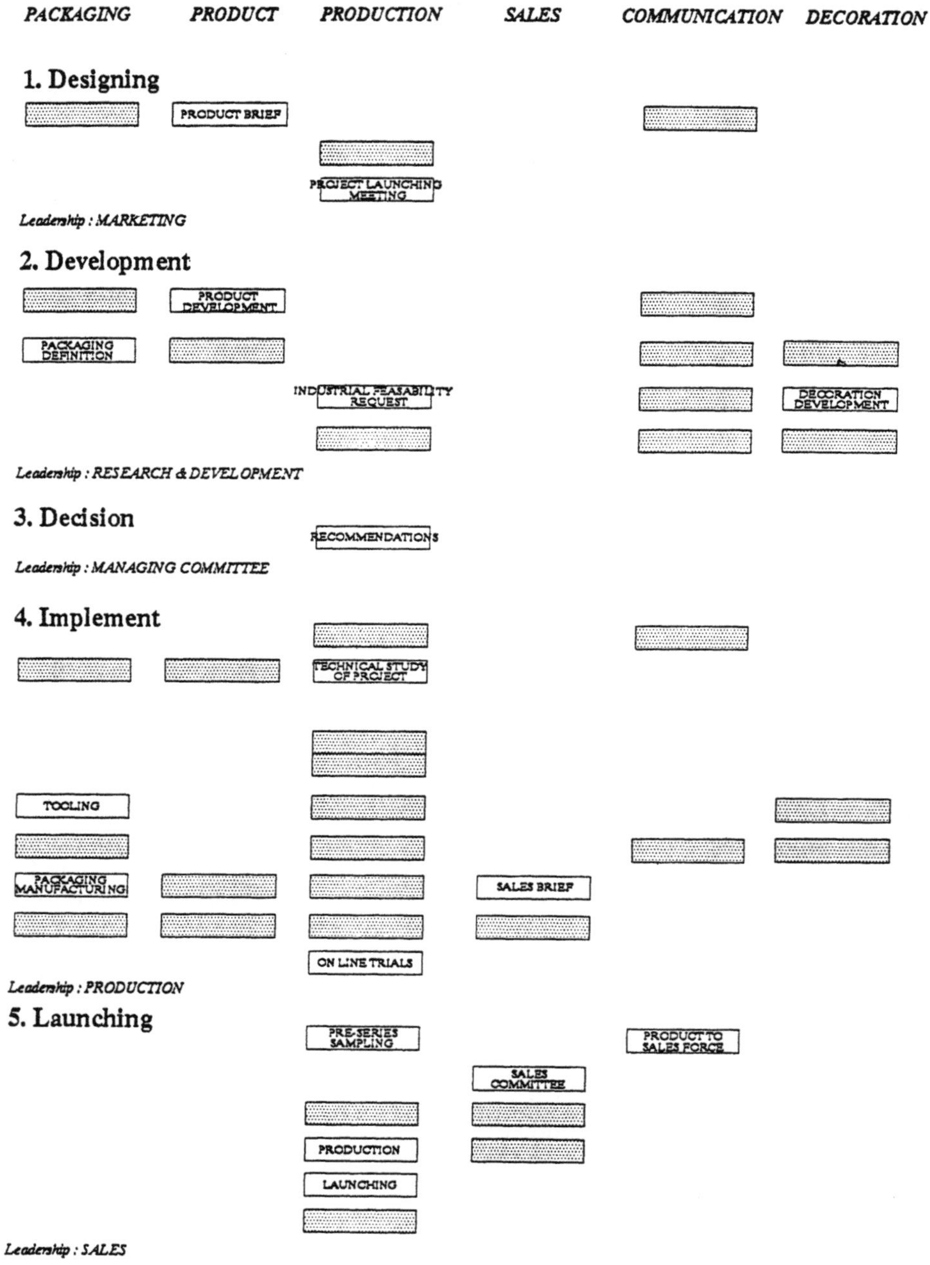

PACKAGING	PRODUCT	PRODUCTION	SALES	COMMUNICATION	DECORATION

1. Designing

PACKAGING	PRODUCT	PRODUCTION	SALES	COMMUNICATION	DECORATION
░░░░░	PRODUCT BRIEF			░░░░░	
		PROJECT LAUNCHING MEETING			

Leadership : MARKETING

2. Development

PACKAGING	PRODUCT	PRODUCTION	SALES	COMMUNICATION	DECORATION
░░░░░	PRODUCT DEVELOPMENT			░░░░░	
PACKAGING DEFINITION	░░░░░			░░░░░	░░░░░
		INDUSTRIAL FEASABILITY REQUEST		░░░░░	DECORATION DEVELOPMENT
		░░░░░		░░░░░	░░░░░

Leadership : RESEARCH & DEVELOPMENT

3. Decision

RECOMMENDATIONS

Leadership : MANAGING COMMITTEE

4. Implement

PACKAGING	PRODUCT	PRODUCTION	SALES	COMMUNICATION	DECORATION
░░░░░	░░░░░	TECHNICAL STUDY OF PROJECT		░░░░░	
		░░░░░			
TOOLING		░░░░░			░░░░░
░░░░░		░░░░░		░░░░░	░░░░░
PACKAGING MANUFACTURING	░░░░░	░░░░░	SALES BRIEF		
░░░░░	░░░░░	░░░░░	░░░░░		
		ON LINE TRIALS			

Leadership : PRODUCTION

5. Launching

PACKAGING	PRODUCT	PRODUCTION	SALES	COMMUNICATION	DECORATION
		PRE-SERIES SAMPLING		PRODUCT TO SALES FORCE	
			SALES COMMITTEE		
		░░░░░	░░░░░		
		PRODUCTION	░░░░░		
		LAUNCHING			
		░░░░░			

Leadership : SALES

Figure 9.7

Today, this approach is commonly and systematically used in this division of EURO Inc. for the development of new products. Training sessions are run to help new staff become familiar with the entire procedure. At the same time, however, none of the other divisions within EURO Inc. have adopted this procedure. Why is that? If concurrent engineering, as it was reinvented and applied in this division of EURO Inc., really made the difference for PA – and it obviously did – why is it that no other division within the firm chose to adopt the same organizational process? It may be worth remembering at this point that the company is structured in a very decentralized way, allowing each division to choose its own operating modes. Still, it is somewhat puzzling to observe that all the other divisions have carefully stayed away from this allegedly remarkable organizational innovation of their colleagues.

We conducted over sixty face-to-face interviews in the firm, both in the division involved with product PA and in other divisions of EURO Inc. We consistently found managers and staff from the former division very happy about the procedure, explaining how it helped channel and smooth out the development processes, how they felt that concurrency (early and permanent involvement of all functions concerned with the project, parallel work) was important, how they skipped many of the formal steps in projects but with everybody at least aware of them. Conversely, we consistently found managers and staff from other divisions either admiring and impressed by the procedure or clearly skeptical or negative but in any case not ready to try to implement it in their own activities.

For example, another division chose to use a rather significant amount of simultaneous engineering while still retaining the usual sequential approach: idea/pre-design/development/industrialization. Marketing keeps a clear leadership of all projects. According to division members, the whole procedure offers a much greater flexibility than the fifty steps described above. That second procedure falls into the 'sequential coordinated teams' category of Figure 9.5. A third division did not adopt the approach of simultaneous engineering nor that of project teams but created a unit to act as a champion for all projects. This unit is in charge of interacting in real time with the different actors in the project – if needed in parallel but more often sequentially – and co-ordinates their actions. This mode falls into the 'shuttle mediation' category. That third division significantly revised that scheme a few months after our field interviews. It was felt that a single champion for all projects means no real championing but purely coordination.

Clearly, if the division of EURO Inc. we first mentioned had really found a significantly more efficient approach for developing new products, several other divisions would certainly have adopted it. This has not been the case. One should thus probably remain cautious about the real merits of the procedure adopted by this division and perhaps more generally about implementation of concurrent engineering, even in the case of inter-functional team work, despite the praise it is given in the literature. Our empirical contribution is therefore presented here as a potential counter-example of what is found in the literature. It is also intended to help introduce some complementary aspects of the issue.

9.4. Crisis, championing, formalization and business development groups

9.4.1. Crisis as a learning mode

Inertia in organizations is a major factor in explaining the often conservative behaviour of firms. Changes, for example the introduction of new procedures, are usually received negatively by organizations. This is mostly due to unlearning/relearning mechanisms which need to be activated. In the case of the product PA at EURO Inc., it was a crisis situation which made it possible to unlock these unlearning/relearning capabilities. The crisis came from the threat represented by a competing innovative product, PX. It led to a new organizational process, relying on concurrent engineering with interfunctional teams, as discussed above. Such change would have probably been very difficult to achieve without the crisis.

We are often given such accounts, emphasizing how real learning comes from the empirical re-discovery of well-known ideas and concepts but experienced under the pressure of a crisis. Cincinnati-Milacron, in the machine tool industry, discovered an interfunctional project team and concurrent engineering under such competitive pressure and thus went through its own management revolution. The other divisions of EURO Inc., not having been faced with a similar crisis, clearly experienced a more limited unlearning/relearning process on this matter. It is worth noting that crises should thus not be considered merely as results of inadequate management but also as opportunities for opening up minds to innovation and progress. Along the same lines as the creative destruction of Schumpeterian changes, crises are needed to unlock unlearning/relearning capabilities of firms.

9.4.2. The role of champions

The literature on the management of innovation tends to assign an important role to the key person who initiates a project, the 'entrepreneur', the innovator, the creator, or more generally the one who brings innovation or change. Burgelman (1984), Roberts (1991), Dougherty (1992), Seurat (1987) or even Peters and Waterman (1983) all give a central role in their innovation model to this mutant, or champion. But, according to others, the word 'champion' should not only refer to the creative person but also to his/her godfather, who plays more political a part, contributing to the success of his godchild's creative ideas.

Moving from this rather idealistic view of innovation to the practical case of project management for the development of new products, the role of the champion is altogether less central and more real. The project does need a driving force, an energy which pushes on, and a co-ordinator. Here is a role for a particular actor, for a project leader or for a function which follows and supports the development through its different steps. Simultaneous engineering goes along well with the existence of a champion, even if the leadership of one function may, in each phase, emphasize one aspect of the project.

It is worth noting however the three different modes encountered at EURO Inc.: the first successively assigns the leading role to each major function but keeps the same champion during the whole of the project's life; the second systematically accepts the marketing group as the natural champion of its projects for new products, while the third creates a specialized unit which in fact becomes the champion for all projects. These procedures are different but each recognizes the pressing need for a champion, a complete co-ordinator and driving force for the developments. It is also worth noting that in practice the most efficient projects are those for which the co-ordinator directly reports to a higher level. We will come back to this issue.

9.4.3. Formalizing the procedure

Since the work of Burns and Stalker (1961) on organic structures allowing lateral interactions, permanent re-definitions, boundaries with variable outlines, some may think that innovation and unstructured 'adhocracy' – after Mintzberg (1979) – are closely linked: indeed coordination mechanisms required by the interactive nature of design and development would operate almost naturally in an organic structure. Conversely, structured organizations with well-defined functions and routines are probably those which most need development processes for new products based on the concept of concurrent engineering. Their reporting systems are closely defined, lead times and commitments are strictly met and the chain of command and the respective roles are observed. One may thus expect that such organizations will tend to formalize concurrent engineering procedures rather heavily. However, one must recognize that the particularly high level of formalization adopted for concurrent engineering by the PA division of EURO Inc. strongly prevented the other divisions from adopting a similar procedure.

The conclusion we draw from this counter-example is the following: if formalizing and concurrent engineering are not contradictory, project management is more comfortable with some degree of freedom within the structures. An approach based on transverse communication, inter-function relations, team spirit and respect for the ideas and constraints of the other actors involved in the project need not be over-formalized. If simultaneous engineering is most likely to be useful for inducing decompartmentalization and integration in the most bureaucratized structures, it would however be erroneous to conclude that the more formalized the process, the more efficient the concurrent engineering. Formalization may simply betray the spirit of simultaneous engineering.

9.4.4. Structuring interfunctional project groups

Figure 9.8 is adapted from Hayes *et al.* (1988), from Midler (1991) as well as from Clark and Fujimoto (1991). It shows how interfunctional project management evolved over the years from simple communication

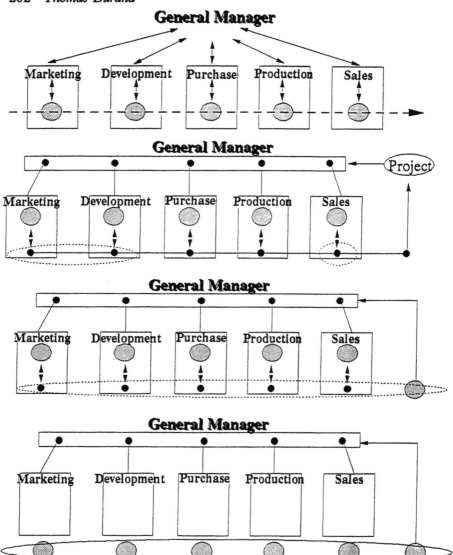

Figure 9.8   Interfunctional project organization over the years

Source: adapted from Hayes, Wheelwright and Clark (1988); Midler (1991); and Clark and Fujimoto (1991)

mechanisms among functional departments, to coordination or project representatives in major functional departments, to heavyweight inter-functional teams coordinated across the departments or even outside the department in an *ad hoc* project group reporting to senior management.

In line with this evolution, we observe that several actors around the firm

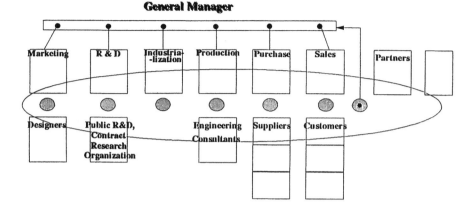

Figure 9.9 Development organization networked interfunctional groups

increasingly play a significant part in development projects as they participate in real time. This is shown in Figure 9.9. In other words some form of concurrency applies in the involvement of suppliers, research contract organizations, clients, engineering consultants, etc. This also happens within alliances among firms co-developing new products and manufacturing processes as partners. The respective involvement of each of these external actors may be more or less important, depending on the type of industry, technological context, rate of change, supplier/client relationships, etc. By recalling Pavitt's (1986) and (1989) typologies of industries one might categorize the degree of concurrency encountered as well as the typical external players involved in development projects:

- **Supplier-dominated industries** (*traditional manufacture*): slow change, no real need for concurrency, strong links with suppliers
- **Production – scale intensive** (*bulk materials–assembly*): internal development, some concurrency especially if strong competitive pressure with some suppliers implication
- **Specialized suppliers** (*machinery–instruments*): strong client involvement with some concurrent engineering
- **Science-based** (*electronics, electrical products, chemicals*): significant concurrent engineering with some public R&D involvement
- **Space, nuclear, transportation**: pipe-line, government-controlled inter-organizational development

This means that the 'concurrent engineering in interfunctional project teams' configuration of Figure 9.5 actually covers settings which become increasingly networked and complex, depending on contexts. Consequently, in many situations, this makes it even more difficult but necessary for concurrent engineering to be adopted as a process.

   With regard to interfunctional project groups, one should stress once more the gains derived from early implication of the various internal and external actors in the project. Not only are design problems going to be solved faster but also each party involved will take part in the debate from the start. Concurrent engineering and team work are indeed designed to generate strong discussion and controversy before design decisions are made in order to limit arguments and vetoes when implementation is supposed to take place.

This has strong implications for the nature of interrelations within the project group. 'One rower and seven helmsmen', that is one active group leader and various passive group members each offering his/her advice is not team work, nor is it concurrent engineering. No problem will be solved, no commitment to the decisions will be obtained. Another implication of the above deals with the status of the project group leader within the organization: his/her position has to be strong enough so that the decisions made by the group will be supported or at least accepted by all functions in the organization and general management. Not only is it a matter of credibility; it is also a matter of effectiveness: concurrency within the project group, but sequential pipe-lining imposed by the rest of the organization lead the interfunctional group to much frustration and strain while little progress is made on the development. Everything depends on the preferences and loyalty of the various group members. They need to commit themselves to the project but should still be in a position to return to their functional department once the project is completed. It is worth mentioning here how many reports claim that the reintegration process is often difficult, especially when project durations are long, eg several years.

Another reason to rely on a heavyweight project manager comes from the uncertain nature of product development. Budget and time constraints are necessary, but no one can know for certain how much a project will cost or how long it will last. Projects are uncertain. Therefore, overruns should be expected both in cost and duration. Deadlines and resource limitations are useful ways of monitoring the progress being made; still some understanding must exist on the part of general management. A heavyweight manager leading the interfunctional team may help in obtaining the necessary acceptance of the inevitable uncertainty attached to the development of new products and the eventual cost overruns and delays incurred.

9.5. Synthesis

We feel somewhat frustrated with regard to the low attention paid to 'real' innovation processes in the literature, as exemplified here by our theme on project management for new products. We also are in some way disappointed by the lack of questioning and debate about the concept of concurrent engineering. We tried first to clarify the concept of concurrency, relating it to structural forms of coordination in organizations. Our empirical work then led us to analyse how this approach was implemented in different divisions of a large consumer goods firm. This case made it possible for us to present another example of the apparently remarkable efficiency of concurrent engineering for speeding up development. However, this case also showed how carefully the other divisions of the same company avoided a similar procedure. We interpret this as a signal: concurrent engineering may not be quite such a winning concept as most of the literature on product development has, since 1988, wanted us to believe.

Based on the case presented, we again came across the role of a crisis as an unlearning/learning booster. We discussed the role of championing and the level of formalization of the procedure using concurrent engineering. We finally focused on the structuring of interfunctional project groups and showed how in certain instances actors external to the firm may be increasingly involved in the groups adopting some form of concurrency in their development processes.

References

Abernathy, W.J. and Utterback, J. (1978) 'Patterns of Industrial Innovation' *Technology Review*, **80**, 7, June/July, 40–47.

Baron, Xavier (1993) 'Gérer des Salariés dans des Structures par Projets', *Personnel* No. 338.

Baron, Xavier and Couvreur, Emmanuel (1992) 'Les Grands Projets, Instruments du Succès de la Gestion des Ressources Humaines?', *Gérer et Comprendre*.

Burgelman, R. (1984) 'Designs for Corporate Entrepreneurship in Established Firms', *California Management Review*, **26**, 3, 154–66.

Burns, T. and Stalker, G.M. (1961) *The Management of Innovation*, London, Tavistock.

Carter, Don (1992) *Concurrent Engineering*, Reading, Mass, Addison Wesley.

Clark, K. and Fujimoto, T. (1991) *Product Development Performance*, Boston, Harvard Business School Press.

Dean, W. and Susman, G.I. (1989) 'Organizing for Manufacturable Design', *Harvard Business Review*.

Dougherty, D. (1992) 'A Price-Centered Model of Organizational Renewal through Product Innovation', *Strategic Management Journal*, **13**, Summer, 77–92.

Hayes, R., Wheelwright, S. and Clarke, K. (1988) *Dynamic Manufacturing*, New York, The Free Press.

Jelinek, M. and Schoonhoven, C. (1990) *The Innovation Marathon*, Oxford, Basil Blackwell.

Kline, S.J. and Rosenberg, N. (1986) 'An Overview of Innovation' in R. Landau and N. Rosenberg (eds), *The Positive Sum Strategy*, Washington, DC, Academy of Engineering Press.

Midler, C. (1991) 'L'Apprentissage de la Gestion par Projet dans l'Industrie Automobile', *Annales des Mines*, October.

Mintzberg, H. (1979) *The Structuring of Organizations*, Englewood Cliffs, Prentice-Hall.

Morris, P.G. and Hough, G. (1987) *The Anatomy of Major Projects*, New York, Wiley.

Navarre, C. (1989) *La Nouvelle Fonction 'Project Management'*, Institute for International Research, Paris.

Pavitt, K. (1986) 'Technology, Innovations and Strategic Management' in J. McGee and H. Thomas (eds), *Strategic Management Research, A European Perspective*, New York, Wiley.

Pavitt, K. (1989) 'Technological Accumulation, Diversification and Organization in U.K. Companies, 1945–1983', *Management Science*, **35**.

Peters, T. and Waterman, R. (1983) *Le Prix de l'Excellence*, Paris, Interéditions.

Roberts, E. (1991) 'Entrepreneurs in High Technology', Oxford, Oxford University Press.

Seurat, S. (1987) *La Coévolution Créatrice*, Paris, Ed. Rivages.

Smith, W.N., Meyer, G. and Hirsig, A. (1982) *Industrial R&D Management*, New York, Dekker.

Teece, D. (1989), 'Inter-Organizational Requirements of the Innovation Process', *Managerial and Decision Economics*, Special Issue, spring 35–42.

10 Rational calculations and information-gathering systems

Harland Prechel

Recent analyses have focused on the economy as the primary catalyst to corporate restructuring and the introduction of new technologies as the solution to problems of inefficiency and inflexibility.[1] The analysis here suggests that, although important, technology is only one dimension of the corporate response. Moreover, technology is best understood in relationship to information-gathering systems and the use of that data to restructure the mode of control to increase organizational flexibility and improve product quality.

Although several researchers comment on the importance of information in the emerging corporate form (eg, Attewell, 1987; Rule and Attewell 1989), few attempt to demonstrate how information is generated and used in the decision-making process.[2] This gap in the literature exists despite the fact that information is the key to action, especially decision making. Several theoretical traditions emphasize the collection and rational calculation of data and its use in the decision-making process. These theorists suggest that historical variation of cost and price calculation is a critical dimension of the accumulation process (Marx, 1981a: 211–12, 1981b: 312; Shumpeter, 1950; Sombart, 1953; Weber, 1978). Several contemporary researchers maintain that rational calculation constitutes a crucial component of organizational structures (Carter, 1985; Clegg, 1990; Cutler *et al.*, 1978; Markus and Pfeffer, 1983). Chandler (1977), for example, argues that the use of accounting information guides the 'Visible Hand' of management within the multi-divisional form.

However, none of these researchers analyze rational calculation and its affect on decision making and the system of control. Although historians have begun to give attention to the structure of corporate accounting and its relationship to decision making, their analyses are limited to corporate structuring during previous historical periods (eg, Johnson and Kaplan, 1991; Johnson, 1991; Temin, 1991). To fill this gap, I will examine changes in the information-gathering system, the use of cost data in the decision-making process, the location and dissemination of cost information and the effects of the information-gathering system on the distribution of authority.

This chapter is divided into three main sections. The first section includes a discussion of dimensions of current concepts of corporate restructuring. The second is an historical analysis of the implementation of information-gathering systems in large US corporations after World War II. This section also discusses how the use of information within the mode of control led to contradictory and irrational action (ie, decision making), which undermined the efficient use of organizational resources. The last section demonstrates how this restructured information-gathering system is designed to both overcome the contradictions within the previous mode of control and to provide the data necessary to implement new technologies successfully.

This analysis suggests that corporate forms evolve. Individuals and organizations learn, corporations are historical entities and corporations must be understood in their historical context (Prechel, 1990a). However, corporations do not evolve at a steady rate. Rather, change is discontinuous and typically triggered by crisis (Benson, 1977; Prechel, 1991a). Moreover, businesses do not always have the best information, and competitive pressures are not strong enough to ensure that only the fittest survive. The result is corporations may be inefficient yet able to survive. However, when competitive pressures intensify, organizational crises emerge which are catalysts to more rapid evolution. At these points in their histories corporations learn at a faster rate and implement what they have learned.

10.1. Information, technology and flexibility

Key dimensions of the 'post-Fordist', 'flexible specialization', 'flexible manufacturing', and 'flexible accumulation' perspectives converge on the idea of flexibility (Harvey, 1991). Flexibility has become the new buzzword with a range of utopian connotations such as the return to craft-work organization and worker's autonomy (eg, Piore and Sabel, 1984). These conceptions of flexibility[3] remain highly abstract and fail to demonstrate, for example, whether this flexibility is highly controlled or if wide parameters of discretion exist. The failure to specify the basis of flexible restructuring masks two issues related to the redistribution of power and authority: (1) different interests are at stake and (2) which interests are served (Pollert, 1988; Standing, 1991).[4]

Moreover, some researchers associate flexibility primarily with computer technology (eg, Zuboff, 1988). This tendency represents an important shortcoming. Computer technologies speed the processing and distribution of information – which may aid in increasing the response rate to organizational dilemmas – but this is not the same as flexibility. *Flexibility* is the capacity to adapt and change. In particular, it entails increased product variability and more rapid responses to changing markets. The distinctive characteristic of flexible technologies is that a machine is programmed to execute a range of operations (Schoenberger, 1988: 252) which makes it possible to use a given machine in the manufacture of a range of product configurations. The change from one manufacturing activity to another is completed by reprogramming the computer that controls the machine. In contrast, the operations completed by traditional mass-production technologies must be adjusted mechanically.

The flexibility and adaptability of the machine, the manufacturing process and ultimately the corporation are dependent on the design of information-gathering systems, which provide the data to configure the machines according to product specifications demanded in the market. In short, computers aid in the access, synthesis and distribution of information. Although important, without adequate information-gathering systems computers can do little to enhance flexibility.[5]

The emphasis on information is not new. Moreover, the demand for information occurs within specific historical conditions. Max Weber (1978) maintained that rational calculation was a defining feature of modern profit-seeking corporations because capitalism demands stable, strict and intensively calculable administration. Rational calculation, which takes the form of cost accounting, provides the necessary information to ensure standardization of the manufacturing process and product quality (Weber, 1978: 224). However, the advancement of rational calculation is historically contingent and occurs at a slower rate 'in the absence of the objective need for it' (ibid.: 106). More recently, Chandler (1962: 9) demonstrated that 'unexpected contingencies or crises' during the decades between 1870 and 1910 resulted in an important shift in emphasis toward a distinctively more purposive system of control, which required increased information-processing capabilities by the organization in order to deliver more precise information to decision makers. In this respect, there is nothing new about contemporary corporate restructuring. Recent accumulation crises simply provide the catalysts to develop more sophisticated information-gathering systems to increase organizational control.

10.2. Information, computers and decentralization versus centralization

Many current explanations of corporate restructuring employ conceptual frameworks that rely on binary categories (eg, inflexibility versus flexibility, centralization versus decentralization).[6] These conceptualizations cause significant distortions. For example, restructured corporations are typically described as decentralized and flexible.[7] Researchers suggest that there has been a sharp break with the past (ie, a 'Great Divide') and that the new technologies being implemented open up the possibility for a reconstitution of labor relations and production systems that entail new forms of worker-cooperative organizations (Piore and Sabel, 1984). This perspective maintains that applications of technologies such as automatic production controls and integrated production complexes are associated with work teams, cooperative decision making, informal networks and participation on the shop floor (eg, Kanter, 1989; Kenney and Florida 1988: 121–58; Piore and Sabel, 1984; Sabel, 1982). These arguments implicitly or explicitly suggest that there has been a shift from centralized rigid organizations to decentralized flexible organizations.

However, neo-Fordists challenge the decentralization argument, suggesting that recent changes in the mode of control are simply mechanisms of extending Fordism. Neo-Fordists focus on the relations of production and suggest that flexible manufacturing systems and automation are simply other instruments of control, de-skilling, and labor degradation (Aglietta, 1979). They maintain that there is nothing new in the capitalist search for increased flexibility and that the substantive evidence for any radical change in capitalism is either weak or faulty (Gordon, 1988; Harvey, 1989; Pollert, 1988; Sayer, 1989).[8] In short, whereas some researchers suggest that authority is becoming decentralized, others interpret corporate restructuring as the intensification of control over the labor process.

These competing explanations exist, in part, because there is a tendency among researchers of corporate restructuring to be satisfied with surface-level analysis and a failure to give adequate attention to the subterranean processes behind corporate restructuring. One of the conceptual obstacles to understanding the logic behind corporate restructuring includes the tendency to associate decision making with authority. Although covariation of these two variables may describe previous historical periods, decision making and authority no longer necessarily covary (Prechel, 1991b). To grasp adequately contemporary corporate restructuring, authority and decision making must be treated as separate variables. The key feature of decentralization is the degree of abstractness of the information flow (also see Stinchcombe, 1990: 114–15). *Decentralization* exists when the controls of a superior level of the organization over an inferior level are highly abstract which leaves discretion with the manager at the lower level.

There are several interrelated ways in which the collection of increasingly precise data and computerization of the restructured corporation provide the organizational capacity to centralize control, while simultaneously decentralizing decision making and increasing organizational flexibility. First, computerization increases the organizational capability to centralize and analyze large amounts of quantitative data. Second, access to more specific data provides the organizational capability to establish *premise controls*, which limit the degree of abstractness of the information, thereby containing behavior. Premise controls place limitations on decision-making discretion which enhances the probability of predictable and consistent solutions (Perrow, 1986: 128). Whereas premise controls historically existed at the higher levels of the organizational hierarchy, computerization makes it possible to analyze data to establish and extend premise controls over previously non-routine production decisions. Third, the centralization of data into a computer system limits the number of independent information sources, which reduce the differentiation of perception and contribute to the standardization of decision making (March and Simon 1958: 127). Fourth, computer linkages between the production sites and centralized computers make it possible to change frequently premise and computer controls and immediately transmit them to the point of production, thereby increasing organizational flexibility. In short, similar to previous organizational arrangements, formal rules accompany decentralization, becoming the basis of more precise control at the lower levels (see Child, 1972).

Hence, the question is not whether organizational decentralization exists. Rather the questions are: what is being decentralized? What makes it possible for decentralization, more precise controls and flexibility to exist simultaneously? And how do corporations maintain control over and integrate highly interdependent manufacturing processes while decentralizing?

10.3. Propositions and the case study

There are several propositions explored here. First, the cost controls based on the information-gathering system between the 1920s and 1970s shaped managerial decisions and actions in such a way that they undermined performance. Second, corporate restructuring entails the revision and intensification of information-gathering systems to overcome the impediments of the previous system. Third, in the restructured corporation top management and a group of experts stipulate the general parameters of a set of more or less coherent and preferred goals for organizational subunits and determine activities of production managers. Fourth, the restructured information-gathering system is the basis of organizational flexibility. Fifth, corporate restructuring is an extension of scientific managerial techniques and principles (ie, measurement, quantification and the separation of conception from execution) to previously unrationalized dimensions of the corporation.

I employed an historical case study method. In addition, I conducted indepth interviews with executives, managers and technicians while the corporation was undergoing restructuring. I selected a corporation in the steel industry because the low quality of steel produced in the US and competition in the global economy resulted in an accumulation crisis in this industry in the early and mid-1980s.[9] Therefore, if corporate capitalism is restructuring the mode of control, it should be readily observable in the steel industry where an extended accumulation crisis existed. Moreover, the steel industry does not have a history of innovation. Hence, if significant changes are occurring in a corporation in this industry, it is probably that other corporations are making similar changes.

10.4. The limits of centralized control

Throughout the early twentieth century Taggert (a pseudonym) had a centralized managerial system. Top management – like the top managers of other corporations (see Chandler, 1962; Johnson, 1991: 49) – was familiar with the company's technology and manufacturing process.[10] Knowledge obtained from non-accounting sources (eg, the craft tradition) allowed top management directly to oversee and monitor a wide range of operating and coordinating decisions. Moreover, because of their knowledge of steelmaking and regular contact with operating management, top managers could monitor the cost-cutting efforts of these managers.

Although top management maintained control over several organizational activities during the first decades of its evolution, there were limits to centralized control. For example, top management could not supervise the various phases of the expanding manufacturing process. To exercise control over operations Taggert – like other corporations – applied scientific management (eg, Taylorism, Fordism) techniques to the production process to increase productivity and control over the labor process (see Braverman, 1974; Clawson, 1980; Edwards, 1979; Stone, 1975).[11] The primary means to ensure control included centralizing quantitative data into planning offices where engineers established rules, reduced jobs to their elemental components and identified and discarded inefficient movements. However, steel manufacturing at Taggert included numerous variables and many permutations of these variables for each product. In addition, each product had unique specifications. Moreover, the corporation's wide product line limited the degree to which bureaucratic controls would be implemented. Establishing and implementing rules governing the manufacture of each product is not only complex, but it restricts the flexibility at the point of production for adjusting the manufacturing process when problems emerge. In short, the complexity of steel manufacturing restricted the degree to which Taylorism and Fordism could separate conception from execution and establish the 'one best way' to manufacture a product with existing technologies and information-gathering systems.

Prior to decentralization, accounting data were used solely to plan and make strategic decisions (eg, reinvestment). However, once top management relinquished direct control over the manufacturing units, it began to use these accounting data to monitor operating costs. The primary form of this control was budgets, which used accounting data to specify operating budgets for each organizational unit. The primary goal of the budgeting mechanism was to harmonize actions within departments with the overall goals of the corporation (Johnson and Kaplan, 1991: 64).

10.5. The information-gathering system and corporate structures

Although numerous state agencies (eg, Securities Exchange Commission, Internal Revenue Service) influenced the way in which the rules of accounting evolved, the public accounting profession's rules for auditing public statements provided the framework for most financial reporting by the 1940s. The accounting rules required costs to be classified in the income statement by the functional area of the business which usually conformed to the divisions and subdivisions within the corporation (eg, sales, manufacturing, purchasing, finance). Rather than identifying costs with *activities* that cause them, this accounting system tended to identify costs with locations where *transactions* occur. It is important to note that these categories do not reflect the underlying categories of work or activities that cause costs (for an excellent discussion see Johnson, 1991: 52–6).

This mechanism to organize accounting information – whether intended or unintended – began to shape the decisions and actions that determine performance results (Armitage and Atkinson, 1990: 141). The budgetary controls based on this information typically identified the costs associated with operating units and allocated budgets to the middle managers (eg, mill superintendents) responsible for those units. These middle managers, in turn, pressured subordinate managers to keep their costs low. This created an incentive system that encouraged operating management to: (1) focus on their subunits and disregard the implications of their decisions on downstream units and (2) maximize output because it lowered per unit costs (for more detail see Prechel, 1991a, 1991b).

In short, the accounting system – which was designed to report financial transactions and results – became the mechanism to monitor operating objectives and the performance of business operations. For the first time, top management used accounting data to control the actions of subordinate managers to ensure the efficient use of labor and resources (also see Johnson and Kaplan, 1991: 140–420; Johnson, 1991: 52). However, little information was available to evaluate the effective use of resources within the operating units. Accounting data merely provided a diagnostic of whether there had been a failure in an operating unit that needed to be discovered and corrected (Armitage and Atkinson, 1990: 141). It provided neither the basis for identifying the failure nor an understanding of what needed to be changed.

However, the abstractness of the data provided manufacturing managers with little information upon which to base these costing decisions. Moreover because these cost data were highly abstract, mill superintendents could not evaluate the cost effectiveness of their own decisions or the decisions of subordinate managers. Transaction-based cost information – rather than activity based cost information – neither identified cost inputs nor established a decision-making criterion that encouraged management to contain total costs.

The inability of the accounting system to provide specific input costs did not go unnoticed. In the early 1990s A.H. Church (1914) – a contemporary of Frederick Taylor – attempted to convince corporate management to develop a product costing system capable of identifying specific costs (wages, materials, indirect shop charges, selling expenses) for each product and to connect those product costs with corporate profitability (see Johnson and Kaplan, 1991: 52–6; Nelson, 1975: 50). However, corporate management did not develop an accounting system with these capabilities.[12]

To overcome the problem of not having the cost information to evaluate the profitability of specific products, like most corporations (Johnson, 1991: 55) Taggert pursued a strategy of manufacturing a full product line. As long as the corporation remained profitable, the profitability of specific products was of little concern. Corporations assessed total profits by comparing the income statement to the balance sheet. That is, corporations developed systems to track the performance of the firm and its units based on return on investment (Johnson and Kaplan, 1991: 58).

However, when corporations began to diversify in the 1920s and 1930s into several industrial markets with a wide range of manufacturing technologies, their inability to specify and evaluate production costs became a concern: there was no way to differentiate between the profitability of distinct product lines (eg, real estate, steel). At Taggert – as at most large corporations (eg, DuPont, General Motors) – the response to this problem was to restructure the corporation by locating product lines in divisions and to decentralize authority. This structure allowed top management to assess the profitability of the product lines (see Chandler, 1962, 1977, 1990).

As the corporation's size and complexity increased in the post-World War II era, additional limitations were placed on centralized control. Coordination of the increasingly complex manufacturing process stretched top management's cognitive capabilities (ie, bounded rationality) which slowed the decision-making process and frequently resulted in underutilizing manufacturing units. As with operating activities, centralized bureaucratic controls could not be implemented to ensure top managerial authority over coordinating activities of Taggert's wide product line. Bureaucratic controls could not govern coordinating decisions because it is difficult to establish rules governing changes in the linkage of the manufacturing facilities when those linkages must frequently change to accommodate a wide product line. As in other expanding corporations, Taggert's top management delegated decision-making authority over coordination activities to the managers of the various operating units, a step which was dependent on personal cooperation among middle managers (see Chandler, 1977).

In short, the technical limitations of scientific management required that the loci of discretion over many decisions was at the point of production, where managers exercised decision-making authority based on their knowledge and understanding of the manufacturing process. Bureaucratic controls could not be specified in such a way that they ensured centralized control over either the manufacturing process or the coordination of the manufacturing units. Control over operating units as initially *decentralized to* the operating units, but it remained *centralized within* the operating units. However by the 1960s and 1970s, as each operating unit expanded, it became necessary to decentralize decision-making authority within subunits because mill superintendents could not supervise all aspects of the manufacturing process.

10.6. Budgetary controls and bifurcate interests among middle managers

During the rapid economic growth of the 1960s and 1970s, the corporation steadily increased its manufacturing capacity. By the late 1960s, the lower and middle segments of the managerial hierarchy expanded to seven levels. Budgetary controls remained top management's primary means for exercising cost control over the production managers who had decision-making authority within the organizational units. These controls determined if production managers remained within their budgets and whether they merited a salary increase.

However, budgetary controls generated a contradiction that undermined cooperation and capital accumulation. A contradiction emerges within a corporation when dimensions of the formally rational mode of control generate a course of action that undermines the corporation's substantive accumulation goal. Budgetary controls shaped the interest of managers in such a way that they resulted in decisions that were in opposition to the profit-making goal of the corporation. The primary contradiction of concern here is between the goals of the manufacturing unit (ie, to remain within its budget) and the substantive profitability goals of the corporation. Contradictions express themselves as crises when they undermine the efficient use of resources and the corporation's capacity to realize a profit (Prechel, 1990a, 1991a).

This contradiction was created by budgetary controls, which bifurcated managers' interests (March and Simon, 1958). Because middle managers were evaluated by their ability to remain within their assigned budgets, keeping costs below their budgets became a substantive goal of the operating units. However, middle-managerial decisions to keep operating costs low within the organizational units often contradicted the corporation's substantive profitability goal because these decisions frequently increased total corporate costs and undermined product quality. For example, if mill superintendents stopped the manufacturing process to reroll defective steel, their operating costs increased, which reflected poorly on their managerial abilities. This system of control encouraged production managers to pass on flawed products to the next stage in the manufacturing process where the manager of the next organizational unit became responsible for the product and the costs associated with it. In short, budgetary controls encouraged these managers to optimize in their area (for more detail see Prechel, 1991a).

Second, the tendency to pass flawed production downstream led to conflict among the managers of the manufacturing units. In some cases, this resulted in open hostility among these managers. This became an important impediment to accumulation because the efficient flow of materials through the manufacturing process was dependent on informal cooperation among the managers of the various organizational units.

In summary, two unintended consequences emerged from using this information-gathering system to establish controls over operating management: (1) passing flawed products through the manufacturing process and (2) hostility and conflict among middle managers. Whereas the first unintended consequence undermined product quality, the second undermined cooperation and the flow of materials through the manufacturing process. In short, the structure of the information-gathering system, and the use of this information to control middle- and lower-level decision makers had the unintended consequences of undermined cooperation, coordination, product quality and, ultimately, profits.

The information-gathering system and the mode of control, however, did not change throughout this period because it was cost effective enough to realize an acceptable rate of accumulation in this oligopolistic industry, where the corporation set prices. Moreover, the information-gathering system could not identify the costs associated with these kinds of decisions.

10.7. Corporate restructuring: from budget controls to cost controls

Competition intensified in the early 1980s as global steel manufacturing capacity exceeded demand, several foreign corporations dumped steel into US markets[13] and foreign steelmakers and domestic minimills were producing lighter, higher-quality steel (Prechel, 1990b, 1991a). Although these trends had been emerging throughout the late 1970s, they did not result in an accumulation crisis until the recessions in the early 1980s when domestic steel demand dropped from 100 million tons in 1979 to 61.5 million tons in 1982.

The internal organizational contradiction between formal and substantive rationality together with the increased economic competitiveness restricted the corporation's capacity to accumulate capital. To regain its competitive position in the market-place, the corporation had to cut costs while improving product quality. However, before costs could be cut Taggert had to identify specific product costs which required a restructuring of the information-gathering system. The comptroller[14] and systems departments were the primary organizational units responsible for restructuring this system. The accounting department was responsible for separating existing cost data from financial data and for restructuring the cost system to identify specific cost inputs, for collecting price data and, together with the systems department, for centralizing these data. The corporation located these data in an expanded centralized computer system where they could be accessed, analyzed and distributed to the appropriate location in the corporation.

Once Taggert centralized these data it created a decision center where experts (eg, metallurgists) analyzed the data to determine the most cost-efficient way to manufacture each product. This new unit – the manufacturing decision center – was elevated to the top of the manufacturing hierarchy, equivalent to the plant manager. Technical experts in the manufacturing decision center used these quantitative data to calculate the most cost-efficient means of producing each product and to establish more precise premise controls in manufacturing them. These premise controls – which were transmitted to production managers – defined the parameters within which decision making occurs, thereby limiting the discretion of production managers. The availability of detailed information simultaneously increased organizational flexibility. If experts in the control center identified a new combination of variables to manufacture a specific product at a lower price, premise controls governing the manufacture of that product were established and transmitted to the point of production.

Similarly, Taggert restructured the systems department and assigned it two new responsibilities. Restructuring entailed the centralization of authority over all computer activities to the systems department. Previously systems personnel were assigned to the managers of the organizational units where they performed support services. The restructured systems department's first responsibility was to centralize all computer activities throughout the corporation and develop a computer system that linked the various organizational units. Second, the systems department was responsible for articulating the relationships between the needs of the computer system and the data-processing activities and the strategic needs of the corporation. This restructuring of the systems department integrated it directly into the managerial hierarchy. In the past, like other corporations, Taggert's systems department was outside the managerial hierarchy and provided service functions to management when called upon (see Mintzberg, 1979). Systems was not considered strategically important and – as was the case for most corporations (see *Business Week*, October 10, 1986, p. 172) – Taggert's top information manager reported to the chief financial officer. In contrast, in the mid-1980s, the general manager of systems began to report directly to the Chief Executive Officer.[15]

The collection and centralization of cost data made it possible to establish more precise and flexible controls over the manufacturing process in two ways. First, more decisions were based on *managerial accounting*: the dimension of accounting that transforms data into decision-making information. Managerial accounting provides production managers with predetermined standard cost data, which can be compared to actual cost inputs. These data were used to determine if variances exist between standard and actual costs. If variances exist, production managers are responsible for determining why they exist and to take action to reduce those costs. By 1987 the corporation located computer monitors at each decision site, making it possible to transmit decision-making information directly from the decision center to the production manager on the shop floor. Second, the specification of costs made it possible to intensify *responsibility accounting*: cost accounting by area of responsibility. Responsibility accounting specified the location in the manufacturing process where cost inputs occurred.

In contrast to the past when only middle managers were held accountable for costs, responsibility accounting identified even the lowest-level decision makers and held those managers accountable for costs within their span of control. Whereas premise controls centralized authority over decision making, Taggert implemented more rules to specify the span of control and lines of authority. In short, these more precise cost data provided the information that made it possible to push decision-making responsibility down the organizational hierarchy, while centralizing control over the decision maker. The more precise information-gathering system became the cornerstone of the restructured mode of control; it provided the quantitative data to establish the parameters for making a 'correct' decision.

Production problems that could not be resolved readily by premise controls were allocated to *managerial teams*, which also use rationally calculated data to make team decisions. Within this structure when a difference between standard and actual costs was identified, management teams investigated the source and collectively made decisions based on the most cost-efficient solution. The centralization of quantitative data and the use of these data in the decision-making process increased cooperation. However, the form of this cooperation was significantly different from generally accepted conceptions of cooperation. Although Taggert introduced cooperative decision making, a 'correct decision' was based on data transmitted from the centralized decision-making centers to the appropriate point of production. The emphasis on team decision-making – together with this predetermined rationally calculated criterion – operated as an *unobtrusive control*: it established a mechanism whereby managers supervised one another to ensure that they employed standardized data collected by the information-gathering system in the decision-making process. This form of cooperation is based on a uniform centralized criterion that ensures standardization of decision making.

Although decisions continued to be executed at lower levels in the managerial hierarchy, many conception functions were concentrated in the manufacturing decision center. By centralizing the loci of decision-making discretion, Taggert created the organizational capacity to move execution down to the level where inputs occur while centralizing the conceptualization and monitoring of those decisions.

10.8. Costs information and technological controls

After specifying costs and more precise spans of control, Taggert implemented more precise technical controls. This phase of corporate restructuring centralized control over coordination of the entire plant into the newly created 'operations control center'. The center cybernetically scheduled orders with similar production specifications to reduce the amount of downtime needed to adjust the manufacturing process to meet different product specifications. This new functional unit transformed steelmaking from batch production toward *continuous processing*, the reconceptualization and reorganization of steelmaking that link operations from initial steelmaking to delivery at the customer's plant. Continuous processing ensures a more efficient flow of steel through the manufacturing process.

In addition, by 1986 Taggert calculated the standards for all significant product characteristics and incorporated statistical process control (SPC) directly into the manufacturing process to improve product quality. Statistical process control and the production computer controls together established a reiterative control system that repeatedly measures the product while it is manufactured. If the manufacturing process exceeds the tolerance limits calculated for a particular product, the production control computer automatically adjusts the technology during the manufacturing process. These technical controls incorporate production decisions directly into the manufacturing process. When the sales department receives an order, they transfer the product specifications to the manufacturing decision center, where technicians program the production control computers to those predetermined standards. Like cost controls, technical controls are based on quantitative, rationally calculated data. They are a means of increasing standardization and ultimately of enhancing substantive goals (eg, product quality).

This centralized mode of control has the organizational capacity to change product specifications minutes before the product is manufactured. When customers call to change product specifications, sales personnel identify the product order and contact the decision center where the new product specifications are transmitted immediately to the manager at the point of production. This mode of control also makes it possible to change product specifications in relation to market conditions. For example, if input costs increase, steelmaking recipes can be altered if technical experts in the decision center develop a lower-cost manufacturing process.

10.9. Eliminating the buffers: more direct top managerial control

Taggert also collected market data that – in conjunction with the cost data – provided the organizational capacity to connect manufacturing more closely with several dimensions of strategic management. First, once Taggert incorporated these data into the information-gathering system, market prices could be compared to the costs for manufacturing each product line which made it possible to match current costs with prices. Second, Taggert used

SPC to analyze statistical variances to identify the tolerance capabilities of a particular technology to determine whether that technology could manufacture a product to meet customers' (ie, market) specifications. Top management used these data to determine which technologies to remove from the manufacturing process. These two dimensions of the information-gathering system provided the organizational capacity to identify its most profitable products and product lines and to make strategic decisions about the products to manufacture and the markets to emphasize. Third, Taggert used data obtained from the information-gathering system to adjust and redefine sales policy as market conditions and profit margins varied on specific products. Similar to what was done in the manufacturing sector, Taggert relocated the loci of discretion regarding sales policy into a sales decision center where production cost and price data – obtained from the information-gathering system – were analyzed to maximize profits through selective marketing. In short, flexibility at this level was dependent on the information-gathering system, which provided strategic management with decision-making information.

Once Taggert identified its most profitable products and implemented the more precise information-gathering system and the computer technology, this restructured mode of control made it possible to transmit the manufacturing specifications established in the centralized decision-making center directly to the shop floor. Moreover, it was possible to assess whether decisions at all levels were consistent with the profitability goals of the corporation. Top managerial control increased because the mode of control conveyed standardized decision-making information directly to operating managers. This intensification of formally rational control reduced the gap between top managerial agendas and activities within each operating unit.

This is in sharp contrast to the past where top managerial decisions were dependent on experience and information obtained from the large staff of middle managers (Chandler, 1962, 1977). The restructured information-gathering system, with computers to aid in the analysis of the data, provided top management and its staff of experts with the information necessary to govern a wide range of organizational activities. This reorganization of the entire managerial system into one hierarchical system more directly connects top managerial agendas to the activities on the shop floor. Whereas the centralization of market and cost data provides the information to establish manufacturing guidelines, the centralized computer system makes it possible to transmit these guidelines directly into the production process or establish the premise of decisions. Restructuring the mode of control by intensifying rational calculation provides the organizational capacity to centralize more conception activities and decentralize more execution activities, simultaneously increasing organizational flexibility and control over more spheres of organizational activity.

10.10. Findings

This analysis demonstrates that Taggert restructured to cut costs and overcome an internal organizational contradiction created by the previous mode of control. The previous information-gathering system and the subsequent budgetary controls shaped the interest of managers in such a way that it generated decisions that maximized subunits' goals. These decisions frequently undermined cooperation between the managers of subunits, lowered product quality and undermined the corporation's substantive profitability goals. The strategy to overcome these constraints to capital accumulation included an information-gathering system that reduced the abstractness of information flows and specified how to use that information. This affected the corporation in several ways.

First, the intensification of rational calculation was the cornerstone of Taggert's restructuring strategy. Restructuring entailed a renewal of emphasis on breaking down the manufacturing process into discrete activities, identifying the costs of those activities, centralizing these data and reconceptualizing how better to unify and integrate the manufacturing process. The more precise quantitative data are cognitive devices that influenced the premise of decision making to reduce differentiation of perception, thereby establishing a uniform decision-making criterion to enhance standardization of both decision making and product quality. In contrast to the previous organizational structure – in which several semiautonomous hierarchies existed – centralization and standardization unified the managerial system into one hierarchical system.

Second, the mode of control was redesigned to ensure that the operative goals of the production units were consistent with the substantive profitability goals of the corporation. Data obtained from the information-gathering system contributed were used to: (1) identify cost inputs and determine the profitability of each product group; (2) eliminate the products and manufacturing units that were unprofitable; (3) establish premise controls to governing manufacturing decisions; and (4) compare the actual costs of manufacturing a specific product to predetermine standardized cost, thus providing a diagnostic tool to determine which activities generated cost overruns. Together the cost-accounting system and more precise spans of control made it possible to locate the manager responsible for cost overruns. This restructured mode of control made it possible simultaneously to centralize authority and decentralize responsibility by ensuring that lower- and middle-level managers based their decisions on standardized criteria established in decision centers. This restructured mode of control placed operating managers at a greater distance from the decision centers, while increasing surveillance over them.

Third, the restructured mode of control increased cooperation among production managers. However, this 'cooperation' occurred within narrowly delineated, formally rational premise controls. Even decisions not subject to premise controls are based on standardized cost data. In those areas of the corporation where premise controls cannot be articulated, team management established an informal structure whereby managers supervised one another to ensure that they employed standardized cost data in the decision-making process. Within these conditions, cooperative team decision making operates as an unobtrusive control.

Fourth, the corporation became tightly coupled in two ways. On the one hand, Taggert tightly coupled production units. The information-gathering system and the application of computer technology provided the organization with the capacity to transform the manufacturing process from batch to continuous processing. On the other hand, Taggert tightly coupled its customers to the manufacturing process. The pivotal organization unit is the manufacturing decision center, which is horizontally linked to the sales decision center and vertically linked to the manufacturing process. Both forms of tight coupling increased Taggert's capacity to adapt to its changing environment by transmitting new product specifications immediately to the point of production.

10.11. Conclusion

The findings here are in contrast to several previous formulations. Rather than associating flexibility with computer technology, the analysis here demonstrates that flexibility and adaptability of the manufacturing process is dependent on the design of information-gathering systems. These data are used to configure the machines according to product specifications demanded in the market. Although computers aid in the access, synthesis and distribution of information, without adequate information-gathering systems computers do little to enhance flexibility.

This analysis also demonstrates that in contrast to previous analysis suggesting that organizations seek to seal off or buffer their core from environmental influences (Thompson, 1967: 19), modern information-gathering systems and computer technology tightly couple the manufacturing process to the environment to facilitate the exchange of resources. In order to compete in the market-place, corporations are creating internal structures that make it possible to be more responsive to their customers. In contrast to previous tightly coupled corporate forms that were rigid and slow to adapt (Burns and Stalker, 1961; Chandler, 1962, 1977), this tightly coupled corporation is flexible because decision-making information can be instantaneously transmitted throughout the corporation. Whereas the logic behind these changes was standardization, the subterranean mechanism to standardize was the information-gathering system. The collection of cost-accounting data made it possible to establish a network of computers that specify parameters that govern decision making in precise detail, while providing the *appearance* of decentralization of decision making.

Rational calculation and information-gathering systems provided the organizational capacity to extend the basic principles of scientific management (ie, measurement, quantification) over more spheres of organizational activity. Taggert's formal controls attempting to establish the 'one best way' to produce each product further separated concept from execution by placing production managers at a greater distance from the loci of discretion. Whereas execution occurred at the point of production, Taggert centralized many conception activities (ie, processing of information, determining what was to be done, authorizing what was to be done) (see Mintzberg, 1979). These formal controls extend scientific management beyond Taylorism and Fordism in two fundamental ways. First, the modern form of scientific management is responsive: it can quickly change and transmit decision-making information and premise controls. Second, whereas previous forms of scientific management were rule-based, rigid and required tall hierarchies, the modern form is flexible: it has the capacity to respond to a wide range of market conditions. These developments are in sharp contrast to recent arguments that suggest that financial tools are restricted to evaluating 'product lines and divisions' (Fligstein, 1990: 226). Cost controls within product lines and divisions are characteristic of systems that emerged in the first half of the century (Chandler, 1962, 1977).

Corporate restructuring is the most recent stage in the progressive centralization of decision-making information and simultaneous centralization of authority (Weber, 1957: 221). When faced with competition, top management progressively tightened the control mechanisms and extended its *authority* – the ability to command effectively (Weber, 1978) – over more spheres of the corporation. This analysis demonstrates that arguments characterizing corporate restructuring as based on work teams, cooperative decision making and participation on the shop floor *mask* the basic relation of subordination that prevails when centralized controls exist. Corporate restructuring represents centralization in two respects since top management is: (1) reasserting control over a wider range of manufacturing activities and (2) shifting authority from production management to experts in the centralized decision centers.

Notes

1. These changes include the oil crises of 1973 and 1979–80, which raised fuel costs in energy-intensive industries. In addition, the success of European and Japanese economies, and the emergence of Newly Industrializing Countries to penetrate markets in the United States increased economic competition, which reduced utilization rates of manufacturing corporations and undermined capital accumulation. Moreover, this increased economic competition undermined the capacity of oligopolistic industries to set prices which was a primary mechanism to ensure an adequate rate of accumulation in the post-World War II era.
2. However, some researchers have analyzed how the use of information affects the transformation of work (eg, Shaiken, 1984).
3. These perspectives are criticized for several reasons. Briefly, flexible specialization is criticized for assuming that the shift in the economy is toward small business and craft production (Smith, 1989). This over-emphasis on small businesses results in an inability to explain transformations in the large organizations that are restructuring (eg, Bethlehem Steel, Boeing, Chrysler, Ford, General Electric, General Motors, IBM, USX). Neo-Fordist arguments are criticized as being locked in a battle with declining Fordism (Perrow, 1991). Rather than continuing within the labor-process tradition that demonstrated how the first factories were developed for control purposes (Braverman, 1974; Clawson, 1980; Edwards, 1979; Marglin, 1974), neo-Fordist researchers emphasize the locational redistribution of jobs in the changing global economy and fail to analyze adequately the internal mechanism of control.
4. Moreover, the current usage of flexibility has been criticized for exaggerating the flexibility of new technologies. Critics suggest that no matter how flexible technology may be, it is still fixed capital which has limited mobility and flexibility (Harvey, 1991; Sayer and Walker, 1992: 200–3).

5. Contrary to the assumptions implicit within several perspectives, the microprocessor and computer technologies are not new forces but merely 'installments in the continuing development of the Control Revolution' (Beniger, 1986, vii). Microchips with the capacity to perform data processing were available in the 1970s.

6. This is especially characteristic of the literature that depicts corporate restructuring as the transition from Fordism to post- or neo-Fordism (Aglietta, 1979; Piore and Sabel, 1984; Harvey, 1991; but also see, for example, Kanter, 1989).

7. There are numerous other dimensions of post-Fordism, including changing consumption patterns, the dwindling power of trade unions and the deregulation of industry that cannot be addressed here.

8. For these reasons several authors refer to this transition as neo-Fordism to reflect the advancement of the same process rather than the transition to a different process.

9. The steel industry did not realize a profit between 1982 and 1986. Although the industry reported a 4 per cent rate of return in 1987, it reported a net loss again in 1988 (American Iron and Steel Institute, 1989). To avoid bankruptcy several large steel corporations filed for protection under Chapter 11 (eg, Wheeling-Pittsburgh, LTV).

10. Until the 1970s, the CEO made regular visits to the manufacturing facilities.

11. Prior to the development of Taylorism, inside contracting was a common method of work organization (see Clawson, 1980).

12. Economists argue that this kind of accounting system was not developed because of the high costs associated with developing and maintaining it.

13. The definition of dumping has varied historically but generally refers to selling steel below prices the US government had negotiated with foreign steelmakers (for more details see Prechel, 1990b).

14. Despite the recent intensification of cost accounting, the emphasis on accounting is not a recent phenomena. For example, in the 1960s the senior accountant's position was retitled Chief Financial Officer in many large corporations (*Business Week*, October 13, 1986, p. 161).

15. A study by Arthur Anderson & Company found that by 1986 40 per cent of 'American's biggest corporations' had chief information officers (*Business Week*, October 13, 1986, p. 160).

References

Aglietta, Michael (1979) *A Theory of Capitalist Regulation*, London, New Left Books.

American Iron and Steel Institute (1989) *Annual Statistical Report*, Washington, DC, American Iron and Steel Institute.

Armitage, Howard and Atkinson, Anthony (1990) *The Choice of Productivity Measures in Organizations: A Field Study of Practice in Seven Canadian Firms*, Hamilton, Ontario, Society of Management Accountants of Canada.

Attewell, Paul (1987) 'Big Brother and the Sweatshop: Computer Surveillance in the Automated Office', *Sociological Theory*, 5, 87–99.

Beniger, James (1986) *The Control Revolution: Technological and Economic Origins of the Information Society*, Cambridge, Harvard University Press.

Benson, Kenneth (1977) 'Organizations: A Dialectical View', *Administrative Science Quarterly*, 20, 229–49.

Braverman, Harry (1974) *Labor and Monopoly Capital: The Degradation of Work in the Twentieth Century*, New York, Monthly Review Press.

Business Week (1986) 'Management's Newest Star: Meet the Chief Information Officer', October 13, 160–72.

Burns, Tom and Stalker, G. (1961) *The Management of Innovation*, London, Tavistock.

Carter, R. (1985) *Capitalism, Class Conflict, and the New Middle Class*, London, Routledge and Kegan Paul.

Chandler, Alfred (1962) *Strategy and Structure: Chapters in the History of the American Industrial Enterprise*, Cambridge, Mass., the MIT Press.

Chandler, Alfred (1977) *The Visible Hand: The Managerial Revolution in American Business*, Cambridge, Harvard University Press.

Chandler, Alfred (1990) *Scale and Scope*, Cambridge, Harvard University Press.

Child, John (1972) 'Organization Structure and Strategies of Control: A Replication of the Aston Study', *Administrative Science Quarterly*, 17, 163–77.

Church, Alexander (1914) *The Science and Practice of Management*, New York, The Engineering Magazine Co., pp. 24–50.

Clawson, Dan (1980) *Bureaucracy and the Labor Process: The Transformation of U.S. Industry, 1860–1920*, New York, Monthly Review Press.

Clegg, Stewart (1981) 'Organizational Control', *Administrative Science Quarterly*, 26, 545–62.

Clegg, Stewart (1990) *Modern Organizations: Organization Studies in the Postmodern World*, London, Sage Press.

Cutler, Anthony, Hindess, Barry, Hirst, Paul and Hussain, Athar (1978) *Marx's Capital and Capitalism Today*, London, Routledge and Kegan Paul.

Edwards, Richard (1979) *Contested Terrain: The Transformation of the Workplace in the Twentieth Century*, New York, Harper.

Fligstein, Neil (1990) *The Transformation of Corporate Control*, Cambridge, Harvard University Press.

Gordon, David (1988) 'The Global Economy: New Edifice or Crumbling Foundation', *New Left Review*, 169, 24–64.

Harvey, David (1989) *The Condition of Postmodernity*, Cambridge, Basil Blackwell.

Harvey, David (1991) 'Flexibility: Threat or Opportunity', *Socialist Review*, 21, 1, 65–77.

Johnson, H. Thomas (1991) 'Managing By Remote Control: Recent Management Accounting Practice in Historical Perspective', pp. 41–66 in Peter Temin (ed.), *Inside the Business Enterprise: Historical Perspectives on the Use of Information*, Chicago, The University of Chicago Press.

Johnson, H. Thomas and Kaplan, Robert S. (1991) *Relevance Lost: The Rise and Fall of Management Accounting*, Boston, Harvard Business School.

Kanter, Rosabeth Moss (1989) *When Giants Learn to Dance: Mastering the Challenge of Strategy, Management, and Careers in the 1990s*, New York, Simon and Schuster.

Kenney, Martin and Florida, Richard (1988) 'Beyond Mass Production: Production and the Labor Process in Japan', *Politics and Society*, 16, 121–58.

March, James and Simon, Herbert (1958) *Organizations*, New York, John Wiley & Sons.

Marglin, Stephen (1974) 'What Do Bosses Do? The Origins and Functions of Hierarchy in Capitalist Production', *Review of Radical Political Economy*, No. 6, 60–92.

Markus, Lynne and Pfeffer, Jeffrey (1983) 'Power and the Design and Implementation of Accounting and Control Systems', *Accounting, Organizations and Society*, 8, 205–18.

Marx, Karl (1981a) *Capital*, Volume II, New York, Vintage Books.

Marx, Karl (1981b) *Capital*, Volume III, New York, Vintage Books.

Mintzberg, Henry (1979) *The Structuring of Organizations*, Englewood Cliffs, Prentice-Hall, Inc.

Nelson, Daniel (1975) *Managers and Workers*, Madison, The University of Wisconsin Press.

Perrow, Charles (1986) *Complex Organizations: A Critical Essay*, 3rd edition, New York, Random House.

Perrow, Charles (1991) 'Organizational Theorists in a Society of Organizations', paper presented at the annual meeting of the American Sociological Association.

Piore, Michael and Sabel, Charles (1984) *The Second Industrial Divide*, New York, Basic Books, Inc. Publishers.

Pollert, A. (1988) 'Dismantling Flexibility', *Capital and Class*, 34, 42–75.

Prechel, Harland (1990a) 'Profit Seeking Organizations: Accumulation, Irrationality, Politics, and Organizational Change', *Mid-American Review of Sociology*, 14, 53–66.

Prechel, Harland (1990b) 'Steel and the State: Industry Politics and Business Policy Formation, 1940–1989', *American Sociological Review*, 55, 5, 648–68.

Prechel, Harland (1991a) 'Irrationality and Contradiction in Organizational Change: Transformations in the Corporate Form of a U.S. Steel Corporation, 1930–1987', *The Sociological Quarterly*, 32, 3, 423–46.

Prechel, Harland (1991b) 'Organizational Control in the Multi-Level Cybernetic Corporate Form', paper presented at the American Sociological Association in Cincinnati, August.

Rule, James and Attewell, Paul (1989) 'What Do Computers Do?', *Social Problems*, 36, 3, 225–41.

Sabel, Charles (1982) *Work and Politics: The Division of Labor in Industry*, Cambridge, Cambridge University Press.

Sayer, Andrew (1989) 'Dualistic Thinking and Rhetoric in Geography', *Area*, 21, 301–50.

Sayer, Andrew and Walker, Richard (1992) *The New Social Economy*, Cambridge, Blackwell.

Schoenberger, E. (1988) 'From Fordism to Flexible Accumulation: Technology, Competitive Strategies, and International Location', *Society and Space*, 6, 245–62.

Schumpeter, Joseph (1950) *Capitalism, Socialism and Democracy*, New York, Harper Torchbooks.

Shaiken, Harley (1984) *Work Transformed: Automation & Labor in the Computer Age*, New York, Holt, Reinhart and Winston.

Smith, C. (1989) 'Flexible Specialization, Automation and Mass Production', *Work, Employment and Society*, 3, 2, 203–20.

Standing, G. (1991) 'Alternative Routes to Labour Flexibility' in M. Storper and A. Scott (eds), *Pathways to Industrial and Regional Development*.

Stinchcombe, Arthur (1990) *Information and Organizations*, Berkeley, University of California Press.

Stone, Katherine (1975) 'The Origins of Job Structures in the Steel Industry', pp. 26–84 in Richard Edwards, Michael Reich and David Gordon (eds), *Labor Market Segmentation: Conference on Labor Market Segmentation*, Lexington, D.C. Heath.

Temin, Peter (1991) *Inside the Business Enterprise: Historical Perspectives on the Use of Information*, Chicago, The University of Chicago Press.

Thompson, James (1967) *Organization in Action*, New York, McGraw-Hill.

Weber, Max (1978) *Economy and Society*, Guenther Roth and Claus Wittich (eds), Berkeley, University of California Press, first published 1921.

Zuboff, Shoshana (1988) *In the Age of the Smart Machine: The Future of Work and Power*, New York, Basic Books, Inc.

11 Information technologies and educational systems in France, Germany and Italy

Pierre Dubois

In the clothing industry and in the information technology industry, as in others, the market had been dominated by producers, in this way guaranteeing standardization and stability of products (and involving long production runs). Instead now there is movement towards a market in which producers, confronted with increased competition, with the internationaliz-ation of trade and with the segmentation and instability of markets, are being driven by a demand that is more exacting, which imposes variation and a short life-span on products (hence requiring medium or short production runs), resulting in a more rapid availability for customers.

The movement from one type of market to another goes through a series of steps and brings about decisive changes. In a producers' market, competitiveness is based on price and therefore achieved through cutting production time (labour costs); in a buyers' market, however, competi-tiveness, while never overlooking the possibility of cuts in production time, depends on control over whole sets of times, by seeking the reduction of these times at every level (design time, tooling-up time, running-in time, ie manufacturing time) and thereby shortening the overall cycle of production (a short cycle from the phase of originating a new product to its actual delivery).

Traditionally, the clothing industry and the information technology industry sought to cut production time, following taylorist principles. In advanced countries there was therefore a movement of sub-contracting abroad in order to lower labour costs. Nowadays, will the need to shorten the overall cycle of production make it possible for advanced countries to retain their presence in these industries?

This chapter, based on field observations of French, Italian and German clothing and technology information firms, examines different ways of shortening times through the introduction of new technical machinery and organizational changes. However most frequently these changes appear in a taylorist world and they can be used in a taylorist manner, so they frequently fail to break the old model. The chapter tries to explain why, in spite of new market pressures, most of the changes do not provide a new competitiveness because power and influence relationships between actors (inside and outside the firms) remain unchanged. Consequently, there is an incapacity by those actors actually and significantly to shorten the overall cycle of production, particularly in the clothing industry.

The chapter also focuses on the links between the design and the implementation of computerized production management systems and the national patterns of educational systems. To what extent do the educational systems of the three countries produce professional abilities, norms, values and patterns of cooperation and conflict that can be used directly in the firms? One consideration is the immediate applicability of educational qualifications within the firm; another is the transmission of general knowledge in school, which, to be sure, has an influence on the social and organizational status of those who have finished schooling but which has no direct application within the company. Another aspect relates to the significance of the education received for status within the company. On the one hand, education and status within the company can be closely related, in which cases inequalities within the company can be justified almost exclusively by reference to different educational achievements; on the other hand, the company can establish its own rules, hierarchy and policy of remuneration independent of educational achievement by favouring length of employment, work performance and other criteria.

11.1. Time and computerization of production management

What is meant by the computerization of production management? Here, it will be taken to mean the assembly and activation of information systems to manage the flows of information that concern orders from customers, the supply of raw materials, production planning, the monitoring of production and the dispatch of finished products to customers. These flows of information involve external flows (relations with customers, suppliers and sub-contractors) just as much as internal flows between different departments of the firm. This definition, therefore, is broader than the traditional one for computerized production planning which is restricted more often than not to the tooling-up at the start of manufacture. Exerting control over information flows has become an essential precondition for controlling markets and technologies and thus for the competitiveness of the firm.

Ironically, the technology of computerized production management did not impose itself in the preceding market system though it could well have been introduced rather easily, if it had been operational and financially viable – as was only partly the case – thanks to the stability of information. The technology seems inevitable given the new market conditions, but, while it has become financially more viable, it is more difficult to introduce because of an ever-greater number of more complex parameters that need to be taken into account: computerization of production management is seen as the only technical system that can handle an ever-growing number of information streams whose life is very short but which must be reliable and freely available, if not in real time then at least in an ever-briefer delayed time.

Computerized production management should increasingly allow the shortening of the overall cycle of design–purchasing–manufacture–delivery to deal with different phases of the cycle simultaneously. In this chapter this aspect will be illustrated by the case of the clothing industry. In this industry, the traditional cycle of a fashion collection was around fifteen months from the moment of beginning the think up models to the very last deliveries to customers. Of these months, only about three months were really devoted to the machining of the product – from running up the thread to running off the garment. Now, the 'Sentier' ('pathway') System has reduced the overall cycle to around a month. None of the firms studied has just-in-time (JIT) systems, that is, steering production from upstream. The short cycle has been much talked of in the French clothing industry,[1] but would the short cycle none the less be a problem for the industrialists in this sector? An inquiry[2] revealed that 71 per cent of professionals in the fashion business reckoned they had a response time equal to that of their competitors; 21 per cent said they had a shorter response time.

11.1.1. Developing models

Model creation is faced with three constraints. (1) There is a need to *manage creation as a permanent activity* – no longer the traditional two collections per year – to speed up the response time to changing demand, creating models on a permanent basis to meet a growth in the proportion of models that are not renewed from one season to the next. The shorter the lifespan of a model, the more efficient one must be in order to cut down on the activity cycle of origination/tooling up/production. The firms studied have not yet quite got there but all are bringing back fewer products from one year to another and already have their 'inter-season' collections and now want to switch over to permanent design creation. Design time, thanks to computer-aided design systems, has been significantly cut down, which can none the less lead to stress or a crisis among the design teams who have been forced to modify their time habits profoundly. (2) *Eliminate right from the start models whose sales would be inadequate*, that means right from the moment of design or from the very first customer contacts by the sales-force (programs are available: 'sketching' methods, the Phebos program, Ariane). (3) *Meet demand with a greater variety of models*: a variety of raw materials and colours for the same article, diversification of the range or of models in a given price range, variation in product families. The work-study department, to estimate the practicability and selling power of newly created models, has to be able to bring into action or to update several computerized data bases in order to fix the planned price of the new model:

- program and data base for manufacturing time (to get an idea of the forecast cost of manufacture);
- program and data base of operating methods (to estimate feasibility and build up the technical dossier for the model);
- program and data base for laying out the garment in separate pieces on the work table (to allow a closer estimate of the length of material in metres necessary to make up the model).

11.1.2. Customer orders and the buying-in of fabrics

The cycle continues by way of the sale of models to various customers. The aim at this level is to get hold of timely and reliable information relating to orders. Ironically, the time left open for the processing of orders and thus for the purchase of fabrics has grown somewhat. An ever-increasing fraction of re-stocking is being added ever more frequently to the traditional sales period with its 'definite orders': customers hold back their orders as long as they can and 'chop them up' right throughout the season to stick as close as possible to actual demand. In the light of orders (just forecast at first then becoming firm), purchases of raw materials (fabrics and trimmings) must be optimized, where optimizing means limiting purchases only to those materials that will be made up (no more possibly unsold articles should be made), holding back their arrival (minimizing stocks of materials) to cut down the risk of having to pay suppliers before the moment products are actually sold. Computerized management of orders and purchasing assumes:

- program and data base on customers with a permanent review of orders received in terms of models, sizes, fabrics and colour;
- program and data base for working out requirements for raw materials, a calculation based on orders and technical data for each model (compare with the data base on setting-out mentioned above);
- program and data base for purchases (orders and supply deadlines).

11.1.3. Scheduling and start-up

Next it is necessary to draw up the production plan in terms of orders and manufacturing times. It consists of working out the number of minutes of work for the season and dividing them among plants in terms of their forecast capacities (forecast development of equipment and staff). This division of the work load is made between the firm's own factories and those of national-level or foreign sub-contractors. The complexity of plans has grown over recent years following the development of industrial strategies (growth of sub-contracting, whether confined to one country or shifted abroad). The practice of several plants for product manufacturing, of sub-contracting and of sending production abroad creates complexity in the flows in which raw materials, part-products and the finished products circulate. Sub-contracting abroad creates a lengthening of the cycle and raw materials have to be ordered more quickly.

Scheduling subsequently tightens up the plan for production deadlines by several weeks and is itself translated into weekly and/or daily product start-ups ('*landements*'). The latter aim to optimize, in terms of priorities, the use of materials (economy of materials), the size of the series to be manufactured (economy of manufacturing time) and the amount of flexibility in times (for going through the manufacturing stage). Cutting-instructions, manufacturing dockets or progress cards, the dates decided for movement to different stages of manufacture and the date for arrival in the warehouse are all linked to these product start-ups.

In order to bring about a proper product start-up, it is necessary to mobilize and activate several date sources; its computerization requires:

- program and data base on customers (compare with remarks above);
- program and data base on supplies (what is the optimal choice to operate for available fabrics in order to avoid running out of stocks);
- program and data base for time/methods/laying-out for scheduling sizes already available (or does the work-study department have to assemble them?);
- program and data base for plant resources (equipment and workforce).

The integration of the preceding computerized applications is somewhat harder to bring about in practice. The overriding problem is that of low reliability for supplier–delivery dates, and this makes the advance preparation of *ad hoc* laying-out schemes and optimal start-ups often impossible.

11.1.4. Manufacturing and monitoring manufacturing

At the manufacturing stage, new market constraints call for a reduction of time allocations through shortening work-in-process times: it has become a question of being capable of making a delivery to a customer in several days, whereas traditionally two or three weeks rolled by between a production order and the point when a series received its finishing touches. Reducing work-in-process times during manufacture amounts to optimizing launch times, using new flexible technologies, setting up a more flexible organization of work tasks, minimizing work in progress, reducing unproductive down-time (waiting times for pieces, handling times, intermediate stock-piling, rectification time for faulty work). During manufacture, movement times have been cut down or can be if need arises (to cope with urgent orders) in all the cases studied. In some cases, they have been reduced by as much as a factor of three or four. Nevertheless, there is always an exception affecting the scale of this reduction in work-in-progress time: sending a part of the production abroad involves an extra delay in manufacturing that can be greater than one or even two weeks.

As it is put into practice, computerized monitoring of production in real time or slightly delayed time makes it feasible to readjust start-ups by frequently recycling products), to keep manufacturing costs as close to forecast costs as possible and to reduce these costs by the close analysis of observed overruns. Monitoring of production is also used to work out pay (and possibly a production bonus). It could also be used – though in fact it was not so used in the firms studied – for a very close check and record of the activity of each wage-earner. Computerized recording of precise production data should also, in theory, make it feasible to verify and update the information in technical data bases.

In order to create computerized monitoring in real time or slightly delayed time, it is necessary to activate and marshall the technical data bases (time/ methods, see above) and the job records for start-ups in order to follow through the completion of a start-up and maybe also to compare time actually worked with the time allowed in the technical data base.

11.1.5. Stockholding and delivery

At the end of the overall cycle the aim is to keep stocks down and thus to cut down stock holding time. The object is also, in a low-stock environment, to have no delivery delays which could mar the firm's image as a serious supplier, leading to cancellations of orders or loss of market share. This has been a cruel disappointment for French clothing industrialists compared to their German and Italian opposite numbers. The French are still inefficient when it comes to delivery dates:[3] nine of out ten manufacturers have trouble with stock-inventory and stockholding times have been cut back everywhere.

At the level of stockholding and deliveries, it is necessary to marshall and activate several data bases as soon as sub-contracting is introduced:

- 'start-up' files to indicate the arrival dates of finished goods, with possible prior allocation of some products to certain customers;
- 'customer-order' files listing the dates and the details of the deliveries to be made to customers and associated programs to flag what is still outstanding (either to be made or delivered) to a given customer, generating delivery dockets, transport-loading documents and customer invoices.

11.2. The features of computerized management systems: the national characteristics

New market pressures demand the management of ever-increasing but short-lived information flows, with ever-shorter deadlines and absolute reliability. They require efficient production management and therefore integrated, computerized management, with an interface of a maximum number of applications. The preceding developments show in effect that an application (program), and the data base that it brings into play, are nearly always used by several departments in the firm. All this can involve recourse to a high-power information system whose data bases are updated if not in real time then at least frequently. What has been happening in the garment industry and in the information technology industry in the three countries?

Eight features shared in common by the cases studied can be identified: a process of computerized production management actually at work; a will to create growing integration in computerized management applications; a speeding-up process in the most recent period; an approach that is progressive but that is sometimes premised on qualitative leaps; a computerization that is neither uniquely 'inward-looking', nor 'outward-looking', a process that is never stable and that is always longer (and therefore always more expensive) than forecast; nowhere has a *totally integrated* computerized information system been achieved – at least one that is operational in all applications and highly efficient.

The example of one French clothing firm is suggestive of the difficulties of implementation of computerized management systems, but there are analogous cases in Italy and Germany. Numerous events, always urgently needing sorting out, made a mess of the implementation timetables. These included harmonization of the two information departments in the 1980s; a sale of plants and a move to sub-contracting forced the finalization or the cleaning-up of certain files; the set-up and need for computer support for a new warehouse; the creation of new departments; and, more recently, the sub-contracting of certain applications to an outside computer company.

Differences between firms and countries can be identified in four areas.

11.2.1. As the years go by integration is ever-closer

Four levels of integration of computerized production management can be defined, with the integration of information flows being specified as the process which interfaces sets of programs and data bases as a condition of their activity. The first level is 'no integration at all'; all the firms studied have gone through this stage, but all have gone beyond it at the present time. The second level of real integration (a beginning of interfaced applications between technical dossiers, customer orders, purchase of raw materials, deliveries and receipt of finished products) is in theory working everywhere. The third level of integration is more seldom met: this consists in interfacing the preceding integrated sets with start-ups, production scheduling and production monitoring. The fourth level of integration links up the preceding level to information systems external to the firm, thanks to added-value communications networks like the Echanges de Données Informatisés (EDI). No firm among those studied had reached this fourth level.

11.2.2. Local-based computing: a viable future or just a relic?

The aim of increasing integration calls for a high-power information system: does it also imply locally based computing? At levels two, three and four of integration, the question still remains. It is possible to make a choice between peripheral devices excluding local applications and more or less 'intelligent' peripherals (network computing and/or micro-computers linked to the central system), which permit access to data managed in the central memory and by processing these data on an off-line basis for local needs.

It is clear that the existence, in the majority of cases studied, of localized off-line computing meets various objectives and has a variety of meanings. It can range from a conscious policy choice for the future (see section on logic of decision facilitation), from a survival purely as a relic from the past (in expectation of fuller integration) and from a 'spontaneous' or undesired process brought by certain system users. The reaction of the latter, keen supporters of off-line micro-computers, can correspond to defensive or aggressive attitudes. They are defensive when the interested parties think they do not have the skills to work on the main-frame system and when they hope that they will do better with micros; they are defensive attitudes when they wish to sidestep any risk of a check on their activity by those higher up the organization. They are aggressive attitudes when they seek to counter the policy of hierarchically organized access to data in the central system, when they seek to begin integration based on the logic of decision facilitation or when they make up for the gaps and slowness of the central information department.

11.2.3. *Prescriptive or participative design?*

Staff involvement and participation can occur upstream from the computerization (*ex ante* participation), it can be a permanent process or it can occur downstream. Three possibilities have been observed. The first is the complete absence of involvement or participation on the part of the users at the design stage. In such circumstances, no project group exists and, once the decision has been taken 'up top', the computer specialists in information technology design the system; certainly the latter develop contacts with the users but always on a one-to-one basis that is also one-sided and sometimes patronizing.

There is a second possibility: taylorist-style participation. Those users who are the most highly qualified and most representative of a given department are summoned by the computer specialists or the organization and methods wizards to yield up their expertise, giving an exact account of their pro-cedures, formulating their requirements and the problems needing solutions, maybe making some suggestions or stating priorities. The designers thereafter get down to work, analysing, simplifying, testing and finally telling the users what they are going to have to do.

The third possibility is that of widened participation. It differs from the last method in as much as, that at different stages of the implementation, the users are associated with the choice of applications to become operational, checking out what is to be done, permanently interacting with the people implementing the system, 'giving the green light' for starting up the appli-cations achieved. In short, through the process of involvement, they become designers themselves.

11.2.4. *A prescriptive logic or a logic of decision facilitation?*

Two operative social logics can be assigned to the computerization. The first ideally aims to take decisions and to stipulate or prescribe solutions for application; the second aims to aid decision-taking, thus preserving a certain freedom of choice and autonomy for the actors, including first-line managers.

The first logic works in line with the pure tradition of scientific manage-ment (analysis, simplification, adaptation of technical tools, specification of tasks). In concrete terms, it is aimed at designing a system of exhaustive information sets that are integrated to form an interfaced whole. Its point of departure is a strongly held underlying assumption that all the information sets required for management can be given clear parameters (modelled, quantified), can be known in real time or in short delayed time and can be managed by an efficient information system – which necessarily will be high-powered. It assumes that a well-conceived information system can permit discovery of 'the one best way' and therefore prescribe rational management decisions, restricting or excluding decisions on the part of actors. By way of this logic, taylorism is seemingly carried to its highest degree of perfection: conception is delegated to the technical system, execution is delegated to human beings.

The second logic works in the opposite way, placing people at the centre of the decision system. To be sure, this logic also tries to take into account all the parameters necessary for efficient management; but it assumes that certain ones cannot be modelled or quantified, or cannot be locked into the information system because they are too unstable or are not available in a short-run period. This logic looks on the information system as a system for facilitating decisions which leaves an area of discretion to the users, their decision-taking being based on information sets provided by the system but based also on their reliable knowledge of information not stored – or not stored yet – in the system.

11.2.5. Classification of firms: the French 'backwardness'

The overall picture is as follows. Using only a small number of cases, any hasty generalization would be foolish, but our results do not run against those of Malsch and Weissbach.[4] There appears to be, into the bargain, a great deal of diversity not only among the countries but also within each country, between industrial branches and within each branch itself. The French and Italian case study firms mark the two extremes of a continuum. In Italy, the trend was towards higher levels of integration, towards more participation and towards the logic of decision facilitation; in France there was a trend towards a lesser degree of integration, towards less participation and towards a more prescriptive logic; the German cases fit somewhere in between.

One explanation can be put forward for the higher degree of integration reached in Italian and German clothes manufacture than in the French clothing industry. The much earlier development of network production in Italy (pulling together a whole gamut of arrangements from sub-contracting to 'sub-contracting of sub-contracting', via the informal economy) and, in Germany, production dispersed abroad. Both of these changes imposed more careful planning of production, in the movement of materials and in finished products. In the French firms studied, sub-contracting or foreign-source production has become a significant proportion of the total only in recent years and is still lower than in the Italian and German plants.

It was also observed that the information technology industry displays a higher degree of computerized integration than the clothing industry. The contrary would have been surprising inasmuch as the computer industry is the technical master of the field; that is to say, it possess the information-handling skills for developing such management systems and sometimes markets its own management applications programs. The gap between the two industries is logical enough because the information technology industry began the process of computerization long before the clothing industry and has even reached the stage of phasing out old systems and the accelerating development of new systems. On the other hand, the information technology industry seems, no more than the clothing industry, to be developing a logic of decision facilitation or a participative process in the design of computerized management systems.

11.3. National differences: explained by the influence of the educational systems?

11.3.1. *The design of computerized production management systems: reproducing or transforming the organization?*

'Grasping organizational reality in full before computerizing' – going back to this basic principle is an obvious step whenever a computerized production management system is designed or updated – but like everything that is 'obvious', it is a long way from being recognized and applied in reality. The principle is, however, clearly stated in all manuals, just as much as the need for a multi-disciplinary approach to organization. In many of the cases studied, it was none the less not followed and this resulted in endless setbacks. It seems clear that the absence of management participation at the design stage is an obstacle to such exact knowledge of organizational realities.

Always supposing that the analysis of organizational reality has been correctly undertaken, two alternatives offer themselves, each having its supporters. The first is to maintain an existing form of organization or make only some marginal change in it (such as rationalizing the flows of information, cutting out duplication, throwing out useless information). The following line of reasoning was regularly to be heard: 'you can only computerize procedures that are fully understood'. This approach, apart from the fact that the statement is self-evidently true even though it leads to the computerization of procedures that are inadequate in themselves, offers certain advantages – the established power-system is not shaken – but also has drawbacks (an incremental adjustment could also fail to be taken at all, blocking computerization).

Above all, and more broadly, it seems clear that new market constraints make organizational transformation inevitable. In the same way, technical success of tightly computerized integration, whether of the prescriptive type or for facilitating decisions, necessarily involves organizational upsets – questioning of departmental boundaries, and possibly the movement from an organization based on stages in a production process to one based on production lines. Market pressures and technical constraints are coalescing to push firms towards organizational change.

While involvement in designing computerization is a precondition of mutual understanding (an end to the dialogue of the deaf and charges of ill-will between computer experts and end-users), it is only one precondition for recasting departmental functions. It seems necessary to move from a type of organization – one that coordinates linear contributions with integration coming from 'on high', has departmental closure at the base and keeps the resolution of conflicts as a high-level line-management preserve – to quite another type: one which permits interfaces between services, horizontal relationships between departments and non-stop interaction. Cooperative relationships, instead of 'departmentalism', have to be established between those in charge of manufacture at shop-floor level, quality controllers, managers of raw materials and production planners. In actual fact, organizational upheavals and hence disruptions of power hierarchies, particularly in clothing firms, were far from apparent – these firms were still very much dominated by members of a family group. For something to happen, it simply isn't enough to want it to happen.

11.3.2. *The educational systems and the ways of introducing computerized production management systems*

One of the conditions of the more successful computerized production management systems in Italy and in Germany, in comparison to France, is the manner of using diplomas and values supported by the educational systems within the companies.

In Germany, in the production control departments, two groups cooperate. On the one hand, older employees with production experience are recruited. The advantage of this group of employees is that they are intimately familiar with the various stages of production; another strength of this group is that it is capable of acting and making meaningful decisions in the event of systems failures. These employees have demonstrated such competence through their work on the shop-floor and by means of more traditional, personally communicated forms of production control and checking. The second group in the production control departments comprises younger, externally recruited employees who have completed a commercial or technical apprenticeship or even have a business or engineering degree. Their knowledge is more abstract and of an inter-departmental nature, and they are often unaware of the actual tasks and problems of the production department. The older employees developed production control procedures in collaboration with their younger colleagues which facilitates the creation of a work-order allocation that is also acceptable to those in production. In the investigated industrial firms, the development of production control systems that are close to the production processes is facilitated by the recruitment both of employees with practical experience in production and of employees with a higher formal education. These two groups share a similarly structured professional space, characterized by a technical education, and it is their common values and experience that make cooperation possible.

In contrast, the situation in the French firms investigated is characterized by a professional, social and even spatial distance between the production control and production areas. This distance creates production control and planning problems. Below and beside the world of the main-frame computers and abstract models of production control planning, another world of PCs with practical production control information has emerged. The organizational and technological separation of production and production control and the minimal connection between the 'general' and 'practical' aspects of production control seem to be not only a reaction of the production chiefs to the 'imperialism' of centralized production control departments but also a response to the limited social recognition granted to 'manual labour' as opposed to 'mental labour'. In France, instead of the tendency toward cooperation and reconciliation within a homogeneous professional arena determined by 'profession' and 'competence' which is observed in Germany, the arenas in which younger, formally more highly qualified employees and the production employees pursue their status and career are less integrated. The clear demarcation between the two populations and the problems induced by it are the result of two clearly separated educational systems and of the hierarchical patterns they perpetuate.

In contrast with the French firms, the computer and production managers in the Italian firms did not establish autonomy over open conflict with each other. None the less, the integration necessary for the functioning of the production line was only achieved when people in the production and maintenance departments developed a common professional foundation ('a solution of daily practical problems') and a corresponding informal relationship based on mutual respect. It was only after the emergence of an informal arrangement giving all parties equal rights that the foremen reassumed responsibility for full use of the facility, the procurement of missing parts, and became involved in reducing the often hour-long stoppages. In Italy, a higher general school certificate is no guarantee of a professional career; the limited impact of diplomas on professional status weakens the competition between the younger program developers and abstractly oriented production control engineers, on the one hand, and the employees on the shop floor, on the other. As a result, although there are no open power struggles and conflicts between production, production control and systems development, there is instead a parallel development of the two cultures, resulting frequently in a year-long isolation of the new information technologies. Once the limitations of abstract, global production control become apparent, there results an intense and informal cooperation similar to that found in German firms.

In conclusion, it can be said that in Italy it was possible only with considerable difficulty to find a common denominator between the problem-oriented, concrete work culture of the production chiefs and the abstract, often academic culture of the technicians in production control and systems development. These difficulties in finding a 'common language' existed in spite of a lack of contempt in the social hierarchy of values for 'manual labour' as against 'mental labour'. In France, the existing hierarchy of values, which distinguishes between 'manual labour' and 'mental labour', favoured the organizational and spatial separation of the production control and production departments, complicating the integration of the abstract and pragmatic concepts underlying their respective tasks. As a result, production often developed its own projects of informatization as against those of the administration, integrating the corresponding computer and production control capacities. In Germany, thanks to the existence of a culturally homogeneous professional bargaining area, there is less possibility of a conflict-ridden integration of the experience-based and the abstract, globalizing aspects of production control. It is not exactly a matter of the national educational system influencing technical-organizational structures but of firms proceeding according to their own internal logic, while utilizing the abilities, values, behavioral and relational patterns embodied in their educational and training systems.

11.4. Conclusion: the case for a system of computerized production management that is integrated and based on a logic of facilitated decision-making

This conclusion begins with a paradox: new market pressures require greater organizational flexibility; computerized production management can be a tool that works in favour of this flexibility because it enables the faster production of reliable information but the closer integration often introduces rigidity and diminishes flexibility. It looks rather like squaring the circle. The paradox has frequently raised comment.

It seemed evident, at the end of the research project, that computerization that is both integrated and prescriptive may present major drawbacks: frequent malfunctions thanks to uncontrolled uncertainties; narrow scope for innovation; limitations in skills and erosion of problem-solving habits; emergence of uncontrolled parallel structures to keep the system operational; diffusion of errors in information (whether introduced willingly or not); and overall frailty. Above all, integrated and prescriptive computerization pursues an unattainable ideal, just as scientific management could never escape a 'work actually-done' hat differs from its 'work-as-should-be-done'. Besides its major drawbacks, it overlooks incontestable facts. In every organization, possession of information is shared and dispersed; every person and every group has an interest in common with others in *sharing* information they possess; and this is to ensure the survival and/or development of the organization. At the same time, every person or every group has an interest to serve in *retaining* information, to ensure individual or collective survival in the organization. Every individual or collective actor is therefore pulled two ways at once: between passing information on and keeping it to themselves. Every computerized information system has to negotiate this dilemma, and only the sort of integrated system which is based on the logic of decision facilitation and the maintenance of actors' autonomy can go safely between its horns.

One last question: 'what seems to be the groupings or coalitions of organizational actors that are equal to the task of driving forward or forcing through computerized production management that is integrated, not narrowly prescriptive, partly decentralized, and designed within the framework of broader employee involvement?' The grouping of actors most conductive to the appearance of computerization of this kind would bring together 'enlightened' senior managers; designers with a different training from the present one – they would be taught that if computerization is going to be effective it should put human beings at the centre of the design process; end-users in a better position to verify step by step the compilation and operation of manuals of work loading and authorized by top managers to carry out this verification; trade-union figures that are committed to be more supportive of certain kinds of 'modernizing projects'. This grouping of actors is probably an unattainable ideal, but it provides some clues to follow.

Notes

1. This chapter is a part of my contribution to the general report of the international comparative research in the garment and in information technology industries: Martin Heidenreich (ed.), *Computers, Communication and Culture, the Introduction and Use of Production Control Systems in French, Italian and German Enterprises*, Bielefeld, 1992, The section on educational systems is an abstract of M. Heidenreich's contribution to the report.
2. Georges Jolles and Jean Bounine, *Un projet pour le Textile-Habillement Français*, a report to the Ministry of Industry, November 1989.
3. Institut Français de la Mode, *Confection 2.000*, April 1990.
4. Th. Malsch and H.J. Weissbach, 'Les technologies d'information entre gestion centralisée et autorégulation. Réflexions sur la mise en oeuvre de la planifaction et de la gestion de la production assistée par ordinateur' in P. Cohendet (ed.), *L'après-Taylorisme. Nouvelles formes de rationalisation dans l'entreprise en France et en Allemagne*, Paris, Economica, 1990.

12 SME competitiveness, new technology, information and formation[1]

Pierre-André Julien

12.1. Introduction

It is an accepted fact today that the dynamism of industrialized economies is based on the innovation and use of new management and production technology in most firms, whatever their size. This is true for both small and large firms. As R. Howard (1991)[2] points out, if small businesses lag behind in competitive terms, this may have a considerable effect on the productivity of larger firms because of the many links between the two.

The important role played by SMEs in national economies is well known, especially as they continue to produce the majority of new jobs (Sengenberger, *et al.*, 1990; GREPME, 1992). However, their contribution is not restricted only to job creation or increasing job numbers. They often also form the basis of economic restructuring in many new economic regions or regions in which the economy was formerly based on traditional, but declining, production (Maglione *et al.*, 1990; Maillat and Perrin, 1992).

In fact, many SMEs are now trying even harder to modernize their production and distribution equipment. This would explain how they continue to be dynamic and also their contribution to the increase in added value and jobs (MacPherson, 1989; Grosnier *et al.*, 1991).[3] However, market globalization[4] or growing economic interpenetration, the formation of economic blocs or large trade zones and increased interdependency between actors within different kinds of networks, etc., are all factors which may perhaps be in the process of changing the conditions which enabled SMEs to be dynamic (the reason for their competitiveness), and will, unless they systematically improve that competitiveness and intensify innovation, affect their surprising economic performance of the last twenty years. However, in their search for information, SMEs are nevertheless restricted by the difficulty of finding good sources and of using the information obtained effectively.

This chapter will examine the issue of the use by SMEs of recent scientific and technological information by, first, analysing the type of information they most need to face up to the challenges of new international competition. It will go on to discuss the principal means at their disposal, namely information networks, and finally, it will identify the basic condition for effective use of information, that is, more technological training, especially at management level.

Table 12.1 Relative significance of the different problems encountered by firms in innovation (%)

Problems	Number of employees						
	10–19 n=75	20–49 n=294	50–99 n=330	100–199 n=264	200–499 n=176	>500 n=112	*
Lack of capital	58.7	47.3	38.8	33.7	29.0	26.8	++
Difficulties in predicting demand	57.3	47.6	49.7	59.1	48.3	50.9	o
Apparent costs of developing innovation	37.3	36.1	32.7	33.3	35.8	30.4	o
Problem of adapting the marketing function	25.3	25.5	27.6	26.5	25.0	25.9	o
Costs of monitoring future applications	29.3	26.9	27.9	20.5	19.3	11.6	+
Difficulties in finding technological information	24.0	20.4	26.1	18.2	22.2	8.9	+
Employee skills	24.0	20.7	21.2	20.1	12.5	12.5	o
Government standards	13.3	8.8	11.2	10.6	13.6	13.4	o

* Significance according to the CHI2 test
o insignificant
+ significant, 90 per cent significant
++ 99 percent significant

Source: A. Kleinknecht (1989), 'Firm size and innovation', *Small Business Economics*, 1, 2: 215–22

12.2. Scientific and technological information

Scientific, innovative and technological information is the key element on which the systematic modernization of both SMEs and large firms is based. It is more difficult for SMEs than for their larger counterparts to obtain that information, given their generally more limited resources and a national information production and transfer structure that is neither adapted to nor oriented towards the needs of small firms. For example, a recent survey in the Netherlands on a representative sample of nearly 2,000 manufacturing firms of different sizes (ten employees and over) showed that the difficulty of finding technological information was one of three parameters in respect of which there was a significant difference between the small and the larger firms in terms of innovation, as can be seen from Table 12.1.

12.2.1. Scientific and technological information as a resource for SMEs

The difficulties in obtaining scientific and technological information seem to explain to a large extent why SMEs lag behind larger firms, relatively speaking, in terms of the use of new production techniques[5] (tangible investment) and in terms of innovation or organized R&D.

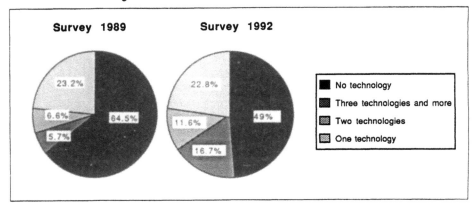

* In 1989, the activity sectors were: plastics, textiles, wooden furniture, clothing, transportation equipment, metal products, mechanical products, electric and electronic products; in 1992, they were: dairy products, textiles, clothing, doors, windows and other turned wood products, household furniture, machining workshops, aircraft and components, automobile components and accessories, electrical products and pharmaceutical products.

Figure 12.1 Penetration of new computerized process technologies in 1989 in all firms in eight industrial sectors, and in 1992 in SMEs in ten industrial sectors in Quebec

Source: CAD/CAM Association, 'Tendances et degré de pénétration. L'informatisation et l'informatisation de la production', Montreal, CRIQ, 1989; J.B. Carrière and P.A. Julien, 'Profil technologique de la PME manufacturière québécoise', Association des Manufacturiers du Québec, September 1992.

The gap in terms of new management techniques is relatively small, and in fact, even as far as new production technologies is concerned, it is closing quickly. Thus, a recent study in Quebec covering SMEs in two very different industries (plastics products and machining workshops) showed that in 1988, some 19.4 per cent of the SMEs questioned had at least one numerically controlled machine, 7.7 per cent had computer-assisted manufacturing (CAM), and 2.8 per cent used a robot. A total of 38 per cent used at least one very modern system.[6] In 1985, this figure was only 17 per cent (Julien, 1991).

In March 1992, a new study carried out for the Association des Manufacturiers du Québec among more than 400 SMEs (with between five and 250 employees) in ten activity sectors showed that rates had risen to 28.8 per cent for SMEs having just one new technology, 11.5 per cent for those having two and 16.7 per cent for those having three or more. Figure 12.1 sets out the results of another study carried out in 1989 among a sample that also included large firms and shows that in a period of just three years the number of SMEs using at least three new computerized technologies had increased at least threefold. Other international studies also show that the penetration of new computerized production technologies in small manufacturing firms with between twenty and ninety-nine employees exceeds 60 per cent (*Statistics Canada*, 1991; Scarlatti, 1991; de Koning and Wennekens, 1991).[7] In short, the presence in SMEs of new management and production technologies, especially the more complex ones, is increasing steadily, and the penetration rate is picking up speed with time. In addition, the lag of SMEs in terms of innovation and R&D is highly questionable.

As regards innovation, for example, studies such as those by CNR/ISTAT in Italy, LATAPSES in France or the IFO Institute in Germany have shown that between 50 and 60 per cent of all SMEs in the manufacturing sector regularly introduced innovation (Ravix, 1988; Archibugi and Cesaretto, 1989; MFRT, 1989). More often than not this was gradual and concerned primarily with the output or improvement of new products (often as a result of special customer requests) but equally the improvement of plant and equipment often purchased second hand or again a particular way of reaching customers. However, the same is often true for large firms. In addition, the proportion of SMEs introducing more radical innovation is apparently about 5 per cent – a higher proportion than in large firms; the SMEs conducting more systematic research apparently spend a higher proportion of turnover than do large firms (Mansfield, 1981; Belhumeur and Nguyen, 1989).

In particular, recent scientific and technological information as a resource is becoming as important as capital, and as strategic as capital, if not more so. It includes various types of scientific data, patents, results of experiments, new products, new plant and equipment or new ways of using old products, equipment or production processes, and also standards, management or procedural methods, new organization forms and so on, depending on their level of production within research organizations and their level of penetration or use on markets and by competitors. New information is in some ways the raw material for the creation and technological change that will bring about internal change and lead to new innovations. It is therefore a central factor in increasing SME competitiveness.

12.2.2. The different types of scientific and technological information

Several types of scientific and technological information can be distinguished. For example, Henri Laborit (1974) speaks of circulating information and structural information. The former is routine and repetitive information which has little economic value. Structural information, however, induces adaptation or transformation of the system which receives it and leads to 'unprogrammed' decisions which encourage change, as explained by H. Simon (1980). It is this second form of information that is relevant to technological change, since it is at the source of innovation and the acquisition of new technologies.

In economics, there are various kinds of structural information. M. Amendola and J.L. Gaffard (1988) consider that there is collective information – which cannot be appropriated by a single enterprise or group – and private information. In the latter case, a distinction can also be made between new or created information, either *controlled* by a small group or by an enterprise, or *shared* between the members of a group of firms or a limited enterprise network.

A high proportion of technological information is of the collective type. It is 'public property' available to all and cannot be controlled or concealed by a few. It consists of scientific and technological information of three basic kinds: that to which access is relatively *free*, that can be found for example in available manuals or in course materials; that which is discussed in the media (specialized or otherwise); and that which reviews the general progress in science and technology. It is thus related to the 'corpus of knowledge and know-how' to which E. Zuscovitch (1985) refers. It is more or less complex, depending on the level of the scientific and development culture of the teaching and research institutions and transfer organizations in an economy. It involves a certain opportunity cost, owing to the time and other limited resources needed for comparing or sorting this highly disparate information and to retain that which may be interesting – in the short or long term – for firms. It is one of the essential factors in the strategy of enterprises, allowing them to adapt and change. However, it often lags behind 'advanced' information or in terms of what is done in the most advanced firms.

Private information is usually the most 'recent'. It is this type of information that allows an enterprise to set itself apart from the others; the information which, applied to products, management, production and distribution, will explain the differences in firms' competitiveness. This information is to a large extent *controlled* by the enterprise or private research centre that created it. It is thus related to innovation and hence to R&D; it often belongs to the world of confidentiality, R&D contracts, patents and licences and hence the legislation by which these are protected. It leads to relatively little trade on the market.[8] Some of this trade is against payment, the extent of which depends upon the expected return on using the information. If the exchange takes place within the system having produced the information, for example between subsidiaries or branches or with foreign partners and on other markets on which the firm producing it is not active, various types of royalties may be paid. This is the most attractive kind of scientific and technological information owing to its novelty and scarcity,[9] and also the most favourable for innovation and the use of newer techniques.

However, this private information may be *shared* among various kinds of restricted groups of firms such as cartels, between customers and sub-contractors, in industrial areas or local production systems, in systems of vertical near-integration but also in technological nurseries or parks, technical centres, etc. This is especially the case where it is produced by public or quasi-public research centres more or less linked to these forms of restricted organization.[10] In these *private groups* (enterprise 'clubs', to use Buchanan's expression), it is supplied in exchange for other information (technological or other) or other services; it is thus a marginal activity in the trading space. The sharing process is of course aimed at reducing costs while establishing a special synergy between the partners in the 'club', allowing each to get more out of this exchange of scientific and technological information. Within these 'quasi-private' networks, the shared information may be incomplete, or at least it is frequently 'wagered' or expects a return, generating obligations which in turn set up a certain solidarity between the members and prevents the information supplied from passing to competing firms outside the group. It generates a revenue distributed more or less unequally between the partners which increases in proportion to the cost for those outside the 'group' to procure that information. In the *quasi-public groups*, such as technology parks or technopoles, involving public research centres or public transfer systems, the information is more available to outside firms, although they incur interpretation and adaptation costs since they are not direct members of the group.

12.2.3. *Sources of scientific and technological information for SMEs*

Access to the various sources of scientific and technological information involves costs, in that such information is too general or badly adapted in the case of public information, or not directly available in the case of private information (and the most attractive information often falls into this latter category). Thus, if SMEs are not involved in a group where useful information is shared, they may be strongly disadvantaged compared with their competitors who are members of such groups. At the very least they may lag considerably behind.

There are a number of indirect sources giving access to new information. These sources vary according to sectors and needs, the type or structure of the economy and the various enterprise organizations. A number of studies have shown that the channels used by SMEs are often related to 'personalized' networks (Meyer and Goes, 1987; Martinet and Ribeault, 1989; MFRT, 1989). However, most firms do not limit themselves to a single source, first because their needs are various and evolving, and second because no one source can provide all the useful and appropriate information needed and be up-to-date at the same time (Planque, 1987). However, it is possible to go much further in the need for variety of sources.

Thus, a recent study in Quebec in the clothing sector showed that these sources varied according to the phases of the information process (Lapointe, 1992). As can be seen from Table 12.2 industrial fairs and exhibitions are most used in the information phase, while suppliers are most used during the evaluation and selection phases. Although less use is made of employees, they are regarded as the most useful in the evaluation and selection phase.

When the information needed is complex, the links between SMEs and the different external sources of information are often formed in a non-linear or iterative fashion. SMEs are wary of a single source; they prefer to check the information they want. For example, they are suspicious of consultancy firms or equipment suppliers, believing they are seeking to impose unsuitable technologies, particularly if it is a question of equipment or software from the suppliers they represent. As regards consultancy firms, it has been shown in the United States that they are used by 35 per cent of manufacturing SMEs but in a rather sporadic way (Griffith and Dorsman, 1987). As regards suppliers, SMEs are also wary of information that is too technical or biased by the desire to sell. This suspicion is also present with regard to public and semi-public research centres or government agencies whose

Table 12.2 Utilization and perceived utility of different sources of information in the different phases of the information process in the clothing industry

Sources of information	Information phase	Evaluation phase		Selection phase	
	Real utilization (%)[1]	Perceived utilization (%)[2]	Perceived utility index[3]	Perceived utilization (%)[2]	Perceived utility index[3]
Industrial fairs and exhibitions	67	17.7	3.48	13.6	3.44
Technical journals	16	11.9	2.40	5.6	3.00
Business journals	4	2.1	1.56	1.2	1.17
Consultancy firms	—	1.8	2.67	0.8	2.50
Technology suppliers and manufacturers	48	22.3	3.43	32.3	4.52
Other suppliers	12	8.9	2.11	1.2	1.17
Personal and business contacts	20	15.9	3.41	30.3	4.00
Employees	4	14.7	4.23	13.2	4.63
Customers	—	1.8	1.33	0.4	—
Public or private training institutions	4	2.8	2.00	1.6	4.00
Average consultation of sources of information	1.68	4.04		2.02	

1. Real percentage utilization indicates that 67 per cent of businesspeople said they used fairs, 16 per cent had recourse to technical journals, etc.
2. Perceived percentage utilization indicates the relative share of utilization of the different sources, weighted by the importance attached to each by businesspeople.
3. Perceived utility is expressed on the basis of a scale from 0 to 5. From 0 to 1.5 is very low, from 4.5 to 5 is very high.

Source: S. Lapointe, 'L'adoption des nouvelles technologies dans le secteur du vêtement. Etude du processus informationnel', paper presented at the ICSB-Canada Conference, Trois-Rivières, Quebec, 14–16 November 1991

specialities do not quite meet their precise needs or whose knowledge may be warped by contact with firms which are too large or too different. Another problem with government institutions seems to be their instability.

In looking for effective sources of scientific and technological information, the development of *bonds of trust*, which can be established only gradually, is necessary if not essential. It must not be forgotten that in information exchanges firms are always afraid of passing on recent internal information which could profit a competitor, whether real or potential. This need for trust is the reason why it is often important that the location of information (or transfer) should be relatively close to the SME, sociologically, geographically and sectorally. This 'proximity' is mainly obtained within or through a network that is trusted (Planque and Py, 1986; Savi, 1988; Sole Parellada and Roca, 1991), unless the information is too specialized and can be found only on a much wider market. However, in this case, it is still preferable for the transfer organization to be close by. Moreover, the fact of referring to a known firm which has had recourse to a good source to obtain an interesting application is a good way of facilitating its use. Most SMEs often function through example, using a reactive strategy, partly imitating others.

The choice among the different sources stems not only from their capability to supply good information and inspire confidence, but also from another factor: cost. For example, for 'high-tech' information and in times of rapid change, the most effective ways of obtaining scientific and techno-logical information are still the patents market, contract research companies, research development organizations or other 'advanced' information channels. Of course, these sources are usually distrusted by or are too 'distant' from SMEs; but in particular the acquisition of this information, which is often 'controlled', may be too expensive or too 'conditional' (limited, for example, to marketing and excluding production) to be attrac-tive. This external controlled information often costs SMEs a great deal in patent rights or other payments and necessitates government aid. This is particularly true when the information obtained must then be adapted to the particular needs of each SME for insertion into its strategy, to be converted into products or new processes; in other words to change from information to development.

It must be added, however, that the significance of overheads in the use of sources of information, as in the use of new production techniques, needs to be qualified since it must be examined from a dynamic standpoint. In fact, the constraint of paying for new equipment is not the first explanatory variable. Or, at the very least, this variable is seen first of all from the aspect of 'the inadequate expected profitability of new machines' for SMEs using systems with numerical control, while for most firms remaining with traditional systems, the owner-managers place almost as much importance on 'inadequate financial resources', the problem of 'too expensive conversion' and 'too great a financial risk' (Julien *et al.*, 1988). It appears that as regards the cost of finding appropriate information, the most dynamic firms will regard it in terms of its potential profitability rather than as an obstacle in itself.

The existence of diverse sources of information is a prerequisite for an effective watch. But the search for effective sources and their development depends also on the dynamism of SMEs, in other words their very openness to new technologies. Such development therefore requires an adequate *technological culture* in SMEs, an interest in and active search for this information through a technological watch and ways and means of processing and converting it into knowledge and applications (particularly the knowledge and skills of the management and key personnel). In short, the development of effective sources of scientific and technological information depends as much on demand as on supply.

12.3. The importance of networks in the information-transfer process

As stated above, a good way for SMEs to obtain information is to go through the information networks available to them. The idea of networks and cooperation among economic agents was unknown until recently and was first developed in 1972 in the United States by G.B. Richardson, who showed that, contrary to accepted economic theory, industrial coordination is present on most markets, so that economic coordination due solely to pricing or to perfect competition is extremely rare and indeed almost non-existent. Such industrial cooperation takes different forms, hierarchic or non-hierarchic such as cartels, subcontracting, near-vertical integration, etc. It was subsequently discovered that networks played a very important role in this cooperation (Thorelli, 1986).

12.3.1. Definition and types of networks for SMEs

Networks are partnerships or groupings – implicit or explicit – comprising economic agents, manufacturing or service firms and institutions, often working in complementary areas. The members of these groups, by building up relationships of trust among themselves, gather together various resources (and especially information) at lower cost, thus reducing the uncertainties of the market in both the short and longer term. They represent what Y. Morvan (1991) calls 'creative communication in a business milieu' which brings about a synergy of the knowledge at network members' disposal, rounding off or speeding their learning process in common or complementary areas.

Networks enable relevant circulating information to be retained, and in particular they permit the most attractive structuring information to be selected and then transformed so as to be more easily understood by participants. They are thus a locus or space in which the circulation of 'free' information is fostered, that information being filtered and adapted to the requirements of the different network members. Once organized into a relatively formal partnership, a network provides access to 'shared' information; and if the partnership is structured in the form of subsidiaries or branches, it supplies – entirely or partly – 'controlled' information.

Networks are more often than not strategic rather than operational and – at least for the newly established firm or the young entrepreneur as yet unattached to one that is solidly structured – often hinge on circumstances. As Rothwell (1990) has shown, the more strategic and long-standing the network, the more efficient it becomes. Networks may include particular suppliers, research centres or other public or private agencies transferring information (or rather, particular members of their staff, to the extent that contacts are often personal), dynamic trade associations, quasi-competitors, subcontractors providing specialities or know-how, or contractors, etc.

Networks take many forms, with more or less flexible boundaries. They are often concentric; that is, where the primary or close network cannot answer a question, another more specialized network can be reached through an affiliate member to obtain some of the information sought and so on until all the information has been obtained. Generally speaking, the primary network is consulted first, even though in most cases it supplies only the most traditional, run-of-the-mill information. Second- and third-level networks are consulted less often but provide more specialized and often more valuable information. Information is a cumulative phenomenon, at the level of learning and sources (from the closest to the furthest, from the simplest to the most complex).

12.3.2. The characteristics of SME networks

The networks to which small – and especially the smallest – firms belong have five notable features. The first is that they are *highly personalized*, as indeed are the firms that belong to them. The owner-manager is at the centre of the information web, although he or she may have to bring in some key staff members where the information is more specialized. B. Johannisson (1989) adds that entrepreneurial networks may be more or less secretive, depending on prevailing standards in the industrial culture concerned.

At the outset, SME networks will usually include just friends, a few clients, a banker, or people with whom the owner-manager was at school or university – not more than between seven and 9.5 individuals on average. A recent survey in Ireland showed that in the early days the people most frequently consulted are employees, followed by professional people with whom the firm is in contact on a regular basis (Birley *et al.*, 1991). Other contacts are more occasional, as can be seen from Table 12.3.

The networks are, at the outset, *informal* (just as they are fairly 'discrete'). Only after a certain time does a network take formal, organized shape, unless the small business concerned is able to join an established network, for example a business club or trade organization. However, even in more formal networks, the owner-manager tends to work only with a few members rather than with all of them; although he or she will use the others when the need arises.

The third characteristic is *flexibility*. Owner-managers build up their networks to suit their own specific requirements and strategies and extend or reduce them as circumstances demand. Network boundaries are vague and extremely supple depending on the information required. It has been shown that the SMEs that perform best are those that best control the boundaries, whereas those that experience the most problems tend to seek all kinds of information all over the place, from people they know and people they meet by chance (Chicha and Julien, 1980). This behaviour would explain why data banks are used so rarely by SMEs and why general dissemination of technical documents among firms by different public agencies is so inefficient, unless they happen to arrive at the right time and provide answers to specific questions.

According to S. Birley *et al.* (1991), the way in which small business networks are structured and used seems to vary according to the prevailing national culture. Italian firms, for instance, apparently call on their personal networks more frequently than their Irish and American counterparts do, as Table 12.4 shows. The same seems to apply to small businesses in Sweden (Johannisson and Johnsson, 1988). Furthermore, in a more complex or 'community-type' environment, such as that of a highly entrepreneurial area, networks tend to be more extensive.

The fourth characteristic of the networks is that they are *multi-functional*.

Table 12.3 Ranking of contacts according to the occupation of network members (%)

Occupation	Ranking of contacts					Total
	1	2	3	4	5	
Owner-managers	3	3	3	4	6	4
Employees[1]	62	64	71	71	71	67
Non-employees[2]	2	3	2	1	3	2
Professors, researchers	3	1	2	2	1	2
Professionals[3]	28	28	19	20	18	23
Government agencies	0	1	2	1	1	1

[1] In the firm
[2] Or retired staff
[3] For example, the banker, accountant, lawyer, and other professional people who advise the firm

Source: S. Birley, S. Cromie and A. Myers, 'Entrepreneurial networks: their emergence in Ireland and overseas', *International Small Business Journal*, 9, 4, 1991

Table 12.4 Average number of hours per week spent by small business owner-managers on maintaining and building up their personal networks

	Northern Ireland		United States	Italy
	Clients	Others		
Established contacts	10.4	6.0 (4.9)	5.8 (8.5)	12.0 (10.7)
New contacts	8.3	4.7 (3.52)	5.6 (8.4)	11.5 (9.4)

Source: S. Birley, op. cit.

The network serves many purposes, in so far as small-business strategies involve the different functions of the firm. Technology watch usually goes hand-in-hand with a watch over competition and over trade. The search for technological information leads on to the search for information about potential suppliers, about sources of financing, about new market openings on domestic and foreign markets, about subcontracting, about training and the emergence of new kinds of jobs and so on.

The fifth characteristic is that, as time passes, networks gradually become *denser and more complex*. In the beginning, A meets B and C separately on a regular basis to discuss business and to obtain additional information in return. Then A introduces B to C, and they are acquainted, respectively, with D and E, who are gradually brought into the network – and so on. In this way the network becomes richer as the diversity and interdisciplinarity or differences in experience of its members increase. The way complexity grows can be seen from Figure 12.2, which represents a typical small business network in a Swedish region.

However, recourse to networks that are other than informal, or to highly complex networks, is not the rule everywhere. Very small firms, or firms which consider that they are in a sheltered position, tend not to form complex, formal networks. Only those that have a competition strategy use the network other than very occasionally. Network complexity – and thus effectiveness – for each firm depends on the effort put into building up the

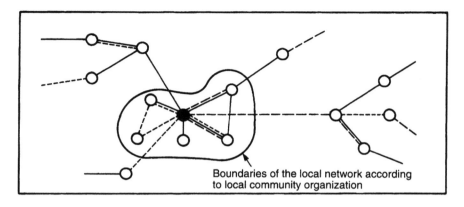

Key:
● = the focal entrepreneur
○ = colleagues and friends or other network members
——— = instrumental links
— — — = effective links
- - - - - = moral links

Figure 12.2 A personalized entrepreneurial network

network and, above all, fitting into it. Surveys show that the more highly developed the firm in technological terms, the more likely it is to be a member of dynamic and complex second- or third-level networks and the more use it will make of those networks to speed its own growth (Rallet, 1988; Grabner, 1989).

12.3.3. Why SMEs use networks

It seems that, to minimize costs, most SMEs turn to organized or formal networks to obtain the scientific and technological information they need; as stated earlier, this is especially true of those who opt for a strategy of systematic change or adaptation to new technologies. There are several reasons for this. First, by definition, obtaining such information calls for personal contacts. Information is akin to a service that is above all intangible: it is of no use unless the message conveyed can be converted into know-how. Furthermore, that service is inseparable from its proposer: the information, especially when it is still quite new, belongs to the person who passes it on and whose participation is therefore required. Another factor is the variability of information: it is seen differently by the person providing it and the person receiving it. The direct contact and dialogue established, based on the relationship of trust that is built up, make it possible to obtain further information, qualified as required. Finally, it must be remembered that information is often a 'perishable' commodity; it cannot always be stored, and because it is subject to rapid change must be passed on equally rapidly.

For these reasons, while information from the written media (trade reviews, etc.) is interesting, it is rarely sufficient on its own; it has to arrive at the right time and be analysed, discussed and so on. Scientific and technological often demands a dialogue. It is rarely simple and must be qualified as required. Only personal contact results in the kind of complexity often needed, in particular since the exchange must include additional information on sources of complementary information, possible yields from its application, potential suppliers and connected services – in other words, the kind of information that is often not included in raw data from information suppliers, or that is not adapted to each individual case.

Third, as observed above, SMEs' resources are slender. To use the example of trade reviews, perhaps the information had already appeared in a previous issue, but the owner-manager was not struck by it because he did not need it at the time. Since SMEs do not have filing and monitoring systems or the means to develop a systematic, large-scale technological watch, and since they may engage in R&D only occasionally, they need antennae to obtain without delay, as soon as it is available, the kind of information they require, and filters to digest it. Networks offer the best chance to do this at the lowest possible cost.

The network's efficiency depends on the participation and the quality of the persons who produce and have access to the most up-do-date and useful information. That efficiency depends on the number of qualified people, the time devoted by the owner-manager to tuning into the network, the density of the interactions among network members and the range of their specialization. In particular, it depends on the level of the management's technological culture.

12.4. Conditions for facilitating information transfer

A firm's technological behaviour is affected by the experience and training of the owner-manager and his or her key assistants, and their individual and collective scientific learning system. Training and experience or learning are therefore a prerequisite for an effective search for and use of scientific and technological information. Such information is truly useful only if it is transformed into knowledge to bring out its full value. Management training (the first vector of knowledge development) or quality is one of the most important characteristics serving to distinguish SMEs that use new production technologies from those that do not. Training should also be extended to the employees who will be required to work with new applications of the information in the form of new products, new machinery or new forms of organization.

For example, in research into the factors distinguishing small firms using new production technologies from the rest, in the same market, we found that five of the ten most important factors (explaining 83.3 per cent of the variance) were concerned with the search for or processing of information (variables 1, 3, 6, 7 and 10) in Table 12.5),[11] and one was concerned with the level of training among the firm's management. In other words, the small firms that use new production techniques are usually those headed by an

Table 12.5 Main variables, by order according to the discriminating analysis, distinguishing SMEs using new technologies from the others, in the plastic products, machining shop and sawmill sectors in Quebec in 1988

1. V141 (source of information: suppliers)
2. ORDIN (use of a computer)
3. V147 (sources of information: industrial exhibitions)
4. PDBAC (owner-manager has an undergraduate university degree)
5. V355 (number of production employees)
6. RAPPOR (market surveys with written reports)
7. ORGREC (cooperation with research organizations)

— R2	: 0.5457	—
— Eigen value	: 1.2044	—
— Canonic correlation	: 0.7292	—
— Wilks Lambda	: 0.4683	—
— % of cases classified accurately	: 82.76%	—

8. IMPOR1 (rate of importation of raw materials, half-products, etc.)
9. EXPOR2 (rate of export outside Quebec and Ontario)
10. COMITE (existence of a management committee)

— R2	: 0.5457	—
— Eigen value:	: 1.2044	—
— Canonic correlation	: 0.7372	—
— Wilks Lambda	: 0.4536	—
— % of cases classified accurately	: 83.33%	

Source: P.A. Julien, J.B. Carrière and L. Hébert, 'Les facteurs de diffusion et de pénétration des nouvelles technologies dans les PME québécoises', *Revue internationale PME*, No. 2, 1988, pp. 193–222

owner-manager who is either better educated or has university qualifications (often in a technical field) or those in which senior staff have better training, use more complex management techniques such as market studies and a management committee and have an effective technological watch. Thus, differences between 'modern' and 'more traditional' firms can be explained by the quality of their internal resources (especially their human resources) and by their mastery of scientific and technological information. The training mentioned above is determined by basic education and also ongoing or *ad hoc* training. It is a well-known fact that ongoing training is much under-utilized in SMEs.

Thus management quality enables the firm to use or even develop the various potential sources of information it needs to ensure its efficiency; that is, to have an effective technological change strategy based on appropriate information sources. It also permits a better selection to be made among available sources.

One indicator for measuring a firm's capacity to seek out and use scientific and technological information is its level of technology watch (associated with its commercial and competitive watch). This watch exists in many of the more dynamic SMEs and may be implicit and/or intermittent or explicit and systematic. It allows the firm to understand market developments, to survey changes in competitors' competitivity and to keep abreast of any new technologies of interest in the process of maintaining or increasing its own competitive capabilities and responding to the needs of innovation when the time comes to apply it. It is based on a selective, mostly iterative search for external information, and presupposes a certain R&D capability to understand, interpret and use the information obtained.

This technology watch is mainly based on a receptive attitude with regard to change but also on an active approach to access to information sources; in other words, on environmental analysis on the one hand, and on consideration of technical change on the other. It is an information process which may vary in its regularity or be systematic and forward-looking and which comprises the selection, analysis and synopsis of information and, lastly, the transfer of the results obtained to the decision-makers for immediate action or a longer-term strategy. A watch therefore depends above all on access to specialized information sources that are not necessarily connected. It is bound to be highly favoured by close links with the technological information networks discussed above which allow information to vary according to the firm's needs and development.

12.5. Conclusion

Training and information are therefore key variables in the process of speeding up SME use of new technologies, and the state has an important role to play here. It must allow the higher education system to keep up-to-date with new technologies and to develop new ways of keeping in touch with SME management. However, it must also be concerned with the production and, particularly the transfer of technological information through its own agencies, through programs supporting private initiative or through the universities, since this type of information is largely in the public domain. Even the most technologically advanced countries are realizing that innovation will not be encouraged merely by stimulating R&D; there has to be rapid dissemination of information from national bodies or international sources. The use of international sources becomes even more important in smaller economies where R&D is necessarily less common than in larger countries. Smaller economies must also make a special effort to stimulate transfer of results from larger countries.

If it is to foster dissemination and penetration of new technologies, the state must develop a clear strategy at the mesoeconomic and microeconomic levels.

- **At the mesoeconomic level:**
  (a) by fostering research and information transfer, especially by systematizing the links between research, development and application of technologies through the intermediary of innovative contexts and 'personal' networks in firms, and through the intermediary of technological and economic networks, or 'dense networks'. The assistance provided should allow the *effective* transfer of technological information, its *assimilation* and, finally, its *management*.
  (b) by multiplying efforts to improve training and to make the supply of complementary generic resources available to SMEs so that they can obtain and use

technologies (basic or risk financing, advisory services in technology management, etc.). If such resources are absent or difficult to obtain, or if they cost too much, this may be a major obstacle to the development of competitivity.

(c) by collaborating with territorial governments to help them play the role of catalysts or stimulators of the development of entrepreneurial energies and local or regional resources, so that a technological culture open to technological information is created – in other words, a 'creative synergy', to use Schumpeter's terms.

- **On the microeconomic level:** by developing various measures to encourage SMEs to establish their own development and competitivity strategies. In particular, the powers-that-be should support measures to improve the capability of SMEs in the search for and processing, evaluation and application of technological information. The authorities should also support measures to help with the introduction and effective management of new technologies.

Technology is not an end in itself; it is a constantly evolving process. It is also renewed within a specific context, depending on very different needs, in an environment that is partly *created* at the initiative of entrepreneurs. It arises out of a great many sources, and circulates via all kinds of channels. The best policies for supporting training and fostering systematic updating of information and its dissemination by networks used by SMEs have not yet been identified. Analysis done so far has been partial, too theoretical or suited more to a big business context. When more is known about all these parameters, it will be possible to improve the transfer of scientific and technological information to SMEs to help them modernize or increase their competitivity.

Notes

1. This chapter is drawn in part from work done for the Organization for Economic Cooperation and Development (OECD) in 1991–2. It binds only the author and not the Organization.
2. According to Howard, for example, the poor competitiveness of American SMEs in sectors associated with transportation products, compared to the Japanese or even the Germans, is the root of the problems experienced by the American automobile industry, since the productivity of the major American car manufacturers now increasingly resembles that of their fellow producers elsewhere.
3. However, this positive development among SMEs as opposed to large firms seems to have marked time in recent years in countries such as Japan and Italy (Griffiths, 1989; Cardone *et al.*, 1990).
4. Prudence is required with the currently fashionable concept of market globalization: first, because the increase in international trade is not new; and moreover, because that increase has slowed down in the last decade, as GATT data show (for example, exports of manufactured goods increased in real terms at an average annual rate of 10 per cent in the period 1960–9, by 7.3 per cent in the period 1970–9 and by only 4.7 per cent in the period 1980–7). In addition, a number of other trends place the concept in perspective. For example, even within new economic blocs, some natural groupings are being recreated within the European Community, such as the links that existed in the fifteenth and sixteenth centuries between Catalonia, Provence and Piemond, or the north–

south relations between border Canadian provinces and American States with the North American Free Trade Zone. At the same time, the number of forms of decentralization of state control and territorial appropriation is increasing, and market segmentation in some places is speeding up.

5. A recent survey by Statistics Canada (1991) shows that in 1989 less than 50 per cent of small Canadian and American manufacturing firms with fewer than 100 employees were using at least one new computerized production technology. This percentage rose to more than 80 per cent among firms with more than 500 employees.

6. Including 'advanced' but non-computerized equipment such as injection moulding, spiral wire winding, double-screw extrusion, etc. as regards plastics, or plasma machining, laser welding, etc., in machining workshops.

7. However, care is needed when making international comparisons. First, survey periods are not always the same, and second, the number of technologies and industries studied may differ. However, such comparisons can provide an extremely interesting overview.

8. As indicated by T. Durand (1989), the supply of technological information 'is often monopolistic and latent because it is rarely formalized'. This information nevertheless does reach the market, after a certain interval, but usually after giving up most of its value and being replaced by even more recent information.

9. It is this that gives the greatest power, a bigger return which is why it is also 'political' in the sense of the term used by W. Ouchi (1980).

10. Indeed, even when research centres are public organizations, many agreements linking them to enterprises can include exclusivity clauses.

11. To these five variables can be added variables 8 and 9, concerning exporting and importing, which also presuppose control of information on international competitors and suppliers, as a number of authors have mentioned.

References

Acs, Z. and Audretsch, D.B. (1990) *Innovation and Small Firms*, Cambridge, Mass., MIT Press.

Aldrich, H. and Zimmer, C. (1985) 'Entrepreneurship through social interaction' in D. Sexton and R. Smilor (eds), *The Art of Science of Entrepreneurship*, New York, Ballinger.

Amendola, M. and Gaffard, J.L. (1988) *La dynamique économique de l'innovation*, Paris, Economica.

Archibugi, R. and Cesarretto, S. (1989) 'Piccole imprese e cambriatorento tecnologico. Modelli teorici e resultate dall indagino CNR-ISTAT sull'innovazione tecnologica nel settore manifatturiero italiano', *Piccola Impresa*, 2, 45–73.

Association CAO/FAO (1989) 'Tendances et degré de pénétration. L'informatisation et l'informatisation de la production', Montreal, CRIQ.

Belhumeur, A. and Nguyen, T. (1989) 'Le processus d'innovation technologique dans les petites et moyennes entreprises manufacturières du Québec', paper presented at the ICSB-Canada Conference, Quebec.

Birley, S., Cromie, S. and Myers, A. (1991) 'Entreprenerial networks: their emergence in Ireland and overseas', *International Small Business Journal*, 9, 4, 56–74.

Cardone, A., Cesarretto, S. and de Marchi, M. (1990) 'Innovative strategies, technological results and competitiveness in Italian firms in the light of industrial policy concerning technological innovation', paper presented at the Séminaire de haut niveau sur les PME manufacturières, OCDE, 2–3 July.

Carrière, J.B. and Julien, P.A. (1992) 'Profil technologique de la PME manufacturière québécoise', report for the Association des Manufacturiers du Québec, Trois-Rivières, GREPME, June.

Chicha, J. and Julien, P.A. (1980) 'Les stratégies des PME face au changement', GREPME, Université du Québec à Trois-Rivières.

Crawford, R.L. and Lefebvre, L. (1986) 'Closing the low-tech gap: smaller firms and manufacturing technology' in P.A. Julien *et al.* (eds), *La PME dans un monde en mutation*, Quebec, Presses de l'Université du Québec, 319–37.

de Koning, A.C.P. and Wennekers, A.R.M. (1991) quoting 'EIM Kleinschalig Ondernemen 1991' in 'Productivity of SME: factors and instruments', paper presented at the International Conference of Lisbon, 1–2 July.

Davis, D.D. (1980) 'Technological innovation and organizational change' in *Managing Technological Innovation*, Jossey-Bass,

Durand, T. (1989) 'Management stratégique de la technologie', *Futuribles*, 137, November.

Falemo, B. (1989) 'The firm's external persons: entrepreneur of network actors', *Entrepreneurship and Regional Development*, 1, 2, 167–78.

Grabher, G. (1989) 'Regional innovation by networking: The case of lower Austria', *Entrepreneurship and Regional Development*, 1, 2, 141–2.

GREPME (Groupe de recherche en économie et gestion des PME) (1993) *Les PME. Bilan et perspective*, Montreal, Edition du Renouveau Pédagogique.

Griffiths, A. (1989) 'Small and medium enterprises and structural change in the 1980's: the case of Japan's manufacturing industry', *The Study of Business and Industry*, (Université Nihon), no. 6, December.

Griffith, J. and Dorsman, M. (1987) 'SMEs, new technology and training', *International Small Business Journal*, 5, 3, 30–42.

Grosnier, P., François and Lehoucq, T. (1991) *Les chiffres clés. Les PME*, Paris, ministère de l'Industrie et du Commerce extérieur and Dunod.

Howard, R. (1991) 'Can small business help countries compete?', *Harvard Business Review*, November–December, 88–103.

Johannisson, B. (1989) 'Network strategies: management technology for entrepreneurship and change', *International Small Business Journal*, 5, 1, 19–30.

Johannisson, B. and Johnsson, T. (1988) 'New venture network strategies', Working Paper no. 18, Université de Vaxjo, quoted by Birley, Cromie and Myers, *op. cit.*

Julien, P.A. (1991) 'Le rythme de pénétration des nouvelles technologies de production dans les PME', *Journal of Small Business and Entrepreneurship*, 8, 3, 21–32.

Julien, P.A. (1992a) 'Petites et moyennes entreprises manufacturières et nouvelles technologies: la situation au Québec', *Revue Internationale de Gestion*, November.

Julien, P.A., Carrière, J.B. and Hébert, L. (1988) 'Les facteurs de diffusion et de pénétration des nouvelles technologies dans les PME manufacturières québécoises', *Revue Internationale PME*, 1, 2, 193–223.

Julien, P.A. and Thibodeau, J.C. (1991) *Nouvelles technologies et économie*, Quebec, Les Presses du l'Université du Québec.

Laborit, H. (1974) *La nouvelle grille*, Paris, Laffond, 1974, cited by M.P. Bes and J.L. Leloulch, 'Transportabilité de l'information technologique dans l'espace', paper presented at the Conference of the Association des sciences régionales de langue française (ASRDLF), Montreal, 3–5 September 1991.

Lambooy, J.G. (1986) 'Information and internationalization. Dynamics of the relations of small and medium sized enterprises in a network environment' in the thematic issue *Les PME innovatrices et leur environnement local at économique* in the *Revue d'économie régionale et urbaine*, 5, 719–31.

MacPherson, A. (1989) 'Small manufacturing firms and Canadian industrial development: empirical and theoretical perspectives', *Revue Canadienne des Sciences Régionales*, XII, 2, 165–86.

Maglione, R., Michelsons, A. and Rossi, S.E. (1990) *Economie locali tra grande e piccola impresa*, Turin, Fundazione Andriano Olivetti.

Maillat, D. and Perrin, J.C. (1992) *Entreprises innovatrices et développement territorial*, Neuchâtel, EDES.

Mansfield, E. (1981) 'Composition of R&D expenditures: relationships to size of firm, concentration and innovative output', *The Review of Economic and Statistics*, November.

Martinet, B. and Ribeault, J.M. (1989) *La veille technologique, concurrentielle et commerciale: sources, méthodologie et organisation*, Paris, Editions d'organisation.

Meyer, O. and Goes, J.B. (1987) 'How organizations adopt and implement new technologies', *Academy of Management Proceedings*, 175–9.

Mills, D. and Schumann, L. (1985) 'Industry structure and fluctuating demand', *American Economic Review*, 75, 4, 758–67.

MFRT (German Department of Research and Technology) (1989) 'Promotion of research and development in small and medium-sized enterprises', Bonn, June.

Morvan, Y. (1991) *Fondements de l'économie industrielle*, Paris, Economica, 2nd edition.

Mouwen, A. and Nijkamp, P. (1986) 'Centre de connaissance et politique régionale', in J. Federwisch and H. Zoller (eds), *Technologie nouvelle et ruptures régionales*, Paris, Economica.

Mussati, G. and Terracciano, C. (1989) 'Il collegamento tra imprese e università nel campo della ricerca e della formazione' in A. Battaglia and R. Valcamonici (eds), *Nella competizione globale. Una politica industriale verso il 2000*, Turin, Libri del tempo Laterza.

Ouchi, W. (1980) 'Markets, bureaucracies and clans', *Administrative Science Quarterly*, 25, 129–41.

Planque, B. (1987) 'PME innovatrices et potentiel d'information et de compétences', *Notes de recherche*, no. 76, Centre d'économie régionale, Aix-en-Provence, February.

Planque, B. and Py, B. (1986) 'La dynamique de l'insertion des PME innovatrices dans leur environnement: problématique et propositions méthodologiques', *Revue d'économie régional et urbaine*, 5, 587–607.

Rallet, A. (1988) 'Les entreprises et l'innovation en matière de réseaux de communication' in *L'innovation dans les entreprises et les régions*, Luxembourg, Atelier interrégional.

Ravix, A.L. (1988) 'Les comportements d'innovation dans l'artisanat de production industrielle: approche régionale et politique publiques d'innovation', *Revue Internationale PME*, 1, 3–4, 277–95.

Richardson, G.B. (1972) 'The organization of the industry', *Economic Journal*, September, 883–96.

Rothwell, R. (1990) 'External networking and innovation in small and medium-sized manufacturing firms in Europe', mimeo, University of Sussex.

Scarlatti, P. (1991) 'Riflessi dei processi di automazione sulla gestione delle piccole e medie imprese nell'area genovese', *Piccola Impresa*, 3.

Sengenberger, W., Loveman, M. and Piore, M. (1990) *The Re-emergence of Small Enterprises*, Geneva Institut International d'Etudes Sociales, BIT.

Simon, H.A. (1980) *Le nouveau management. La décision par les ordinateurs*, Paris, Economica.

Sole Parellada, F. and Roca, B. (1991) 'Evolution et contraintes dans la configuration résiliaire d'un milieu: le cas de Barcelone', Report for GREMI III, Université Polytechnique de Catalunya, October.

Statistics Canada (1991) 'Les indicateurs de l'activité scientifique et technologique 1989', no 88-002, **1**, 4.

Thorelli, H.B. (1986) 'Networks: between markets and hierarchies', *Strategic Management Journal*, **6**, 37–51.

Tinacci-Mossello, M. and Dini, F. (1989) 'Innovation et communication sociale dans les districts industriels', *Revue Internationale PME*, **2**, 2–3, 229–53.

Zurkovitch, E. (1985) 'La dynamique du développement des technologies', *Revue économique*, **36**, 5, 897–915.

Index